A HISTORY OF BRITAIN

A Narrative for the Middle School

GENERAL EDITOR

DENIS RICHARDS, M.A.

Principal of Morley College
Formerly Senior History and English Master, Bradfield College,
and Scholar of Trinity Hall, Cambridge

VOLUME IV

BRITAIN 1714–1851

Britain 1714-1851

DENIS RICHARDS, M.A.

AND

ANTHONY QUICK, M.A.

Headmaster of Bradfield College
Formerly Assistant Master, Charterhouse

LONGMAN

LONGMAN GROUP LIMITED
Longman House
Burnt Mill, Harlow, Essex, U.K.

First published 1961
Eleventh impression 1981

ISBN 0 582 31488 7

Printed in Singapore by
Ban Wah Press Pte Ltd

CONTENTS

MAPS

ACKNOWLEDGMENTS

The illustration on p. 295 is reproduced by gracious permission of H.M. The Queen.

For permission to reproduce other illustrations we are indebted to the following:

Associated Rediffusion for p. 362; the Assay Office, Birmingham for p. 135; the Museum and Art Gallery, Birmingham for pp. 319, 363; Mrs. Barrett and the Oxford University Press for p. 217 from the *Oxford Companion to Music*, 1938, edited by Percy Scholes; the Syndics of the Cambridge University Press for p. 114; J. Allan Cash for p. 389; the Marquis of Cholmondeley for p. 18; Lt.-Col. J. N. Chaworth-Musters for p. 228; Mr. Gilbert Davies for p. 127; the Family Welfare Association for p. 269; the FitzWilliam Museum, Cambridge for p. 224; the Guildhall Library for pp. 109, 354; *History Today* for pp. 62, 162, 247, 332; *Illustrated London News* for p. 285; the India Office Library for p. 332; A. F. Kersting for pp. 234, 390; the Mansell Collection for pp. 157, 268, 278, 280, 337, 340; the National Buildings Record for p. 81; the National Gallery for pp. 222, 225; the National Maritime Museum for p. 54; the National Museum of Wales for p. 139; the National Portrait Gallery for pp. 38, 107, 121, 141, 143, 159, 160, 165, 174, 215, 218, 377, 382; Nottingham Museum and Art Gallery for p. 238; the Parker Gallery for p. 155; the Oxford University Press for p. 271 from Young, *Early Victorian England*, the Proprietors of *Punch* for p. 361; *Radio Times* Hulton Picture Library for pp. 263, 266, 289, 301, 303, 358; Rathbone Books Ltd. for p. 88; Crown copyright Science Museum, London for pp. 115 (top), 140, 276, 282, 284, 345, 346; Photo Science Museum, London, for p. 350; the Trustees of Sir John Soane's Museum for p. 221; the Trustees of the Tate Gallery for pp. 8, 227, 387; Mr. F. Sherwood Taylor for p. 113 from *An Illustrated History of Science* published by William Heinemann, Ltd.; *The Times* for p. 372; the Victoria and Albert Museum for pp. 6, 96, 206, 237, 239, 240, 241, 357, 385, 393, 396 (these photographs are Crown copyright reserved); Messrs. H. E. Wingfield & Co. for p. 351.

Illustrations on pp. 10, 25, 35, 57, 62, 74, 76, 85, 87, 93, 94, 95, 98, 100, 102, 123, 131, 133, 134, 150, 162, 177, 209, 230, 247, 249, 251, 267, 275, 307, 338, 343, 379, 395, 397, are reproduced from subjects in the British Museum, and illustrations of pp. 185, 374, from books in the Cambridge University Library.

The portraits included in the chart on p. x are details of larger pictures and are reproduced by permission of the following:

The National Portrait Gallery for George I, George II, and William IV; the Trustees of the Wallace Collection for George IV and Victoria; the British Museum for George III.

THE HANOVERIANS

James I

STUART LINE   Elizabeth, m. Frederick Elector Palatine

(Three sons
d. childless)   Sophia, m. Ernest Augustus of Hanover

GEORGE I m. Sophia Dorothea of Celle
King 1714-1727

GEORGE II m. Caroline of Anspach   one other
King 1727-1760

Frederick, Prince of Wales, m. Augusta of Saxe-Gotha
d. 1751

five others

GEORGE III m. Charlotte of Mecklenburg-Strelitz
King 1760-1820

four others

nine
others

GEORGE IV m. Caroline of   **WILLIAM IV**   Edward, Duke of Kent
Prince Regent   Brunswick   King 1830-1837   d. 1820
1811-1820   m. Adelaide of   m. Victoria of Saxe-Coburg
King 1820-1830   Saxe-Coburg

VICTORIA
m. Albert of Saxe-Coburg
Queen 1837-1901

Frederick
Duke of York
d. childless
1827

Charlotte, m. Leopold of Saxe-Coburg   d. childless
d. 1817   (later Leopold I of Belgium)

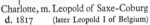

CHAPTER ONE

GREAT BRITAIN IN 1714

1. *England and Wales*

'POOR Peggy too has frequent returns of her illness. She would receive benefit if the old fashioned thing called summer would make its appearance.' So wrote an English gentleman in the early eighteenth century. Although there seems to have been little alteration in the weather since then, in other ways the changes that have come to these lands during the last two and a half centuries have been enormous. They far exceed those that had taken place in the previous thousand years, and if by some magic we could transport ourselves back to the Britain of 1714 we should find ourselves in a very strange place indeed.

There were far fewer people. Accurate figures are Population difficult to obtain, for the first census was not taken till 1801, but the population of England and Wales in 1714 can be estimated roughly at 5½ million, of Ireland at 2 million, and of Scotland at 1 million. In other words, the population of the entire British Isles at this time was no larger than that of Greater London today. It was disease—notably consumption, smallpox, dysentery, typhus and typhoid—rather than war that stopped any increase in the population, and it is probable that only one out of every four children born in High London lived to reach the age of five. The figure for the death-rate new towns that were beginning to rise in the north was no better, though chances of survival in the countryside were greater. One of the early governors of London's Foundling Hospital, which was built by private charity in 1742, tells us that out of the 1,384 children received in the first fifteen years it was 'very remarkable that only 724 died in all this time'.

The
countryside

The great majority of Englishmen and Welshmen still lived in the country, and farming was still the country's most important industry. In some areas the countryside has changed little since 1714; the familiar chequer-board of field and hedgerow which we think so typical of the English

'Enclosed'
farms

countryside could already be seen in counties in the south and east such as Hertfordshire and Surrey, and also in the west in the valleys of the Severn and Wye. In these areas, groups of fields were tilled by individual farmers helped by wage-earning labourers. There was, however, a broad band of country stretching from Dorset and Hamp-

Open-field
districts

shire right across the centre of England to Yorkshire and Lincolnshire where the fields were still unenclosed, and where the villagers farmed strips within these fields as in medieval times. Outside the three or four great fields the land was common and could be used by the villagers to graze their cows, geese and pigs. In addition the villagers usually had small allotments around their cottages, in both enclosed and unenclosed areas.

Wasteland

Much of the higher land throughout England and Wales nowadays used for hill farming was waste, and even as low an area as the Cotswolds was completely uncultivated and afforded only very poor pasture for sheep and cows. On the other hand, the great forests of England had been over-

Forests

felled and were fast disappearing. Sussex still produced its much-prized oaks from the Weald and Ashdown Forest for the dockyards of the Thames and Medway, but ever-increasing quantities of timber had now to be imported from the Baltic and America.

Welsh
agriculture

Wales, like England, lived mainly by farming. But there were no open fields, for this system had been introduced into Britain by the Anglo-Saxons, who had never penetrated into the heart of Wales. Large estates were on the increase at the beginning of the eighteenth century, but these were broken up into hundreds of smallholdings and it was the peasant smallholder who was mainly responsible for tilling Welsh soil.

Social
classes in the
countryside

In England the countryside supported several different classes of people. There were peasants, tenant farmers, freeholders or yeomen (a name sometimes also applied to the larger tenant farmers), squires, nobility. The differences in wealth and rank between them were very great. The peasant's income might be as little as £7 a year. The Duke of Newcastle, one of the foremost landowners, had an annual income in 1714 of £40,000.

The great men's homes—many of which can still be seen —were scattered throughout the land, and some of the best known were being built at this time. The great palace of Blenheim at Woodstock was being constructed for Marlborough; so was Castle Howard in Yorkshire for the Earl of Carlisle. Both were designed by Sir John Vanbrugh, playwright and wit as well as architect, and both had vast parks—for nearly as much care was given to the laying out of the parks as to the actual building of the houses. These huge mansions were but two of many, for this was the golden age of the landed aristocracy. Neither nobility nor the much larger class immediately below them, the gentry, were however 'closed castes'. It was always possible for a merchant to buy an estate, become a landowner, and marry his children into much more exalted circles than those into which he himself had been born. *Great country houses*

The nobility not a 'closed caste'

Agriculture was not the only industry of the countryside. Spinning and weaving, especially of wool, was carried on in tens of thousands of homes throughout the country—for the factory was still the exception rather than the rule. Defoe, who, besides writing *Robinson Crusoe* and many political pamphlets, has left us a very interesting record of his travels in England at this period, noted as a great curiosity a factory 400 feet long at Derby for manufacturing silk thread. It was run by water power from the Derwent. Before Defoe's visit an engineer eagerly showing round visitors had slipped into the river; he was carried straight beneath the great water-wheel, jammed it, was released as the pressure of water increased, and was finally pulled out at the far end of the mill-race, by some miracle completely unhurt. *The cloth industry*

The West Riding woollen industry is a good example of a manufacture done in the home. Defoe, who had crossed *West Riding woollens— Defoe's description* over the moors from Rochdale to the Upper Calder valley and almost lost his way owing to a freak snowstorm in August, came upon a great scene of activity. As he rode down to Halifax, he found many large villages in the valleys, and houses dotted all over the hillside. For miles around, white patches could be seen near the houses—the cloth that was being dried and stretched out of doors. Each house had its own stream of water from the hill and many their own coal-pit. Within, everyone was at work at the loom or the dye-vat or preparing the cloth. Each family kept a horse or two for collecting their wool and for taking their cloth away to market at Halifax, already an important centre in the industry—as were Leeds, Bradford, Huddersfield and Wakefield. To Halifax, too, went the clothiers in September or October to buy two or three large bullocks. These they killed, salted, and hung in the smoke of their chimneys, to be assured of meat throughout the winter.

Early 18th-century roads

Defoe travelled over atrocious roads. Even for the traveller on horseback they were difficult in rainy weather, for they turned into quagmires. Men and horses were drowned in the potholes of the Great North Road during these years. On some routes there was a strip of hard surface four feet wide, sufficient for a rider or line of pack-horses, but quite inadequate for coaches, which had to plunge into the morass beside it. By these the aged and infirm had to travel. Even the coaches that carried the post could never average more than three or four miles an hour, and for the mail to travel between Edinburgh and London took six days and nights.

Livestock on roads

Especially near London the roads were much worse because of the quantity of livestock driven over them. Vast numbers of cattle, sheep and poultry reached the tables of Londoners in this way. They had to be moved into the London area before October, otherwise they became stuck in the mud; it was reckoned that 150,000 turkeys alone gobbled their way every year into the city down one of the main roads from Suffolk. However, a special four-tier cart had just been invented which could carry as many as a hundred turkeys and could with luck do a hundred miles in two days and a night. This was a speed record for the period.

Highwaymen brought another peril to the traveller. This was the time of Dick Turpin, but he proves on investigation to be a disappointing figure. His famous ride to York is a groundless legend, and though he committed one or two robberies on the road his main occupation was cattle-stealing. There were, however, many others, and highwaymen came close to London to haunt places like Wimbledon Common and Epping Forest. Highwaymen

Britain's real highways were the sea and the rivers. All bulky and heavy goods had to be carried by water. Fortunately by 1714 many rivers were navigable, and later in the century canals were to extend further the range of water-borne transport. London, for instance, was supplied with flour and wood that came down the Thames from the Wey, which had locks as far as Guildford, and with corn that barges brought down the Thames from Abingdon. And when the iron manufacturers of Shropshire wanted to send their pig-iron to Chester, a distance of about fifty miles, they sent it right down the Severn (which was navigable as far as Welshpool), round Wales, then up the Dee. This journey of some 450 miles by water was cheaper and more reliable than the direct journey of fifty miles by road. Transport by river

The small ports, nowadays in decay or used only for fishing, enjoyed in the eighteenth century a flourishing trade. The biggest of the coastal trades was in coal from Newcastle to London; it all came to London by sea and was known there as sea coal. This traffic kept many harbours down the east coast busy, including places such as Ipswich and Whitby which built and manned the ships. It was, however, a dangerous trade. Between Flamborough Head in Yorkshire and Winterton Ness in Norfolk the ships left the coast and sailed direct. But if they were caught by an easterly gale there was only one refuge, the Humber. Sometimes disaster overtook them. In 1692, 140 vessels of a fleet of 200 northward bound for Newcastle were caught by a north-easterly gale and destroyed among the treacherous shoals of the Wash. Cromer Bay with its dangerous rocks Transport by sea—the coal trade

A Country Inn Yard, 1747

From an engraving by William Hogarth. Amid clamour of horn and bell, the stage coach prepares to depart. In the background an election mob chairs a candidate.

was another of the hazards of this area. It was known to mariners as 'the Devil's Throat'.

On the west coast, too, colliers were at work. There was a big trade between Whitehaven and Ireland, and Swansea exported coal to places like the inland port of Bridgwater, in Somerset. Here some of it was transhipped to barges which could carry it on to Taunton. From South Wales, too, were exported lead and iron as well as coal, though as yet Welsh production of all these was still on a small scale.

Considerable though they were, the risks and rewards of the coastal traders were small compared with those of the merchants and sailors who traded across the oceans. These played for very high stakes—and won, with dramatic results for the history of Britain. It was to her world-wide commerce as much as to the Industrial Revolution that Britain owed her enormous prosperity and influence in the nineteenth century. In 1714 the foundations of her trading empire were still being laid, but besides the major colonies in North America there were already several British settlements in the West Indies (including Barbados and Jamaica), in India (the East India Company's posts at Bombay, Madras and Calcutta), and in West Africa (Gambia). All these maintained a valuable trade with Britain, to whom West Indies sugar and Indian tea, silks and spices were already items of particular importance.

The towns that were growing fastest at this time were those concerned with trade across the oceans to America, Africa and Asia. The chief were Liverpool, Bristol and London. Docks had already been built along the banks of the Mersey, and by the end of the century Liverpool had 78,000 inhabitants and was the third town of England. Bristol was only a little smaller, while London was in a class by itself. Through these ports there was already a big flow of tropical and semi-tropical produce, including cotton and the tobacco, sugar, rum, spices, tea and coffee now being bought by more and more people.

London was already a giant and had a population of about 600,000. In 1714 there can have been no other town in Britain with a population of more than 50,000. Yet its

Overseas trade

Colonies

The fastest-growing towns

London

area was small compared with modern London. The district round Victoria was still the Tothill Fields, Chelsea was a village, and there was no building west of Park Lane and practically none north of Oxford Street. Marylebone, like Paddington, was a separate village. Eastward the building line extended farther north, but Islington was not yet joined to London. Hoxton and Shoreditch were largely built up, and building down the Thames reached as far east as Limehouse. Poplar and Blackwall, the East India

Old London Bridge

From a painting by Samuel Scott. The houses on the bridge were demolished in 1 ?
and the bridge itself was replaced in 1831.

Company's depot where all their ships docked, were still just separate from the main built-up area.

    On the South Bank, building stretched in a narrow strip from Deptford to Vauxhall. One bridge alone connected the two banks—old London Bridge, 100 feet downstream from the present bridge. It was covered with houses which were built right over the roadway so that crossing London Bridge was like walking through a tunnel with a few patches of light where there were gaps between the houses. Beneath, the piers took up so much room that the water could not flow freely between them. On a full ebb-tide there was a

London
Bridge

five-foot drop between the east and west side—to shoot the fall in a boat needed such skill that it was rarely attempted except at slack water. The bridge in fact acted like a weir. There was an incessant roar, and people rigged up water-wheels on the arches nearest the banks to make use of the power.

There were many other sights in London—and in other towns too—that would astonish a modern Englishman. He would be appalled by the squalor. Outside the area rebuilt after the Great Fire many of the streets were narrow, with gables projecting above so that they almost met, and almost all were filthy. Gutters and drains from upper storeys poured their contents down into the streets—into which housekeepers and even butchers threw their refuse. The whole place stank. Drains sometimes ran down the middle of the road, and the smell of the Fleet Ditch, the remains of a stream, was especially notorious. Water and the contents of the drains often seeped into the cellars. A petitioner in 1766 recalled that in his father's house in Spital Square the water had been three or four feet deep in the cellars, and that to draw the daily beer the servants used to punt themselves along in a washing tub from the stairs to the barrels. *London squalor*

The houses of the great and the prosperous were vast and concentrated in the west-end, already the fashionable quarter. Whitehall Palace had been largely burned down in William III's reign, and was no longer in use as a royal residence, but there were two big royal palaces at St. James's and Kensington. The majority of London inhabitants, however, lived in very cramped conditions either in the City or to the north and east of it. It was common for working-class families—as often in Moscow today—to live in a single room. Garrets and cellars all held their share of humanity, and some of the poorest found shelter in the common lodging houses at twopence a night. When they rose in the morning, many had no idea where they would lay their heads at the end of the day. *Housing conditions*

The man of today would have been surprised, too, by the insecurity of life. Not only was there great risk of falling an early victim to some fatal disease, but buildings often *The risks of London life*

Night: London, 1738

From an engraving by Hogarth. Note the fire in the distance, a coach robbery, a publican watering down beer, two drunks, destitute people sleeping in the street, the excess of taverns, and the slops descending from an upper window.

collapsed and buried their inhabitants. When on one occasion in 1718 a man ran into a London tavern with urgent news, it was instantly assumed by those inside that he had come to tell them that the building was falling. Nor was there an efficient fire service or police force, and the maze of narrow streets and alleys afforded excellent cover for criminals. Of these, one of the most outstanding was Jonathan Wild, who organized gangs of thieves, and stationed one on each of the main London roads. At the same time he opened an office near the Old Bailey to help citizens recover their stolen property—and here he sold back to them the property of which his men had robbed them. Eventually, justice caught up with him, and in 1725 he met his well-merited end at Tyburn.

Crime—Jonathan Wild

The manufactures carried on in London were numerous. There was an important silk-weaving industry in Spital-fields, various metal trades in Clerkenwell and Shoreditch, and a considerable production of luxury goods of all kinds, including jewellery. But it was commerce rather than industry that brought London its great prosperity. The centre of the port of London was The Pool, the stretch of river from London Bridge to Limehouse, and in this small area Defoe claims on one occasion to have counted more than 2,000 sea-going ships. These included neither the East Indiamen nor the ships of the Navy, which did not come up as far as this. Along both banks of The Pool the same observer noticed a long line of quays with ships busy loading and unloading. The whole sight was a striking glimpse of that vast sea-going commerce on which, more than on anything else, depended the fame and wealth of London.

London manufactures

London a great port

2. Scotland and Ireland

Since the Act of Union in 1707 Scotland had been ruled by the same ministers and parliament as England and Wales. She sent forty-five members to the House of Commons and, in addition, sixteen of the Scottish peers sat in the House of Lords. But she retained her own legal system and her own established religion—Presbyterianism.

The Act of Union, 1707

Growth of
Scottish
trade:
Glasgow

The greatest immediate advantage of the Act of Union to Scotland was that it enabled her to share in England's trade across the oceans. At the beginning of George I's reign Glasgow had only just started her commercial contacts with America and was a town of only 12,000 inhabitants. However, by the 1770s she had deprived Liverpool and Bristol of the lion's share of the American tobacco trade, and by the end of the century had a population of 77,000. Edinburgh in 1714 was twice the size of Glasgow and with her university and law courts was the centre of Scottish society, but she was not to develop at anything like Glasgow's speed. Her population was extremely proud and independent, and in the years following the Act of Union staged a number of riots against the government.

The Lowlands

The Highlands

In the Lowlands rural life was not unlike that of the poorer parts of northern England, though methods of farming were old-fashioned. In the Highlands, however, an utterly different life was led, a life that had not changed for centuries. The clans still dominated the country. In many areas English was not spoken. The government had little real power and there were no roads, the post between Edinburgh and Inverness being taken on foot till 1755. The man who mattered was the clan chieftain, to whose hereditary powers of justice—including the right to inflict sentence of death—the whole clan was subject. These Highlanders had the virtues of great courage and loyalty, but in other ways had less to recommend them. Their agriculture was primitive; in places where they used a horse they tied the harrow to its tail, and they expected the women to do the hard field-work while the men put their energies into fighting, raiding and cattle-stealing. The soil was poor, rents were comparatively high so that the chief and his retinue could exist in idleness, and most of the population spent their lives in terrible poverty and hardship. Yet Charles Edward Stuart, the Young Pretender, wandered for five months among the Highlanders in 1746 with a price of £30,000 on his head and no one betrayed him. Honour, even if sometimes an odd form of it, meant more to them than money.

Ireland was in a far less fortunate position than Scotland, Ireland for England openly treated her as an inferior. Dublin, the centre of government, was the second city of the British Isles, but the Parliament there had little power and the real governors of Ireland, the Lord Lieutenant and the Lords Justices, were appointed from England. The Control by England Lord Lieutenancy was often given to English politicians as a consolation prize. Few of them took the job seriously—indeed two of the eighteenth-century Lords Lieutenant never even bothered to cross to Ireland. As to trade, the Irish were forbidden to export their better woollen cloths to England, and both England and the colonies were closed to their cattle, sheep, butter and cheese—their main products. Everything, in other words, was regulated so that there could be no competition with English industries.

Five-sixths of the Irish population were Roman Catholic, Restrictions on Roman Catholics yet no Catholics were allowed to hold government office, and except in the west it was practically impossible for them to own land. Office and land-ownership were for the most part the privilege of the small ruling class of Protestants— the members of the Church of Ireland (i.e. the counterpart in Ireland of the Church of England). Not surprisingly, many of the more ambitious Roman Catholics left the country and sought service in Europe. Two Russian field-marshals in the eighteenth century were Irish, as also were at least five Austrian generals. Spain at one time had five Irish regiments, and the Irish Brigade of the French Army established a great reputation, turning the tide of battle more than once against the English.

Unambitious Irishmen stayed at home and wrung a The Irish peasantry miserable living from the soil. Their clothes were in tatters and great numbers lived in hovels made from wood or unmortared stone. In poor seasons when other food failed they bled their cattle and consumed the blood mixed with sorrel. The rents they paid went in all too many cases to England to keep absentee landlords in luxury. Those who could not pay their rent were evicted, and Ireland was notorious for thousands of wandering beggars who had given up hope of regular work and spent many of their nights in the open.

Ulster

This was the general countryside scene over much of Ireland. In Ulster, however, there was some prosperity. Here the population was Protestant, with many of Scottish descent. Though they were excluded from most official positions because they were Presbyterian, they did not suffer the same handicaps in business as the Catholics, and during

The linen industry

the eighteenth century the linen industry round Belfast became increasingly important. Needless to say, it was allowed to flourish because there was no linen industry in England with which it would compete.

3. *The Political Situation in 1714*

Importance of the monarch

The year 1714 makes a convenient starting point to this volume because in that year died Queen Anne, the last of the Stuarts. In those days a change of monarch was an event of great political importance, for the monarch still had a large share in the day-to-day government of the country. The few ministers normally met in the royal presence and were dependent on the royal favour, and the number of civil servants was extremely small. The two Secretaries for State, for instance—one for the Northern Department and one for the Southern Department—dealt with practically all matters within their areas, including foreign, colonial, naval and military affairs, yet their entire staff was only twenty-four, including caretakers. Like the other ministers—of whom the First Lord of the Treasury and the Chancellor of the Exchequer were now among the most important—they relied for their influence not on a well-organized party in Parliament or the advice of an efficiently organized civil service department, but on the support of the Crown.

Act of Settlement, 1701—the Hanoverian succession

The last of Anne's many children had died in 1701, and in that year an Act of Settlement vested the succession in the Electress of Hanover (a granddaughter of James I) and her heirs. This lady having died shortly before Anne, her rights had descended to her son Prince George, now

Elector of Hanover.[1] There was, however, another candidate, or Pretender, for the English throne—Anne's half-brother, James Edward Stuart, the son of the displaced James II by his second and Roman Catholic marriage. James Edward had been proclaimed James III of England by Louis XIV at Versailles. But Louis was beaten in the great European war known as the War of the Spanish Succession, which lasted from 1702 to 1713, and with his defeat vanished the best chances of the Pretender. Moreover, the Pretender remained firmly Roman Catholic, and this alone made him quite unacceptable to the majority in Britain.

The Pretender, James Edward

So everything pointed to George of Hanover as Anne's successor—everything, that is, except the interests of the Tories, who had captured office from the Whigs in the closing years of Anne's reign. The Tories had ended the war by making Britain desert her continental allies, including Hanover, and George was furious with them. While the Whigs were clear that they wanted the Hanoverian Succession, the ideas of the Tories were thus muddled. They had no common policy—which was not unusual, for neither the Whigs nor Tories at that time had the unity or close organization of a modern political party. Most Tories probably favoured the Hanoverian, yet their normal belief in strict hereditary succession and the fact that he was offended with their party led some of them to consider the claims of the Pretender. In the closing years of Anne's reign the Tory leaders, Lords Oxford and Bolingbroke, had negotiated with James Edward and tried to persuade him —in vain—to renounce his religion. Towards the very end the vigorous and determined Bolingbroke, tired of his colleague's hesitations and seeing ruin staring the Tories in the face if George came to the throne, had persuaded Anne

The Hanoverian heir offended with Tories

Tory views on the succession

Oxford and Bolingbroke negotiate with Pretender

Dismissal of Oxford and death of Anne

[1] The rulers of Hanover were known as Electors, since, in common at this time with the rulers of eight other German States, they had the right to elect the head of the Empire—as the Holy Roman Empire was now usually called. In fact, the right to elect meant little, since the ruler of Austria had for long been regarded as the automatic choice for Emperor.

Bolingbroke unprepared for action: Proclamation of George I to dismiss Oxford. But within five days Anne was dead, and Bolingbroke had had no time, if such had been his intention, to organize opposition to the Hanoverian. Though it would mean the end of the Tory spell of power, there was nothing for it but to proclaim George.

So it came about that when the Bishop of Rochester, an extreme Tory and supporter of the Pretender, announced his intention of going to the Royal Exchange and proclaiming James III as King of England, Bolingbroke refused to join any such party, saying that their throats would all be cut. 'England', he said, 'would as soon have a Turk as a Roman Catholic for a king.' Thus the Bishop's determination came to nothing, and the Hanoverian was peacefully proclaimed as George I throughout the land: so peacefully that he could remain in Hanover another six weeks, arranging the affairs of the Electorate, before setting out for his new, greater, and much more troublesome inheritance.

CHAPTER TWO

THE AGE OF WALPOLE

1. *The Rise of Walpole*

IT was a fine September evening in 1714 when George I at length landed at Greenwich and walked across to the impressive palace designed by Wren, which stands to this day. With him there came many followers from Hanover. They included his two main German advisers, his two Turkish servants Mustafa and Mohammed, and his two chief lady-loves—nicknamed the Elephant and the Maypole on account of their figures.

All these were people of political importance, for they were in close contact with the king. A harsh, masterful man of fifty-four, reserved and stiff in manner, George was by now too set to welcome new advisers. Nor did he encourage a lively social life at court, having divorced his wife and imprisoned her in a castle in Germany (where she died thirty years later). He took his meals by himself in the vast rooms of his palaces, attended only by his two Turks. His main amusements, apart from his ladies and the pleasures of the table, were music, gambling, and cutting out paper figures.

As king, however, George had the power to make or mar the fortunes of any British politician. The king still had much freedom in his choice of ministers, and there was keen competition to obtain office from him—for office brought great opportunities for enrichment, and the vast range of honours and posts at the royal disposal usually gave the king's ministers a comfortable majority in Parliament. So it was only natural that all those with very high ambitions in politics should be gathered at the quayside at Greenwich to greet the new king. Among those waiting was a squire from Norfolk who was destined to become for twenty years the

most powerful man in British politics. His name was
Robert Walpole.

Thirty-eight years earlier Robert Walpole had first seen
the light of day in the Manor House at Houghton, in
Norfolk. In that county his family formed one of those local
connections which had great influence in eighteenth-
century politics. It was with the support of powerful local

Country Life Ltd.

Houghton Hall

A modern photograph of Sir Robert Walpole's home in Norfolk. He
inherited a modest manor-house and transformed it into this stately
classical mansion.

relations that his father, Colonel Robert Walpole, had made
good a claim to one of the parliamentary seats of Castle
Rising, a 'rotten' borough nearby, after disturbances in
which the parson had to take refuge in the church steeple.[1]
In this part of Norfolk, however, the Walpoles were out-

---

[1] 'Rotten' boroughs were towns which had once been important
enough to justify having two representatives in Parliament. By the
eighteenth century they had lost their importance, and most of their
population, but retained their M.P.s.

shone by the Townshends, whose great house at Rainham was close by—for the Townshends were peers, the Walpoles only squires. The two families were nevertheless very friendly and shared the same political views, and the patronage of Viscount Townshend was Walpole's main support in the early days of his political life.

Third in a family of nineteen, Robert was sent to Eton and then to King's College, Cambridge. On the death of his elder brother, however, his father recalled him from the university so that he might train him to take over the estate. The next year Colonel Robert found his son a wife, the daughter of a Baltic timber merchant, who brought with her a handsome dowry of £7,000—of which Colonel Robert retained two-thirds. A year later Colonel Robert was dead, and young Robert, aged twenty-four, had succeeded to all his property and responsibilities—including the seat in Parliament. *Father and son*

It was in 1701, in the closing months of the reign of William III, that Walpole came up to take his place in Westminster. From the start he showed himself to be, as Townshend became, a firm Whig. He soon made his mark in London society: pleasant in expression, if short and plump in body, he was a good companion who enjoyed his food and drink and was soon admitted to the most select of the Whig clubs, the Kit Kat. The main difficulty of these early years was money: he was always in debt, and in 1702 he had to make over his seat at Castle Rising to an uncle— but fortunately another uncle soon helped to bring him back as member for King's Lynn. If he could get office, however, the money difficulty would be solved. From a minor post in 1705 he progressed in 1708—after an election feast at which he stood his supporters some fifty gallons of port—to the important office of Secretary of War. But with the growing unpopularity of the War of the Spanish Succession Queen Anne gradually dismissed her Whig ministers, and Walpole was even thrown into the Tower by his opponents on a charge of bribery. By 1714 he was out of the Tower, had learnt much of politics, and had high hopes of royal favour in the new reign. *Robert Walpole's early career*

A Whig
Ministry,
1714

The king's choice of ministers was now keenly awaited. Would they be Whigs or a mixture of the two parties? In outlook the strongest point of difference between the two parties—which were only very loose groupings, not closely organized bodies—was that the Whigs really believed in the toleration granted in 1689 to Nonconformists, while the Tories still resented it. It was true that the Whigs had also made a special point of defending the Hanoverian succession, but most Tories too had welcomed George—it was only Bolingbroke and a few other extremists who had tried to secure the throne for James Edward Stuart, the son of James II.

Nevertheless, the king's choice fell almost entirely on the Whigs—including Townshend and Stanhope, a soldier turned politician, as the two Secretaries of State. Walpole was not forgotten: the king granted him the office of Pay-

Walpole,
Paymaster
General

master General of the Forces. This was a minor post, but most valuable, for its holder received the pay for all the Forces. While the money was in his account he normally invested it and took for himself any profits that might be made.

Walpole
attacks
Tories·
flight of
Bolingbroke

In the new Parliament of 1715 it was Walpole who led the attack on the Tories of the old Ministry. Threatened with impeachment, their leaders grew desperate, and Bolingbroke fled abroad to take service with the self-styled James III. They were planning an invasion in the south when the Earl of Mar, encouraged by Jacobite riots in several British towns, raised the standard of revolt for James in Scotland.

The '15

The rebellion of 1715—or 'the '15' as it is popularly called—was soon over. On the same day in November an Anglo-Scottish Jacobite force was completely routed at Preston, and at Sheriffmuir an indecisive engagement between Mar and government forces under Argyll ended, according to popular report, by both sides running away. James himself landed in Scotland at the end of the year, but seeing that the position was hopeless—for Mar's force was dwindling as rapidly as Argyll's was increasing—soon left with Mar for France. By April the rising had been totally suppressed both in England and Scotland, and George I was safe. For its complete failure the most important reasons were the incompetence of the Jacobite leaders, the vigour of the Whig government, the lack of support from France —Louis XIV died just before Mar took up arms—and the steadfast and honourable refusal of James to abandon his Roman Catholic religion.

Walpole's reward for the zeal with which he had denounced the Tories both before and after the rising was the office of First Lord of the Treasury and Chancellor of the Exchequer. He did not enjoy it long. With the Tories completely discredited after the '15 because they could be labelled Jacobites, the Whigs could afford to indulge in internal quarrels, and Lords Stanhope and Sunderland soon drove Townshend from the ministry. Walpole felt obliged to resign at the same time, but the two statesmen were not prepared to take their exclusion lying down. They decided to make thorough nuisances of themselves in the hope that the government would take them back, if only to keep them quiet. Walpole threw all his energy into a violent attack on the government's measures, making an exception only in favour of a scheme he had fathered when in office—a Bill to set up a sinking-fund for the reduction of the National Debt. The amount to which this debt had grown—£54 million—was then a great worry to all statesmen. Today it stands at £27,000 million—and people hardly feel any concern.

Walpole's speeches against the government were so powerful and persuasive that the results were soon seen in the divisions in the Commons. He even attacked—though unsuccessfully—the Septennial Act, which had been passed with his approval in 1716 during the Jacobite crisis to extend the maximum length of Parliament from three to seven years.[1] Eventually, to avoid further trouble, the government found it advisable to recall both Walpole and Townshend, though neither to major office.

Walpole's promotion—

—and resignation

Sinking Fund

The Septennial Act, 1716

Walpole returns to the ministry

---

[1] The Septennial Act remained in force until 1911, when the maximum length of Parliament was reduced to the present figure of five years.

In 1720 an unexpected crisis broke on the heads of the Ministry—a crisis from which Townshend and Walpole were to draw great advantage. The South Sea Company had been formed during Anne's reign by Robert Harley. It was mainly a finance company, though it had obtained a monopoly from the government for trade with South America and the Pacific Islands, and of the slave-trade with Spanish America. In 1720 the directors of the Company persuaded the government to agree to a grandiose scheme. In return for an extended monopoly over South Sea trade, the South Sea Company was to try to take over the whole of the National Debt. It was to do this by offering South Sea stock to investors in place of their Debt stock. On the Debt stock which it thus gathered, the Company agreed to accept from the government interest first at 5, then at 4 per cent, instead of the 7 or 8 per cent which the government had been paying to the Debt stock holders. The government thus stood to gain by greatly reduced annual payments of interest. For the Company to gain, it was essential that the price of their stock should be driven very high, so that people were willing to accept a very little South Sea stock in return for a great deal of Debt stock. To achieve this, rumours were spread of the great riches to be had from South Sea trading, the directors of the Company lent money to investors to purchase their stock, and all possible tricks were employed to set prices rising. In all this several ministers, including the Chancellor, were involved, and there was a good deal of bribery to get the whole scheme accepted and under way.

Unfortunately it succeeded too well. A mania for South Sea stock seized the British public, who thought they were on to an extremely good thing. In March 1720 the price of £100 of South Sea stock was £183; by June it had reached £1,050. Moreover, other stocks had risen in sympathy, and a vast wave of speculation was sweeping the country. In the prevailing atmosphere, many companies were floated with no sound economic basis—there was, for instance, a 'company to trade in hair', a 'company for settling the Tortugas', a 'company for wheels of perpetual motion', and even a 'company for a design which will hereafter be promulgated'. People were willing to buy shares in anything, and a crash was bound to come. During August, as 'mushroom' companies failed and people began to take a more hard-headed view of South Sea prospects, £100 of South Sea stock sold for £800. By the end of September it was worth no more than £300.

A few fortunate men—including Walpole—sold out in time. Thomas Guy made the magnificent profit of £180,000 from his dealings, and used it to found his hospital in London. But many faced utter financial ruin. There was an outburst of indignation all over the country and the government found itself under heavy fire. The chief ministers seemed helpless; Stanhope died of apoplexy, and another shot himself; and only Walpole seemed to have the energy and confidence to cope. By luck rather than good judgement he was one of the few members of the government not implicated in the South Sea scheme, and he came to the rescue both of his colleagues and of the Court—for George I and his ladies were also heavily involved. He produced a plan to sort out the affairs of the Company, managed to restore something like one-half of their previous income to those who had given up their Debt stock, and at the same time limited the criminal investigation to as few as possible. His opponents gave him the name of 'Screenmaster General'. By 1722, as a reward for his efforts, he was again First Lord of the Treasury, with his friend—and future brother-in-law—Townshend once more as Secretary of State. And it was now Walpole who was the leading partner.

Walpole sorts out the wreckage

Walpole chief Minister, 1722

2. *Walpole in Power (1722–42)*

Once firmly in power, Walpole succeeded in staying there till 1742. He was the leading minister and had more influence than many later Prime Ministers, although he did not hold that office—which did not exist at that time, and in fact has never officially been created but, like so many British institutions, has only 'grown up'. By his long period of rule Walpole pointed the way not only to this important

Growth of Prime Ministership and Cabinet

future development but also to another—that of the modern Cabinet.

Under the early Stuarts the day-to-day government of the country had been in the hands of the Privy Council. After the Restoration this body had become too large for efficiency, and a smaller committee of the Privy Council, known as the Cabinet Council—over which the monarch also presided—took most of the decisions. But from 1717 onwards, King George I, partly owing to his ignorance of English and partly owing to a deadly quarrel with his son Prince George, who had previously acted as interpreter, ceased to attend the meetings of the Cabinet Council. Thus the leading minister increased his power. Moreover, another development took place during Walpole's period of office. Once he had established himself he made it a practice to call together his closest friends in the ministry to discuss plans so that they could act in unison when the Cabinet Council—which included the Archbishop of Canterbury and the main officials of the royal household—met to take decisions. From these two changes springs the small Cabinet of today, with the Prime Minister and not the Monarch in charge. Walpole himself was all the more powerful in that George I, besides knowing little English, cared little for British affairs, and was only too anxious for his ministers to do all the work. He went off to Hanover whenever he could, and was most annoyed if summoned back—as he was over the South Sea Bubble.

Walpole dependent on royal favour

How did Walpole succeed in staying in power for so long? In the first place, because he managed to keep the king's favour. This gave him great power, for the king appointed bishops—who had a vote in the House of Lords—as well as judges and officers in the armed and civil services; as long as Walpole was the minister to whom the king listened, it was Walpole's men who got the jobs. So all those ambitious for public office, or the easy money that often went with it, were anxious to please him.

Walpole's control of Commons

This helped him in turn to keep control of the House of Commons. He did this partly, it is true, by the power of his speeches, which were delivered in a direct, rustic, 'no-

Walpole addressing the Regency Council, 1740
From a sketch by Joseph Goupy.

nonsense' style well calculated to appeal to the country squires on the benches. Moreover, he continued to sit in the Commons, because it was the more difficult House for the government to sway, when he might easily have accepted a peerage and sat in the Lords. Nevertheless, it was also by the use of this royal patronage, including its use to influence elections, that he kept his hold over the members. To see how, we must glance at the system of representation in the House of Commons, which had not been changed much since the Middle Ages and was quite unlike that of today.

Representation— counties and boroughs

In the first place, each county returned two members— except the Welsh and the Scottish,[1] which had only one. This accounted for 120 members. The other 430 came from the boroughs, which also sent two members each, except in Scotland and Wales, where they were combined in groups returning only one member.[2] These boroughs that returned members had been selected either because they were important in the past or because they could be easily influenced. The two fishing villages on either side of the Looe Estuary each returned two members; so too did those classic examples of 'rotten' boroughs Old Sarum (in Wiltshire), where there was now not a single house, and Dunwich (in Suffolk), most of which had disappeared under the sea. On the other hand, neither Manchester nor Leeds, already becoming towns of considerable size, had their own members.

The vote

In the counties all those could vote who owned freehold land of forty shillings annual value—a fair number. But in the boroughs possession of the vote was largely a matter of luck. At Gatton in Surrey all men had the right to vote, but at one time there were only six houses and one voter. At Bath there were only thirty-two electors. At Droitwich the vote was the privilege of those with a share in the local salt-mine. In very many boroughs the right to vote was confined to the Mayor and Corporation; and in a few so-called 'pocket' boroughs there were no electors at all

---

[1] Some Scottish counties were grouped and had to share a member.

[2] Edinburgh, however, had one member to itself.

except one—the 'owner', who appointed the Member of Parliament. In other boroughs the right to vote was exercised only by the holders of certain houses; and yet elsewhere it was extended to all those who had a hearth, and who were popularly known as 'potwallopers'.

Because the voting was done not by secret ballot but by open announcement on platforms known as 'hustings', the borough elections, and to a lesser extent the county elections, could often be controlled by the local landlords. Walpole had owed his original entry into politics to his family's local power in Norfolk, and he now made it his business to extend his tentacles wherever he could. It was for this reason that he persuaded the king to appoint the Duke of Newcastle as Secretary of State in 1724. Newcastle was timid, fussy and wavering, but he was the foremost election manager in England; he specialized in Sussex, Nottinghamshire, Yorkshire and Lincolnshire but had influence outside and was worth between sixteen and eighteen seats. Those who supported him in elections, Walpole repaid by granting them the offices and places that were at his disposal. It was an intricate system made possible by the comparatively few families in public life—one member in the eighteenth century discovered he had fifty relatives in Parliament!

This has often been described as a system of corruption, and so indeed it was. But as there was still nothing like a closely organized modern political party, politics had to be run in some other way. The eighteenth century system was a perfectly natural result of the contemporary respect for property, birth and influence. The great family in a district regarded it as a right that at least one of the two local parliamentary seats should be reserved for its representative, and other people usually accepted this fact. The seat, in other words, came to be considered almost as a piece of family property—which if not occupied by a member of the family could be temporarily leased to someone else. Similarly the right to vote, which depended in most places on a property qualification, was commonly regarded as a form of property, and the exercise of the vote as something for which an

Elections

Walpole extends his influence

Duke of Newcastle

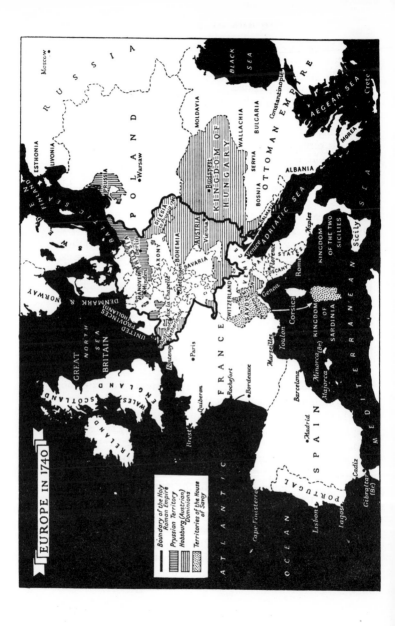

EUROPE IN 1740

Boundary of the Holy
Roman Empire

Prussian Territory

Habsburg (Austrian)
Dominions

Territories of the House
of Savoy

adequate return should be secured—if not a direct payment, then at least the continuing favour of one's landlord or employer or the government. All this did not mean that when the members got into Parliament they were necessarily more corrupt than members appointed under a more democratic system. In the absence of any strong party organization they voted mainly in accordance with their personal feelings, and usually most of them felt it to be both their interest and their duty to support the government. But when some great national issue or crisis arose, there were never lacking a large number of M.P.s whose attitude was decided from the principles of the matter rather than from considerations of self-interest.

So it was his great influence not only with the king but also with Parliament that enabled Walpole to remain in power for twenty years. It has often been said that he acted by the light of two maxims—'Every man has his price' and 'Let sleeping dogs lie'. The first gave him power, the second governed his policy once he got it. There is much truth in this. Walpole had a low opinion of human nature and his aims were not heroic. Coarse in language and gross in figure—he weighed over twenty stone—he was, as he himself said, 'no saint, no Spartan, no reformer'. His main objects were, in fact, severely practical: to preserve peace, encourage trade, keep taxes low, and otherwise maintain the existing state of affairs with the minimum trouble. He was, however, a first-class administrator, and his policy gave England something which she needed badly after all the alarms and strife of the previous century—a period of peace and stability at home. By the end of his life Jacobitism was nearly dead and the settled conditions in England gave great encouragement to commercial expansion at home and abroad. *Walpole's principles and aims*

Stability

Walpole's desire for peace is seen in his foreign policy. Britain's relations with the continental countries after 1714 are complicated and are made more difficult to understand by the connection between Britain and Hanover. In general, however, after the death of Louis XIV British policy was marked for some time by friendship towards France and *His peace policy* hostility towards Spain. Louis XV was still an infant, the French regent wanted as little trouble as possible, and the British wanted to keep 'James III' out of France. Hostility towards Spain was of course traditional, especially in matters of trade with America, and the Spaniards naturally wished to regain Gibraltar and Minorca. There was fighting between the two countries before Walpole came into power, and then again, owing to Townshend's impetuous direction of foreign policy, in 1726. Walpole disliked this policy and in 1729 he succeeded in concluding peace with Spain against Townshend's wishes.

English hostility to Spain

Walpole makes peace (1729) and quarrels with Townshend

This was a serious affront to his brother-in-law. Townshend was annoyed, too, at the way Walpole had now outstripped him in control of the ministry, and was stirred to jealousy by the magnificent new house that Walpole had constructed at Houghton, so eclipsing Rainham. So he resigned, and threw all his energies into farming—where he earned his immortal name of 'Turnip Townshend'. After this resignation Walpole was in an even stronger position than before. He kept England clear of continental entanglements and was able to declare proudly on one occasion after the outbreak of the War of the Polish Succession in 1733: 'Fifty thousand men killed this year in Europe, and not one of them an Englishman.'

England neutral in War of Polish Succession

A threat to Walpole's power—the accession of George II, 1727

During all these years, from 1722 to 1733, Walpole's position was only twice seriously threatened. The first occasion was on the death of George I in 1727, when everyone assumed that Walpole's career was ruined—for George II detested his father and his father's ministers. The quarrel was of old standing, the final break having come when George I forced young George to appoint the Duke of Newcastle as godfather to his eldest son. The prince did this with an ill grace and at the christening deliberately stamped on the goutiest of Newcastle's toes. The fussy Duke, mishearing the prince's accompanying remark, imagined himself challenged to a duel and complained to the king— whereupon the infuriated monarch clapped the prince under house arrest and then banished him from the Court. After that, all the discontented politicians flocked around

Leicester House, the new residence of the heir to the throne, waiting for George I to die.

Now their hopes were fulfilled and at first everything went according to plan. When the news of George I's death arrived from Hanover, Sir Robert Walpole went straight to inform the prince. The prince, a soldierly, pompous, precise, energetic and conscientious little man of thirty-one, was in bed. The only answer he gave to Walpole's enquiries about the measures to be taken was, 'Go to Chiswick and take your directions from Sir Spencer Compton.' But Compton was a man of extraordinary incompetence whose only pleasures were money and eating. He failed hopelessly even in his first task of preparing a speech for the king, and it soon became clear that rejoicing over Walpole's fall was premature. Moreover, Sir Robert had an invaluable ally in George II's Queen Caroline, whose considerable intelligence, allied to striking features, a well-made figure, fair hair and clear pink skin, made her a far more attractive and impressive personality than her husband. Finally Walpole tipped the scales in his favour by offering to raise the annual grant given by Parliament to the king for his household expenses. The move was decisive, and his opponents retired defeated.[1] *Queen Caroline— an ally of Walpole*

Walpole survives

On the other occasion on which Walpole ran into serious trouble it was the support of Parliament, and not of the king, that Walpole lost. Finance was his speciality, and the trouble arose over the Excise Bill he introduced in 1733. Excise was a tax levied on goods wherever they were sold, while Customs were levied only at the ports. Soon after he came to power, Walpole had experimented with this tax; he had introduced it for tea, coffee and chocolate, in addition to the Customs duty; and he had also set up bonded warehouses where merchants could store these goods and *Another threat— Parliamentary opposition to Excise Bill, 1733*

[1] The relationship between George II and Queen Caroline was amusingly expressed in a popular ballad of the time:

'You may strut, dapper George, but 'twill all be in vain:
We know 'tis Queen Caroline, not you, that reign—
You govern no more than Don Philip of Spain.
Then if you would have us fall down and adore you,
Lock up your fat spouse, as your dad did afore you.'

B*

then re-export them without paying any duty. This had proved an efficient method of collecting tax and the aim of the Excise Bill of 1733 was to extend the system to tobacco; wine was to follow. In this way Walpole could obtain a necessary increase in revenue without resorting to methods that he disliked, such as increasing the land tax or raiding the sinking-fund.

Unfortunately for Walpole, Excise was an extremely unpopular tax, mainly because it was difficult to evade. The only taxes in the eighteenth century that worked properly were those, like the land or window tax, which could not be escaped. As for the ordinary Customs duties, cheating these was a national industry at the time. It has been estimated that half the brandy and two-thirds of the tea 18th-century which entered the country were smuggled and that 40,000 smuggling people were engaged in the occupation. They were much better organized than their rivals the coastguards, and they carried out their operations under cover of darkness. An estuary or cove was chosen; as soon as the ship anchored, boats rowed out; the contraband was landed and loaded on horses; and by morning it was miles out of reach of the few coastguards of the district.

By Excise and bonded warehouses Walpole would have done much to check frauds on the revenue. It was a good scheme but, as the Exciseman was so very unpopular in the country, Walpole's enemies saw in it an excellent opportunity to discredit him. Discontented Whigs banded together with the Tories under the leadership of Bolingbroke, now returned from exile, and accused Walpole of tyranny. They said that no one would be safe from the Excise officials, who were armed and had wide powers of search: the Bill would destroy the great English tradition that every man's home is his castle. The agitation was Walpole extravagant, but it was successful. Walpole withdrew the withdraws Excise Bill Bill, raided the sinking-fund with increasing frequency, and gave up any idea of reforming the finances.

The An incident in connection with smuggling also caused Porteous Riots Walpole trouble in Scotland. In 1736 two Scottish smugglers were sentenced to death at Edinburgh. One escaped, but the other was executed, and the citizens showed their sympathy for the victim by hurling abuse and stones at the City Guard, who had been turned out to prevent interference. Its commander, Captain Porteous, annoyed at the insults, thereupon ordered the guard to fire at the crowd, with the result that several were killed. This led to the arrest of Porteous, his trial for murder, and condemnation to death. Then there arrived a reprieve from England. It did not, however, save Porteous, for a mob, sprung from nowhere, marched by night to the Tolbooth prison where Porteous was confined, burnt down the gates and dragged him out. By the light of flaming torches they put a noose round his neck and hanged him in his nightgown and cap on a dyer's pole. Those responsible were never traced and the government tried to bring in a Bill inflicting extremely severe punishments on Edinburgh—including cancellation of its charter, the disbanding of the City Guard, and the imprisonment of the Provost. Against this, Scottish opinion united successfully, and in the end the city was no more than fined. Over the whole incident Walpole suffered bitter criticism in Scotland and permanently lost the support of several Scottish M.P.s.

About this time Walpole also greatly offended various quarters in England by an effort to limit the widespread drinking of gin. The mania for gin was the most serious social problem of his time, and by 1743 the country was consuming over eight million gallons of gin and other British-produced spirits each year. Scenes of utter squalor such as those recorded in Hogarth's print 'Gin Lane' were all too common, especially in London. Here there were at least 6,000 shops that sold it, and in one London parish one house in every five was engaged in the trade. 'Drunk for 1d., dead drunk for 2d., straw for nothing', was a notice everywhere displayed. Parliament had earlier encouraged the manufacture of gin, for it used up the surplus corn in years of plenty, but in 1736 Walpole's government passed an Act which put a duty on spirits and forced retailers to buy a £50 licence. Riots promptly broke out. The Act could not be enforced, and only three licences were ever bought.

Walpole and gin-drinking

In fact, the rate of spirit-drinking increased, and it was not till nearly ten years after Walpole's fall that an effective measure was passed against it.

Attacks by writers   To attacks on Walpole by smugglers and gin-drinkers there were also added attacks by writers. Bolingbroke, who had forsworn the Pretender and had been allowed to return to England, founded a periodical, *The Craftsman*, the main object of which was to criticize and abuse Walpole. Dramatists, too, especially Henry Fielding, joined in the hunt, and John Gay's *The Beggar's Opera*, the greatest theatrical success of its day, depicted among other characters two quarrelling rogues, Peacham and Lockit, whom spectators immediately recognized as Walpole and Townshend. Finally, Fielding's attacks on the king and the ministry resulted in Walpole's passing the Licensing Act of 1737, which limited the presentation of plays to two theatres in London and made it illegal to present any play before the general public without previous licence from the Lord Chamberlain.

The Beggar's Opera

Fielding

Licensing Act, 1737

Walpole's influence, already shaken by criticism, suffered a further blow with the death of Queen Caroline in 1737. In particular his foreign policy came under heavy fire. Many—including a young group in the Commons who called themselves the 'Patriots', and were nicknamed by Walpole the 'Boys'—disliked his peaceful attitude towards Spain and wanted stronger measures taken against her. They complained that George and Walpole thought only of keeping Hanover safe from attack in Germany, when they should have been thinking of building up the Navy and capturing trade from Spain. Such a policy would mean incurring French hostility as well, for since 1733 France had been allied to Spain by an agreement known as the 'Family Compact', both kings being Bourbons; but this did not deter the critics. A special grievance against Spain at this time was that the Spanish authorities were trying to stop the important illegal trade which had sprung up between British ships and Spanish America, for the Spaniards considered that all trade with their colonies in America should be their own preserve. Their cutters intercepted and

Renewed English hostility to Spain

The 'Family Compact'

Gin Lane

From the famous satirical engraving by Hogarth. Above the arch in the bottom left corner runs the advertisement: 'Drunk for a penny, dead drunk for twopence, clean straw for nothing'. In the whole scene of death, violence, drunkenness and disease, only one person flourishes—the pawnbroker, to whom a carpenter is pledging his tools and best coat. In a contrasting print Hogarth depicted the happiness and prosperity of 'Beer Street'.

searched British ships and many were the stories told of Spanish arrogance and cruelty on these occasions.

In 1738 feeling in Britain grew more bitter. Much was heard of the story of Captain Jenkins, who claimed that as long ago as 1731 he had had his ear cut off by the Spaniards when they had boarded a ship of which he was the master. Gradually the demand for war with Spain became so vigorous, especially among sailors and merchants, that it could not be resisted. Newcastle and other members of the Cabinet had long pressed for it, and finally in 1739 Walpole gave way and war was declared on Spain. To Newcastle he remarked: 'It is your war and I wish you joy of it.' Of the general public he said: 'They are ringing their bells now: they will soon be wringing their hands.'

All the same, Walpole stayed on in the ministry, so loath was he to lose power. But the Fleet was in poor condition, there was no clear plan of campaign, and the war brought Britain little advantage. It soon became merged in a greater conflict, whose origin and course will be described in the next chapter. Meanwhile the lack of success further discredited the ageing Walpole, and in 1742 he resigned his office and took a peerage, becoming the Earl of Orford. He died three years later—£40,000 in debt. In private life he had always spent lavishly. He had transformed Houghton into one of the most imposing houses in England, built a hunting lodge at Richmond, kept two packs of hounds, made a great collection of paintings, and regularly spent something like £1,000 a year on wine. However important a position he had held in public affairs, and however great his tasks in striving to foster peace and prosperity over twenty years, he had never turned his back on his early life as a squire. He munched his red Norfolk apples in Parliament, and it was the letters from his huntsman in Norfolk that he opened first.

The War of
Jenkins's
Ear, 1739

Little
success

Walpole
resigns,
1742

CHAPTER THREE

THE ELDER PITT AND THE STRUGGLE FOR EMPIRE

1. *Pitt, Britain, and Europe*

ONE of the 'Patriot Boys' in the Commons who had distinguished himself by the power and energy of his attacks on Walpole was William Pitt. He was the grandson of Thomas Pitt, a merchant and buccaneer who had made a fortune in India, by first defying, then serving, the East India Company. *Thomas Pitt*

William Pitt inherited all his grandfather's restless energy and independence. Tall, he stood erect and was famed for his courtly manners. He had a thin face with a long nose and hawklike eyes, so fierce that when he was angry or speaking in earnest few men could look him in the face. Unlike Walpole, he had no skill in handling other politicians, for he was cold, haughty and aloof. But—also unlike Walpole—he had a daring and ambitious policy for Britain. He foresaw a great destiny and untold wealth for his country if only she would concentrate on her true interest—the trade of Africa, Asia and America. He saw, too, that only by force could this be won and successfully maintained against such rivals as France and Spain. *William Pitt* *Colonial trade*

'I know that I can save this country and that I alone can', Pitt was to declare. These are the words of a genius or a madman. Perhaps the two are often not very far apart. Certainly this was so in Pitt's case, for there was a black side to his temperament. After periods of excitement there were times when utter despair took hold of his mind. The number of these fits increased in his later years and the depression became insanity. During his long illness in 1767 he would sometimes sit for days in his little room in the top storey of his Hampstead house, resting his head on the *Genius— —and madman* table. He could not bear anyone to be with him, not even his wife, to whom he was devoted. Meals were left at a hatch outside the room and he collected them after the servant had gone. Yet to this man more than to any other

William Pitt, 1st Earl of Chatham

A portrait from the studio of William Hoare. Note the dominating 'Pitt nose'.

we owe the building up of a great British Empire. He was a giant who dwarfed the other politicians of his day.

After being educated at Eton—which he loathed—and at Oxford—where he considered going into the Church— Pitt had entered Parliament in 1735 for the family borough of Old Sarum. His views made him hostile to Walpole and in 1739 he launched a bitter attack on an agreement that Walpole had made with Spain. In no uncertain tones he called for war. 'When trade is at stake . . . you must defend it or perish', he declared. He got his way—but even after the fall of Walpole he received no office in the government. *Pitt attacks Walpole*

By this time, in addition to fighting Spain, Britain had become involved in a big continental war for which Pitt had no use. This struggle, known as the War of the Austrian Succession, had broken out in 1740. At this time there were two major continental powers in Europe—France and Austria (whose Habsburg ruler also held sway over most of Hungary, Bohemia, the southern Netherlands and northern Italy). This ruler was also normally the Emperor of the Holy Roman Empire, the ancient and powerless organization which was the only bond of union between the hundreds of small German States. The latest occupant of this position, the Emperor Charles VI, had died in 1740. He had no son, but before his death he had persuaded the monarchs of Europe, despite the general law in central and western Europe barring women from the throne, to recognize his daughter Maria Theresa as his successor in all his hereditary dominions. She could not, of course, become the head of the Holy Roman Empire, but Charles hoped that for this position the Electors would choose her husband. *War of Austrian Succession, 1740-48*

In the event Charles's precautions availed nothing, for no sooner was he dead then Frederick the Great, King of Prussia—by this time among the most powerful of the many German states—coolly seized the Austrian province of Silesia. Soon most of Europe was at war, for the other vultures gathered round and a coalition under France was formed to divide up the territories of Maria Theresa. Britain was dragged into the conflict on the Austrian side because George II as Elector of Hanover could not look without concern at the growth of Hanover's neighbour Prussia. Moreover, George had promised to uphold the succession of Maria Theresa, and not only Hanover's but also Britain's interests demanded in the long run opposition to any great increase in French power. *Prussia seizes Silesia, 1740* *Britain supports Austria*

The war
against
Spain
('Jenkins's
Ear')
Meanwhile the war with Spain had brought little comfort to Britain. Various strokes in the West Indies had failed completely, and apart from the capture of Porto Bello in the Panama Isthmus the only expedition to encounter considerable success was that of Commodore Anson, who was sent out to the Pacific to attack Spanish trading and treasure ships. His orders were to sail westwards to Manila, and then proceed home by completing the journey round the world. He had a highly adventurous voyage. His little squadron was scattered by terrible storms while rounding Cape Horn, and only three vessels reached the agreed place for linking up again—an uninhabited island off the coast of Chile. By this time about half his men were dead and most of the remainder so sick with scurvy that they had to be carried ashore. Nevertheless, after refitting, he captured a town on the coast of Peru and a treasure ship, and then proceeded to cross the Pacific. He reached Macao, in China, and then cruised in the Philippines, where he secured another great prize, the annual Manila galleon stuffed with pieces of eight and pure silver. After this he put back to Macao, where his 'red haired barbarians', as the Chinese called the English, caused some concern, and thence returned home by way of the East Indies and the Cape of Good Hope. Only his own ship, the *Centurion*, completed the voyage, which had lasted nearly four years. It brought back treasure valued at over £600,000.

Anson's
voyage,
1740–44

In general, the ministers—of whom the most prominent by 1744 were Henry Pelham and his brother Thomas Pelham, Duke of Newcastle—were now giving less and less thought to the Spanish war and more and more to the struggle on the Continent. They poured out money in subsidies to Austria and to any German prince who would fight France and her allies. English troops, too, were engaged on the Continent, and there were several English regiments in the army which George II—the last British monarch to command a force in the field—led to victory against the French at Dettingen. At this time Britain and France were still officially at peace, but they declared war the next year, 1744.

British
subsidies
to Allies

Dettingen,
1743

The Ministry's conduct of the war was by no means to the liking of Pitt. He considered that Britain was pouring out her resources in a way that could bring her no benefit. 'Neither justice nor policy', he declared, 'required us to be engaged in the quarrels of the Continent. . . . It is now too apparent that this great, this powerful, this formidable Kingdom is considered only as a province of a despicable Electorate.' Instead, Pitt wanted France to be fought like Spain, at sea and in the colonies. He was all for Britain's capturing France's trade and leaving the Continent to its own squabbles. For long, however, the government paid no heed to him—least of all the king, who not only owned the 'despicable Electorate' but also much preferred it to England. *Pitt's policy*

A crisis in 1745 at last brought some recognition to Pitt. British troops were fully engaged on the Continent, and had just suffered a defeat—though no loss of glory—at Fontenoy, in the Austrian Netherlands, when Charles Edward Stuart, son of the Pretender, landed at Moidart in western Scotland. He arrived with only seven men, yet such was the attraction of his handsome figure, his adventurous spirit and his gracious demeanour that he won the hearts of the Highlanders and within a few weeks was in control of the Highland area. His cause made no appeal at all to the Presbyterian majority of the Lowlands, and more Scotsmen enlisted against him than for him. However, he was helped by the incompetence of the government general, Sir John Cope, who failed to make full use of the roads and forts which General Wade had been building in the Highlands in the preceding twenty years. Charles Edward—'Bonnie Prince Charlie'—finally defeated Cope in five minutes at Prestonpans, near Edinburgh, and now the Lowlands too were his. *The '45* *Charles Edward* *Prestonpans*

Thinking that only extreme boldness could succeed, the 'Young Pretender' then decided to march on London. He reached Derby on December 4th, and London was in panic on Black Friday, December 6th, when the news reached the capital—which was protected only by a camp at Finchley. At Derby, however, Charles's advisers forced him to turn back. German, Dutch and English troops hastily *Retreat from Derby* brought from the Continent were gathering to attack, and apart from 300 recruits in Manchester practically no English had rallied to Charles Edward's standard. Nevertheless, he managed to defeat the government forces again at Falkirk. But a few months later saw the end. On Culloden Moor the Duke of Cumberland—George II's younger son —utterly defeated the remains of Charles's army, and then proceeded to take a terrible revenge on the homes and persons of the rebels. Charles himself finally won his way back to France after wanderings and hair-breadth escapes which have become part of Scottish legend.

Culloden. 1746

The results of the '45 were twofold. In the first place the rising showed that Jacobitism was dead except in the Highlands, but that trouble could be expected as long as the Highlanders retained their ancient ways. So the government decided to go to the root of the matter and break up the clan system. The wearing of the kilt or tartan was forbidden, and the clan chiefs were stripped of their right to hold courts and demand military service. Schools were set up and more roads built, and within a few years most parts of the Highlands had adopted the more civilized life of the Lowlands.

Results of the '45

In the second place the crisis gave a severe jolt to the Government. The Pelhams began to feel that they needed more strength, and that Pitt alone could provide it—for he enjoyed great popular support, especially among the merchants of London. By threatening to resign, together with all their principal colleagues, the Pelhams therefore forced George to accept Pitt as a minister, though the best office they could get for him was Paymaster General. This could well have destroyed Pitt's fame in the country as a patriot; but he declared that he would take no profit from the public funds assigned to his care, placed them in the Bank of England instead of in a private account, and kept his great reputation unblemished.

Pitt, Paymaster General

In his new position Pitt at once displayed his characteristic energy. He pressed the Pelhams for a bolder war policy, and especially for an attack on the French colony of Canada, but they would not listen. The war dragged on,

and eventually a peace treaty was signed in 1748 at Aix- Treaty of Aix-la-Chapelle, 1748
la-Chapelle. By this all territory was restored to those who
had held it in 1740 except for Silesia—which Frederick of
Prussia managed to keep. As far as Britain and France were
concerned, the treaty was more a truce than a peace and
overseas it was quickly broken.

Even when Henry Pelham died in 1754 Pitt was offered
no higher office. Thwarted, he openly opposed some features
of the policy of the Duke of Newcastle, who was now the
main figure in the ministry. Newcastle promptly retaliated Newcastle dismisses Pitt
by having him dismissed. His career seemed ruined, but
like Sir Winston Churchill nearly 200 years later he was
rescued from hostility and neglect by his country's mis-
fortunes. In 1756, after preliminary hostilities in several
places, the Seven Years War broke out. Earlier in the year
Prussia and Britain had come to an agreement for mutual
support in protection of their territories, after which the
old rivals France and Austria had allied and secured the
support of Russia. Following this reshuffle of the alliances—
a change so dramatic that it has often been called 'the The 'Diploma-tic Revolu-tion'
Diplomatic Revolution'—a European war soon developed
in which Britain and Prussia were ranged against France, Seven Years War, 1756–63
Austria and Russia. But a series of disasters for Britain,
including the loss of Minorca to the French, rapidly
plunged the government into extreme unpopularity, until
Newcastle resigned and George II was forced by public Disasters: Newcastle resigns, 1756
opinion to call in Pitt. Even so, Pitt's first ministry was a
failure, because he could not command sufficient support in Pitt in charge—
the Commons. So in 1757 he allied with Newcastle. —forced to ally with Newcastle, 1757
Although so dissimilar, the two made an extremely success-
ful partnership. Newcastle managed Parliament; Pitt
managed the war.

At last in real power, Pitt seized his opportunity with
both hands. Though he remained in office for less than five
years, in that time he transformed the history of Britain.
His policy had three main objects: to secure British Pitt's war aims
supremacy at sea, to seize France's overseas trade and
possessions, and to keep Frederick in the field—for Pitt
had a great admiration for the clever and unscrupulous

Prussian king and knew that he had the only army in Europe capable of beating the French. Pitt succeeded brilliantly in all three aims. With regard to the third, despite his earlier criticism of continental entanglements he gave large subsidies to Frederick, who repaid support by managing to resist three countries each with an army larger than his own. With regard to the second aim, the capture of Dakar and Senegal from the French in 1758 won for Britain a valuable African trade in gum and slaves; and still greater triumphs, as we shall see, rewarded British arms in America and India.

Command of the seas

But it was on the success of his first aim, that of driving the French navy from the seas, that the whole of Pitt's policy depended. To this end, British squadrons blockaded the main French fleets in Brest, Toulon and Rochefort. This was an extremely tough job, especially in winter and heavy weather, for the ships tossed like corks and there were neither comforts nor even decent food. In fact Admiral Hawke, who in 1759 was blockading the large French squadron in Brest, was moved to write to the authorities at Plymouth: 'The beer brewed in your port is so excessively bad that it employs the whole time of the squadron in surveying it and throwing it overboard. . . . A quantity of bread will be returned to you, though not altogether unfit for use, yet so full of weevils and maggots that it would have infested all the bread come on board this day.'

Yet on men condemned to these conditions, and for the most part still recruited by the Press Gang, depended the whole safety of the country. For the French intended to invade England, and were striving to link up their blockaded fleets. Their scheme was checked at every stage. The Toulon fleet managed to emerge, only for Admiral Boscawen to

Lagos, 1759

catch and defeat it off Lagos. Then came the turn of the Brest fleet, which slipped out while Hawke was sheltering from a gale. He was soon in hot pursuit, and at 2.30 on a stormy November afternoon action was joined. The French

Quiberon Bay, 1759

turned for refuge amidst the shoals of Quiberon Bay, but though in perilous waters Hawke pressed on, saying to his protesting pilot: 'You have done right in warning me of the danger. Now lay me alongside the enemy.' At four o'clock, in the gathering gloom, three of the French ships struck their colours. The gale continued, blowing fiercely from the west, and during the night five more of the French ships were lost among the breakers, besides others disabled. When day dawned, the Brest squadron was shattered, and for the rest of the war there was no serious challenge to the British fleet. *British naval supremacy*

2. *India and North America*

From the days of Alexander the Great to the sixteenth century, there was very little direct contact between Europe and India. It was after the great voyage of Vasco da Gama in 1497–8 that the Portuguese began to establish missionary and trading posts. The Dutch, British and French were not slow to follow, and all three nations gradually acquired trading settlements, mostly on lease from Indian rulers. By the early eighteenth century the various struggles in Europe had resulted in France and Britain becoming much more important powers than Holland or Portugal, and the French and British were accordingly the two chief competitors for the Indian trade. So far as Britain was concerned, all trading rights were in the hands of the East India Company, whose main settlements or 'factories' were at Surat and Bombay in the north-west, Madras in the south-east and Calcutta in the north-east. The biggest French settlements were at Pondicherry in the south-east and Chandernagore near Calcutta. *The Portuguese in India* *British settlements*

For most of the first half of the eighteenth century, life pursued its normal course in the European settlements. The greatest enemy was disease, and in one year 460 of the 1,200 English in Calcutta were buried within six months. Then the situation changed, and the English began to think not so much of the threat from cholera as the threat from the French. One reason for this was the renewed Anglo-French fighting in Europe, but even more important was the lack of central government in India. Aurungzeb, the last great *Danger from French*

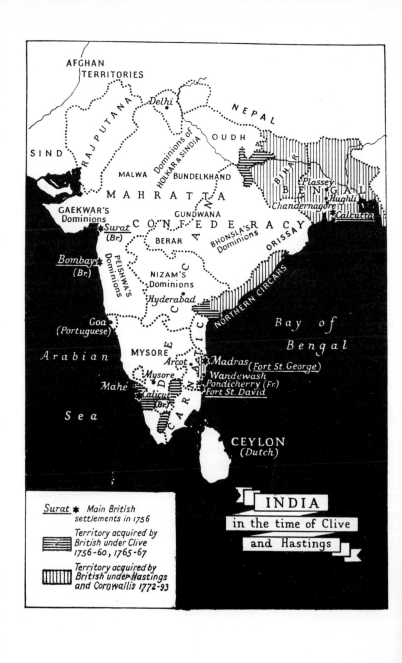

AFGHAN
TERRITORIES

Delhi

NEPAL

RAJPUTANA

OUDH

SIND

Dominions of
HOLKAR & SINDIA

MALWA

BUNDELKHAND

BIHAR

BENGAL

Plassey

MAHRATTA

GUNDWANA

Hughli

Chandernagore

GAEKWAR'S
Dominions

Surat
(Br.)

CONFEDERACY

Calcutta

BERAR

BHONSLA'S
Dominions

ORISSAY

Bombay
(Br.)

PEISHWA'S Dominions

NIZAM'S
Dominions

NORTHERN CIRCARS

Goa
(Portuguese)

Hyderabad

Bay of
Bengal

Arabian

MYSORE

CARNATIC

Arcot

Madras (Fort St. George)

Mahé

Mysore

Wandewash
Pondicherry (Fr.)
Fort St. David

Calicut
(Br.)

CARNATIC

Sea

CEYLON
(Dutch)

INDIA

in the time of Clive

and Hastings

Surat ★ Main British
settlements in 1756

Territory acquired by
British under Clive
1756-60, 1765-67

Territory acquired by
British under Hastings
and Cornwallis 1772-93

figure among the Mogul Emperors (a Muslim dynasty which had ruled most of India for two centuries) died in 1707, and under his powerless heirs and successors the central government collapsed utterly. Uncontrolled from Delhi, and beset by foreign invaders from Persia and Afghanistan or the marauding Mahratta chieftains from the western uplands of India, each local Indian governor began to set himself up as an independent power, and to enlarge or defend his territory as best he could. It was Dupleix, the governor of Pondicherry, who now saw the possibilities of exploiting this situation in the interests of France. *Weakness of Indian central government* *Dupleix*

After the news of the Anglo-French fighting in the War of the Austrian Succession reached India, a French expedition from Mauritius captured the East India Company's settlement at Madras. Dupleix at once stepped in and assumed control, but he was forced to return the town to the English at the peace. However, he was now set on securing French predominance throughout southern India. His chosen means was to put the disunity of the Indians to good use by interfering in their quarrels. By 1751 he had successfully interfered in two disputed successions, and placed his favoured claimants on the thrones of the Deccan and its subordinate territory the Carnatic—two of the largest states in the south. The influence of Dupleix was now immense, and of course threatened ruin to the British, who might soon find themselves excluded from southern India.

It was left to Robert Clive, a twenty-five-year-old officer of the East India Company who had recently abandoned the ledger for the sword, to revive the flagging British fortunes. Only one town in the Carnatic was still held by the candidate recognized by the British, and this was on the point of falling. To create a diversion, Clive set out from Madras with a force of 200 Europeans and 300 sepoys— European-trained Indian troops—and marched on Arcot, the capital of the Carnatic. The garrison panicked, and he entered the fort without striking a blow—only to be promptly besieged by the forces of the Nawab and his *Clive at Arcot, 1751*

French allies. Nevertheless, Captain Clive and his little band, a few hundred men against 10,000, held out for fifty days and repulsed all attacks. In the end the besiegers drew off. From this time onwards Clive and his superior commander were able gradually to extend operations until Dupleix's Nawab was killed and the 'British' claimant *British control Carnatic* ruled over the Carnatic. All the efforts of Dupleix failed to turn the tide, and within two years he was recalled to France in disgrace.

After a spell at home, Clive, now wealthy and famous, returned to India in 1755 as Governor of Fort St. David, near Pondicherry. He had not long been there when danger *Bengal* came from an unexpected direction—Bengal. The British in Calcutta had then far less experience of the fighting to which those in Madras had become accustomed; but now a new and tyrannous Nawab of Bengal quarrelled with them and seized Calcutta. Those of the settlers unfortunate *The 'Black Hole of Calcutta'* enough to be captured, 146 in all, were shut up for the night in a twenty-foot square garrison prison—from which twenty-three emerged alive in the morning.

When news of this deed and the fall of Calcutta reached Madras, the Council there was in a difficulty, for war in Europe was known to be again imminent and they feared the arrival of a French expedition. Nevertheless, within forty-eight hours they had decided to take the bold course and send Clive north. After a long and difficult voyage by *Clive retakes Calcutta* sea he invaded Bengal, retook Calcutta, and drove out the French from the neighbouring settlement of Chandernagore —for by this time war was declared in Europe. Before long, matters came to a head with the Nawab. Clive bribed the Nawab's commander-in-chief with the offer of the throne, *Plassey, 1757* and then set out to face his enemy. At Plassey, inland from Calcutta, Clive's force of 1,000 British and 2,000 sepoys attacked the levies of the Nawab, 55,000 strong. Within two hours, and for the loss of twenty-two lives among the victors, the whole vast host was scattered and vanquished. *British control Bengal* Bengal lay at Clive's mercy. Before long the Nawab was dead and Clive's nominee ruled in his place.

All this was much more the work of Clive and the men

on the spot in India than the achievement of the home government. Nevertheless, Pitt's despatch of reinforcements to the small naval squadron in Indian waters proved invaluable, and helped to turn the scale against the French fleet which at last arrived to reinforce Pondicherry in 1758. After this the British forces in the south, under Colonel Eyre Coote, also reinforced by Pitt, were able to meet and beat the French at Wandewash. It was a decisive battle Wandewash, because all the European troops in the south on both sides 1760 were engaged, and it led soon afterwards to the fall of Pondicherry, the last major French stronghold. From that Capture of time onwards, though the French were to recover their Pondicherry settlements purely as trading posts, they were not allowed to fortify them, and were never again able to contest the supremacy of their British rivals—a supremacy which now stretched along the whole east coast from the Carnatic to Bengal, and far inland as well.

*   *   *   *   *

In 1740 it seemed as if the bulk of North America might The French fall into the hands of the French. Though settled only at in North America comparatively few points, they claimed the whole vast area from the Alleghanies to the Rockies, and from Hudson's Bay (which was British) to the Gulf of Mexico. In fact, however, their actual power rested on two great rivers, the St. Lawrence and the Mississippi.

The centre of French rule was the colony around the St. Canada Lawrence, known as Canada. It included their two main towns, Quebec and Montreal. These and the mouth of the St. Lawrence were guarded by the French fortress of Louis- Louisburg burg on Cape Breton Island—which was taken by the British colonists during the War of the Austrian Succession but returned at the peace. Thousands of miles away far down in the south at the mouth of the Mississippi lay the other main French colony, based on the settlement of New Orleans. Connecting these two widely separated colonies New Orleans was a trading route used by canoes—up the Mississippi and the Ohio, overland to the Great Lakes (the canoes were carried), and then down the St. Lawrence. This trail, guarded by a few scattered French forts, lay right across the path of any British expansion into the interior from the east coast. Moreover, its advance posts, by Lake Champlain, seemed to point the way to an eastward movement which would carry the French to the sea and split the British colonies in twain.

The French in North America were soldiers, explorers, missionaries, hunters and traders, often on good terms with the Red Indians. They were adventurous and energetic but *The British in North America* very few in number. By contrast, most of the British colonists on the east coast were farmers, and they were settled much more densely—in fact they outnumbered the French by some fifteen to one. They were, however, completely dis- *Thirteen coastal colonies* united. The thirteen separate colonies, including the newly founded Georgia in the extreme south, had thirteen separate governors and thirteen separate assemblies, all of whom were liable to quarrel with each other. There were, more-over, very real differences between the colonies. In the north, New England was Puritan and democratic; in the south, Virginia and the Carolinas were Anglican and aristocratic; in between, New York still had a substantial Dutch population and Pennsylvania was full of Germans and Quakers.

French resist British move westwards By the early 1750s the British colonists were beginning to push westwards across the Alleghanies into the Ohio valley. Determined to keep the mountain line as a barrier to British expansion, the French sent military forces and drove them out. For a time only the Virginians showed any enterprise in trying to break the ring, but even so Colonel George Washington, the able young Virginian *Fort Duquesne* commander, was unable to take Fort Duquesne, the French strongpoint newly built in a commanding position on the Ohio.

Braddock's expedition, 1755 Next year the British made a more determined effort. General Braddock and regular troops had arrived from England. Braddock was a brave soldier, but unfortunately he believed that battles should be fought according to established rules. He might have been successful in Europe, where the rules were known, but he failed disastrously in the forests of America—where they were not. Braddock was marching through the forest seven miles from Fort Duquesne when he was attacked by the French and their Indian allies. The English formed line and fired several volleys with great precision but without much effect, since the French and Indians were sheltering behind trees. Soon a murderous fire was spread on the British from every quarter. The unfortunate soldiers did not know what to do. They could not see the enemy; they could only hear the blood-curdling whoops of the Indians. When some of the British tried to take cover and snipe from behind trees, Braddock in a fury pulled them back into the line. Soon the day was lost, Braddock had died of his wounds, and the French and the Indian war-bands were free to raid far and wide into the British colonies.

At this stage the outbreak of the Seven Years War in Europe brought the certainty of hostilities on a much larger scale. It was not till Pitt attained power that the British achieved any success; but when success came, it came in full measure. By the end of 1758 he had accomplished two of his objects. Louisburg, sentinel over the mouth of the St. Lawrence, had fallen to a combined military and naval expedition under General Amherst and Admiral Boscawen; and a force of colonists and Highland regiments, pushing through the Alleghanies, had taken Fort Duquesne, sentinel over the Ohio valley.[1] Only a third movement, a thrust up the Hudson from New York against Fort Ticonderoga (on Lake Champlain) and Montreal, had as yet shown little profit. *Outbreak of Seven Years War* *Capture of Louisburg and Fort Duquesne, 1758*

The next year proved decisive. With Louisburg fallen, Pitt could aim a direct attack at Quebec up the St. Lawrence, while other movements converged overland on Montreal. Despite strong opposition he gave the military command of the Quebec expedition to James Wolfe, an officer of only thirty-two, who had distinguished himself in the fight for Louisburg. Admiral Saunders was in charge of the naval side. In the summer of 1759 the fleet and *Wolfe*

[1] Fort Duquesne was renamed Fort Pitt, and has now become Pittsburgh.

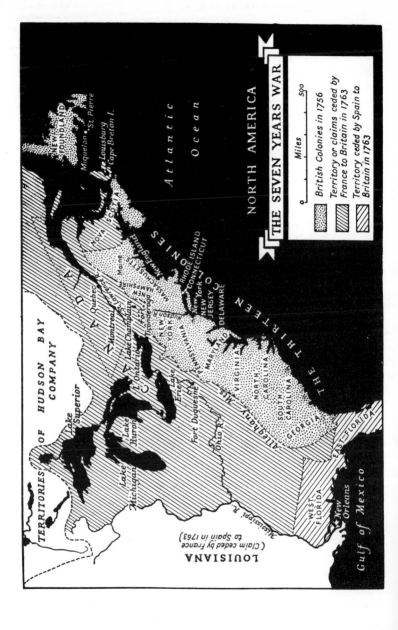

THE SEVEN YEARS WAR

NORTH AMERICA

Miles
0   500

British Colonies in 1756

Territory or claims ceded by
France to Britain in 1763

Territory ceded by Spain to
Britain in 1763

Atlantic Ocean

NEWFOUNDLAND
Miquelon St. Pierre
Louisburg Cape Breton I.

NOVA SCOTIA

Maine
NEW HAMPSHIRE
MASSACHUSETTS
RHODE ISLAND
CONNECTICUT
NEW YORK
NEW JERSEY
DELAWARE

Montreal
Quebec
Lake Champlain
Ticonderoga
Fort Edward
Hudson R.
Lake Ontario
Lake Erie
Fort Duquesne
Ohio R.

PENNSYLVANIA
MARYLAND
VIRGINIA
NORTH CAROLINA
SOUTH CAROLINA
GEORGIA

THE THIRTEEN COLONIES

TERRITORIES OF HUDSON BAY COMPANY

CANADA

Lake Superior
Lake Michigan
Lake Huron

LOUISIANA
(Claim ceded by France
to Spain in 1763)

Mississippi R.

New Orleans

WEST FLORIDA

EAST FLORIDA

Gulf of Mexico

transports left Louisburg and by a superb feat of navigation
arrived off Quebec without losing a ship. But Montcalm,
the French commander, was fully prepared and held an
almost impregnable position. The citadel of Quebec stood
on a cliff on the north side of the St. Lawrence. The river-
bank upstream was protected by high steep cliffs, the river-
bank downstream by lesser cliffs and the main French camps.
Wolfe quickly seized a large island—the Ile d'Orleans—
somewhat downstream of Quebec, and some points on the
shore opposite the town; but on the vital north side of the

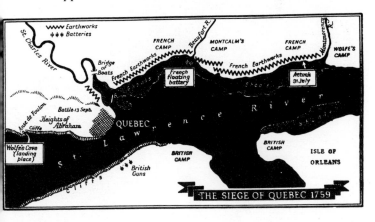

river his attacks against the French forces holding the downstream defences made no progress at all. Two months had
passed and Wolfe was broken in health and on the point of
despair when his men reported finding, upstream from
Quebec, a small cove from which a track led up the face of
the cliffs to the plain above. On the night of the twelfth of
September, after having marched the bulk of his men along
the south bank and then ferried them upstream of this
point, he drifted down with them in small boats to the cove
and led them up the cliffs to the Heights of Abraham, the
plateau on which Quebec stands. Meanwhile, Admiral
Saunders delivered a feint attack on Quebec itself from
directly across the river. Concentrating on this, Montcalm

found out too late that Wolfe had mustered a force on his weakest side. The French commander now had no option but to emerge from his defences and face battle in the open, which was what Wolfe desired. On September the 13th the skill and discipline of the British infantry proved too much for the French. The British troops held their fire until the enemy was within decisive range. Then, in the words of the

The Landing above Quebec, 1759

From an engraving by P. C. Canot. This shows the landing at Anse du Foulon with Wolfe's men in rowing boats coming down from farther up river while a bombardment and subsidiary attack is launched from the shore opposite Quebec

historian of the British Army, 'with one deafening crash the most perfect volley ever fired on a battlefield burst forth as from a single monstrous weapon, from end to end of the British army'. The French broke, and a few days later Quebec surrendered. The death of both Wolfe and Montcalm gave still more of a memorable quality to the battle, which in effect decided the fate of Canada.

Capture of Quebec, 1759

The next year, 1760, saw the end. After an anxious winter in Quebec the beleaguered British garrison was reinforced, and could then emerge to take its part in a triple movement against Montreal directed by General Amherst. The three wings of the attack linked up punctually. Montreal fell, and Canada was no longer a colony of France but of Britain.

Capture of Montreal, 1760

Nor was the capture of Canada, as we have seen, the only great success of the years 1759–60. In India there were the conquests of Clive and Coote, at sea the victories of Lagos and Quiberon Bay, in the West Indies the capture from the French of Guadeloupe. Everywhere, except in Germany where fortunes still fluctuated, British arms, guided by the war-making genius of Pitt, stood triumphant. But though the minister's foes abroad were reeling, at home a very different danger suddenly threatened him. It had taken many years for George II to accept and trust Pitt. He had at last learnt to do so, with remarkable advantages for his country. And now George II had suddenly collapsed in a fit and died. In the hands of his grandson, the young George III, now rested the fortunes of Britain's great war minister.

1759–60: years of victory

Death of George II, 1760

CHAPTER FOUR

GEORGE III, THE KING'S MINISTERS, AND JOHN WILKES

George III

GEORGE III—George II's grandson—was only twenty-two when he came to the throne. His father, Frederick, Prince of Wales, had died nine years before George II, and is remembered by posterity only for his quarrels with his parents and the verses unkindly written on his death:

> Here lies Fred,
> Who was alive and is dead:
> Had it been his father,
> I had much rather;
> Had it been his brother,
> Still better than another;
> Had it been his sister
> No one would have missed her;
> Had it been the whole generation,
> Still better for the nation:
> But since 'tis only Fred,
> Who was alive and is dead—
> There's no more to be said.

George III was to reign for sixty years, longer than any other British monarch except Queen Victoria. In his later years he exercised no power, for he became mad and a regent had to be appointed. At his accession, however, it was a very different story. What his precise intentions were in 1760 is a question which has long been debated by historians and on which there is still no certainty; but one or two points at least seem tolerably clear. The first of the Hanoverians to be really British—'I glory in the name of Britain', he proclaimed in his first speech to Parliament—he was determined to be an effective king and not to be confined in his choice of ministers to the political sets who had monopolized office under George I and II. He seems

His principles

in fact to have nourished 'patriot' ideas of appointing the best men irrespective of their political grouping, and of bringing greater purity into political life. This last he could do by seeing that the hundreds of posts, sinecures and pensions within the royal gift were not regarded primarily as a means of purchasing loyalty to the leading minister of the day.

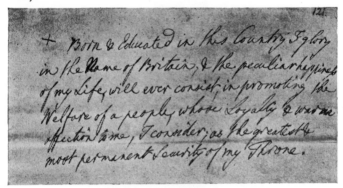

'I Glory in the Name of Britain'

A famous passage, written in his own hand, which George III inserted into the draft of his first speech to Parliament. From the manuscript in the British Museum.

At any rate it is clear that, within what was legally correct, George did his conscientious best to exercise fully the remaining royal powers. He wrote endless letters—often two or three a day to the leading minister—put innumerable comments on state papers, and personally made a high proportion of the appointments within his patronage, especially in the Church. In his zeal he often started work at 6 a.m. To this virtue of industry he added—unlike nearly all his relatives—a blameless private life. Yet he did more damage to Britain than did either of his predecessors. He was mentally very slow and retarded and was full of narrow prejudices. Pitt, he thought in 1760, was 'the most ungrateful . . . and dishonourable of men'; and of one of his later ministers he said: 'I would rather see the devil than

His industry—

—and faults

George Grenville.' All his trust at the beginning of his reign
went to the Earl of Bute, a good-looking and well-informed
Scotsman who had been the head of George's household,
but who was completely lacking in both political experience
and prestige.

George III

A silhouette cut by his daughter, Princess Elizabeth.

George's feelings towards Bute in fact amounted to
devotion. He had earlier admired Pitt, with his 'patriot'
views, but was bitterly aggrieved when Pitt allied with
Newcastle and refused to be guided by Bute. In 1760,

shortly before his accession, George wrote to Bute: 'Whilst my Dearest is near me, I care not who are the tools he may think necessary to be in Ministry provided the blackest of hearts is not one of them.' 'My Dearest' was of course Bute; 'the blackest of hearts' Pitt!

As soon as George became king he accordingly appointed Bute to a ministerial post and made it clear that Bute was in many ways his own mouthpiece. But though Bute, as one critic put it, 'would have made an excellent ambassador in a court where there was nothing to do', he was ill-fitted for the hurly-burly of Westminster. He became one of the Secretaries of State, only to find himself still more at loggerheads with Pitt, who naturally resented his loss of influence within the ministry. The issue came into the open when both George and Bute, as well as most of the rest of the ministry, opposed Pitt over the question of war with Spain. Details of the renewal of the Family Compact between France and Spain had been intercepted, and Pitt prophesied that Spain would shortly be entering the war on the French side. He urged that Britain should forestall this by an immediate attack on Spain. George and Bute, who were keen to conclude peace, refused to agree, and Pitt promptly left the ministry. 'Being responsible, I will direct and will be responsible for nothing that I do not direct', he told the Cabinet—and resigned. Shortly afterwards Bute and the others saw that Pitt's view was justified and war was in fact declared on Spain; but this did not restore Pitt to the ministry. And soon Newcastle, alarmed at Bute's determination to stop subsidies to Frederick of Prussia and withdraw troops from Germany, also resigned.

Having parted with his grandfather's ministers, George III could now make Bute the First Lord of the Treasury and officially, as well as actually, his leading adviser. King and minister were alike eager for peace; but meanwhile the British forces, still animated by the spirit of Pitt, were securing some remarkable successes. During 1761 and 1762 British expeditions took not only several of the West Indies, including Martinique, from France, but also Havana and Manila from Spain. By the end of 1762, however, George

Bute

Resignation of Pitt—

—and Newcastle

Bute leading minister

and Bute had agreed with France on the main terms of peace, and in 1763 the Peace of Paris brought hostilities between the two countries to a close.

Peace of Paris, 1763 By this treaty Britain made great gains. Canada, Nova Scotia, some of the smaller West Indian islands, and Senegal were all officially ceded to her by France, as well as Florida by Spain. Minorca was recovered. Yet the Peace was bitterly criticized at the time, and with some justice, for Bute in his haste gave away far more of Britain's recent conquests than was necessary. To France he returned the two richest West Indian islands, Guadeloupe and Martinique, as well as the great harbour of Dakar in West Africa and the French settlements in India. To Spain he gave back Manila and Cuba in exchange for Florida. When the treaty was debated Pitt was ill, but scorning his sickness he had himself carried to the Commons. His arrival caused an immediate hush. Clothed in black velvet, he entered on crutches; his face was white and lined, his legs swathed in bandages to relieve his gout. He spoke for three and a half hours and was forced to deliver parts of his speech sitting down as he had not the strength to stand. Bitterly he attacked the government for its concessions to France and its desertion of Frederick, an act which left Britain without **Pitt's attack fails** any powerful ally on the Continent. But his effort was in vain, for many thought that to insist on retaining more French territory would only make another war inevitable—and in any case the government had spent a large sum of money on making sure of a majority in the Commons. So swiftly had George III found it necessary not merely to adopt but to exceed the methods of the despised and displaced Newcastle!

Bute resigns Nevertheless, Bute became more and more conscious of his great unpopularity, and very shortly he insisted on resigning, much to the king's grief. The next seven years **Short-lived ministries, 1763–70** saw a series of short-lived ministries; for Newcastle's political system, which had secured a steady monopoly of power for the great Whig families, was now broken, and as yet there was nothing equally stable to take its place. To achieve stability, George had to find a leading minister

who would see eye to eye with him and still command a
regular and reliable majority in Parliament—a task which
needed skill and some sort of popularity, and for which
corruption alone was insufficient. It was not, in fact, until
1770 that George found a leading minister entirely to his
liking who was also popular with Parliament—Lord North. Lord North
During the intervening years he employed men of diverse
connections—for the former Tory families could no longer
be regarded as disloyal to the Hanoverian dynasty, the
Whigs consisted of at least three different factions, party
divisions had become very blurred, and the king's support
and patronage usually secured a majority in the Commons
for his chosen minister. These various ministers, and later
Lord North, had two main problems to face. One was the
American colonies, of which more later. The other was
John Wilkes.

*　　*　　*　　*　　*

John Wilkes, M.P. for Aylesbury, first came prominently Wilkes and
into public notice through his newspaper, *The North Briton*, *The North*
Briton
in which he hurled abuse at Bute over the Peace of Paris
and even sneered at the king. In No. 45 of the paper he 1763
excelled himself by implying that it would be sacrilege if
George attended a thanksgiving service in St. Paul's. The
son of a rich London distiller, and as ugly as he was bold,
Wilkes was a notorious rake and a member of a club—the
Hell-Fire Club—whose proceedings shocked even the
eighteenth century. At one of its meetings he caused
consternation by releasing a dressed-up baboon which he
had smuggled in. His wit, as well as his humour, was
robust. When the Lord Chancellor, Thurlow, a keen supporter of George III, said, 'God forget me when I forget
my sovereign', Wilkes was heard to murmur, 'God forget
you! He'll see you damned first.' But though far from being
a copy-book character, Wilkes was a strong believer in
liberty and got immense satisfaction from annoying what he
proclaimed to be tyrannous authority. Disliking his attacks,
and especially those in No. 45, the king and his ministers
therefore decided to arrest him and put him on trial for

seditious libel. But the arrest was carried out in a very questionable way—the warrant was a general one to search out the authors, printers and publishers of the paper and

John Wilkes in 1763

From an engraving by Hogarth, who sketched Wilkes as he awaited trial. The artist has added a reminder of Wilkes's slogan 'Liberty', and has shown two issues of the *North Briton* which specially offended George III— Nos. 17 and 45.

Trial for
libel—
acquittal

did not name any particular individual—and Wilkes denied its legality with such success that he was acquitted in court and got a large sum in damages from the Secretary of State, who had issued the warrant.

Wilkes had struck a blow for liberty. Thenceforth 'general' warrants were illegal. He had become the hero of the hour, for he made an appeal to classes outside the small circle that ran politics in the eighteenth century—classes which were becoming increasingly important through the development of trade. Members of these classes—small traders, artisans, clerks—were now beginning in much larger numbers to read the newspapers which had sprung up so vigorously during the century, and many were displaying a keen interest in politics. Wilkes put his case with great skill to these new readers, and 'Wilkes and Liberty!' became a national slogan. However, George soon spurred the government to take further action against him. An obscene poem had been found among his papers when he was arrested: and for having this printed with footnotes ascribed to a bishop, he was expelled from Parliament and faced with a charge of impious libel. Seeing no escape, Wilkes fled to Paris. By this time he had also suffered various attempts on his life and been gravely wounded in a duel in Hyde Park.

In Paris Wilkes lived a gay life for four years. The government began to hope that the country had forgotten him, but they were mistaken. His memory was as fresh and his popularity as high as ever, when he returned to England in 1768 in time for a general election. He had been declared an outlaw in his absence, but so slow were the authorities to act on his return that he was able to secure his election as M.P. for Middlesex—a county with a large number of 'forty-shilling freeholders' and no predominant local family —and to have a holiday at Bath without disturbance. Eventually he sent his footman to ask the sheriff to be good enough to arrest him. In court he then successfully contested the sentence of outlawry, but could not reverse the verdict over the impious poem. Back in prison, however, he was just as much a menace to the government, for he was the idol of London and the provincial towns. Portraits of him appeared in shop windows, on decorated trinkets, and were even dangled outside ale-houses.

As a convicted felon, Wilkes could not legally sit in the Commons, and Parliament hastened to expel him. But he

C*

put himself up again at the subsequent by-election and was
re-elected a second and then a third time. Finally, at the
fourth election, when the Middlesex electors had insisted on
returning him yet once again, Parliament was driven to
declaring his opponent elected, though he had polled only a
fifth of Wilkes's votes. This was absurd. Moreover, it was
dangerous because it showed the country how little either
king or Parliament cared for popular opinion. The whole
affair was immensely significant, for Wilkes—who later
scored another great success by claiming, and winning, the
right to report parliamentary debates—had brought discredit to George and his ministers, and had aroused
opposition to the existing system of government among
classes who before had taken little interest in politics.

Re-elected
but
Parliament
accepts his
opponent

Crown and
Parliament
discredited

CHAPTER FIVE

THE LOSS OF THE THIRTEEN COLONIES

1. *The Quarrel with the Colonists*

MUCH the most serious problem in the first half of George III's reign was America. In 1763 Britain had the greatest possessions in the world. Within twenty years the wheel of fortune had turned almost full circle, Britain had lost all her original thirteen colonies on the Atlantic shore of America, and her empire lay in ruins. *The American colonies*

Why did Britain lose all her North American possessions except those recently acquired from the French? To begin with, there were certain underlying causes which would sooner or later have brought on a crisis between Britain and her colonies. In the eighteenth century most people still thought that colonies existed entirely for the benefit of the mother country. The trade of the British colonies, as of all colonies, was regulated to this end. In general, they were legally entitled to export products only to Britain or British colonies and were supposed to import all their wants from the same sources. Moreover, laws were passed by the English Parliament which made it impossible for the colonies to create certain industries, notably the manufacture of woollen cloth. These were to remain the monopoly of the mother country. *Reasons for conflict* *Trade restrictions*

Some of these trade restrictions naturally irritated the colonists and led to smuggling and evasion. In addition there was a further source of trouble over the power of the elected colonial assemblies. The colonists regarded these as their Parliaments; but most Englishmen considered that they were little better than town corporations, and that the British Parliament should control the colonies. The British representatives in the colonies were the Governors, most of whom were appointed by the king. They were responsible for the enforcement of the laws *Governors versus Assemblies* passed by the king and the British Parliament. In these circumstances the Governors and assemblies often came into collision, the assemblies being particularly difficult about internal taxation. This they claimed they should control. In fact, the principle that taxation should not be imposed without the consent of elected representatives— 'No taxation without representation', as the cry soon went —had long applied in practice in the colonies. For this principle the English had fought during the seventeenth century and they had no intention of abandoning it when they crossed the seas.

Disputes about taxation

Further, the conditions in America produced men with a very different outlook and way of life from that of most Englishmen. Independence and hard work were the qualities above all cultivated in America. Most of the inhabitants of the northern and middle colonies were farmers and they were practically all freeholders. There was no point in accepting a subordinate position when any man of energy and courage could carve out a farm of his own from the virgin lands farther west. The frontier, with its cheap and plentiful land, was a standing invitation to the poorer American. The result, except in the south, was a society far more equal than that of England. The financial rewards of a professor of mathematics were not very different from those of an industrious house carpenter or bricklayer, and these in turn might earn almost a third of what was due to the Governor of the colony. So in these middle and northern colonies there were no extremes of poverty and luxury. Only in the south was there a real aristocracy: in the old lands of Virginia around the James and York rivers and in Carolina there were planters who owned 80,000 acres and as many as a thousand slaves.

The American way of life

Greater equality

The difference in outlook between British and Americans was increased by the facts that the latter were educated in their own schools and universities, where there was little class distinction, and that few came across to England. The result was a race of men who were out of sympathy with European life. The Americans tended to think the English arrogant and full of flummery and nonsense—as indeed they were on occasions, such as when English commanders during the Seven Years War treated all English officers as senior to all colonial officers, whatever the ranks and experience of the latter. On the other side, the English tended to think the Americans simple and rather boorish. All told, the forces gradually driving England and her colonies apart were extremely powerful.

Moreover the Americans were becoming strong enough to defy England. After the Seven Years War the colonists no longer needed British protection against the French, and by the time the War of Independence broke out the population of the thirteen colonies had risen to $2\frac{1}{2}$ million, about a third of England's. The chief weakness of the colonies was their complete lack of unity, but this was cured when the British ministers decided to adopt a tough policy. The colonists soon became so indignant that they managed to sink their own differences and unite against Britain. *American strength*

The decisive step which soon led to the War of American Independence was an attempt in 1765 by the British ministers to impose a tax within the colonies by Act of the British Parliament. This policy was not unreasonable, for Britain had spent much money on the defence of the colonies during the Seven Years War, and the colonies resolutely refused to provide any adequate sum for this purpose. But the attempt was novel, for previously the British Parliament had only regulated the external taxes or customs duties, which were supposed to be in the interests of imperial trade. It was also unwise, for it provoked widespread resistance— a surprise to the many ministers who were completely ignorant of American affairs. *George III's ministers decide to tax colonies directly: the Stamp Act, 1765*

One of the few prominent politicians in Britain who understood America was Pitt. Early in 1766 in one of his greatest speeches he denounced this new tax, known as the Stamp Tax, by which all the colonists' contracts and other legal documents had to bear stamps of varying value. It seemed for a moment that all might be well. New ministers had taken office, and they gave way and repealed the Stamp Act—though they accompanied this by an unwise declaration that the British government had the right to tax the *Stamp Act repealed* colonies if it wished. And even George III so far changed his mind as to call on Pitt, for whom he had now once more conceived a great admiration, to form a ministry. In agreeing, however, Pitt accepted a peerage, becoming the Earl of Chatham. This destroyed some of his prestige as 'The Great Commoner' and weakened his influence in the House of Commons, but much worse was to follow. Within a month Chatham was suffering from one of his mental attacks. His condition slowly deteriorated, and for almost two years he paid no attention to business—until in a lucid interval in 1768 he repudiated all the steps that his colleagues had taken in his absence and resigned office.

Ministry of Pitt (Chatham)

His illness

Meanwhile, Chatham's colleagues had undone whatever good had followed from the repeal of the Stamp Act. Since the colonies would not accept direct internal taxation, the ministers had decided to raise a revenue from them, for their own defence, by imposing new customs duties on a variety of articles, including tea. Opposition promptly blazed forth again in America, and before long a new minister, Lord North, had removed all the duties except that on tea—which was kept on purely to show the colonists that the right to tax them existed. However, encouraged by all the choppings and changings and ministerial irresolution of the last few years, the colonists refused to be shown. And when in 1773 the East India Company were allowed to send their tea direct to America instead of via England, there at once occurred the famous episode of the Boston Tea Party. Thinly disguised as Red Indians, some local patriots boarded the first Indiaman that sailed into Boston, the capital of Massachusetts, and flung all the tea into the harbour. And tea sent to other ports fared little better.

Indirect taxes on colonists— withdrawn except for tax on tea

Boston Tea Party, 1773

Spurred on by the king, whose agent he was quite prepared to be, the able and charming but altogether too easygoing Lord North now decided to take strong action in the interests of law and order. General Gage, the commander-in-chief of the army in America, was made Governor of Massachusetts, the centre of resistance, and ordered to concentrate his forces at Boston. The port was closed, and

Action against Massa-chusetts

the colony's powers of self-government largely removed. The ministers imagined that this would soon bring Massachusetts to heel. They were wrong, for Massachusetts was by no means alone in her resistance. Support poured in from the other New England colonies, and as a result of invitations sent out by Massachusetts the first Continental Congress was held at Philadelphia, the capital of Pennsylvania. All thirteen colonies were represented with the exception of Georgia, for they all realized that their turn would come after Massachusetts. Moreover, some of them had been further irritated by the Quebec Act of 1774, which had extended the southern boundary of Canada to the Ohio and so cut off the central colonies from their hinterland. In general the Congress was markedly anti-British. It voted to boycott trade with the mother country, but as yet made no attempt to decree independence. *The Continental Congress* *American trade boycott*

In April 1775 Gage received orders to bring Massachusetts to heel by the use of force. Before long he sent out troops to prevent some military stores at Concord falling into the hands of the resisters. In the course of the operation a skirmish took place at Lexington, blood was shed, and the War of American Independence had begun. Soon afterwards the Continental Congress in its second meeting at Philadelphia officially organized armed resistance, adopted the New England forces as its own army, and appointed George Washington as commander-in-chief. It was not, however, until more than a year later, on July 4th, 1776, that Congress finally approved the Declaration of Independence, cutting all bonds between Britain and the thirteen colonies and calling into being a new organization—the United States of America. *Force against Massachusetts* *Lexington, 1775* *Congress organizes official resistance, 1775* *Declaration of Independence, July 4th, 1776*

Washington was one of the Americans' greatest assets. He was born of a good family in Virginia, a great stronghold of the 'patriots'. His appointment secured the full support of the southern colonies in the fight for independence. Washington had left school early—he always had difficulty with his spelling—and by the age of sixteen he was already at work surveying the Alleghany mountains. It was an arduous life and a good apprenticeship for *George Washington* campaigning. In the Seven Years War, he was one of the most vigorous colonial officers and at the age of twenty-two was in action with the French on the borderlands between the British colonies and Canada. With his considerable experience he was thus a wise choice for commander-in-chief in 1775. As a general he proved to be competent rather than brilliant, but as a leader and statesman he was quite outstanding. He was never irritated by the distractions to which Congress and the colonial assemblies subjected him. He never gave up hope in defeat or when his soldiers deserted him. He was the rock on which the American cause was built.

2. *The War of Independence*

Nature of American war

The War of American Independence was unlike any other war the eighteenth century had seen. It was a war half civil, half national. At the beginning Americans and British were alike subjects of the same king, and even after 1776 many Americans did not repudiate their loyalty to George III. A very large section—possibly as much as a third—opposed the Declaration of Independence. Known as the Loyalists, they gave the British forces considerable help, over 30,000 taking up arms in support of the king. That they were not more effective was due partly to their lack of a vigorous policy, partly to the barbarity with which they were treated by the rebels—for those who refused to renounce the king were pelted with muck and then tarred and feathered. By ruthlessness of this kind the rebels early acquired control of practically all areas. At the same time it cannot be denied that on the American side the war was a national one—when Gage's troops issued from Boston they found the whole countryside in arms against them. As a war it proved to differ sharply from the standard European war fought by professional soldiers with the inhabitants taking little part. The British failed to grasp the consequences of this difference quickly enough—which was one of the reasons why they lost.

The Loyalists

There were other unusual features. The distances were vast, the numbers engaged comparatively small. The colonies lay 3,000 miles across the ocean from Britain and a good voyage would last four or five weeks, a bad one as many months. The distance between Georgia in the south and New Hampshire in the north was a thousand miles. There were few roads and most of the country was wooded. The conditions were ideal for guerilla action, and that was very largely how the Americans fought. Vast distances, small numbers

The conflict was marked by three main British efforts to re-establish control. During the first, in 1775, the British under Gage concentrated in Boston and attempted to subdue New England. For their part the New Englanders tried to seize Canada. Both were unsuccessful. The main British efforts: (1) Against New England, 1775

The second attempt began in 1776 when General Howe, who had succeeded Gage and had been forced to abandon Boston, launched an attack on the middle colonies. Here the British fared better than in New England. Howe had an army twice the size of that of the previous year and the area was full of Loyalists. He won a battle on Long Island and occupied New York, but Washington and his army escaped. The Americans were dejected and many of Washington's troops deserted, but Howe failed to follow up his successes. He took over eight weeks to cover the thirty-five miles from Long Island to White Plains, where he fought an indecisive battle with Washington. He then settled down to winter in New York. (2) Against middle colonies, 1776–7 Howe occupies New York

The next year saw a more ambitious plan, still directed against the middle colonies. General Burgoyne was to lead a force south from Canada down Lake Champlain and into the Hudson Valley, and Howe was to send a force from New York to support him. But at the same time Howe himself planned to attack Philadelphia, the seat of the American Congress, from the sea. With Howe's own scheme all at first went well, though he was so leisurely that he did not sail from New York until nearly the end of July. He landed his troops in Chesapeake Bay, defeated Washington at Brandywine, and captured Philadelphia—from which Congress hastily fled. But he had not been able to Howe captures Philadelphia leave behind in New York enough troops to make possible the other attack in conjunction with Burgoyne—who by this time was in difficulties.

Burgoyne had won a considerable success when he destroyed the American flotilla on Lake Champlain and recaptured Ticonderoga from the colonists. Once he had to leave the lake, however, he found himself in heavily wooded country with practically no roads. The transport of artillery and supplies became a major problem, and he took ten weeks to cover the fifty miles from Ticonderoga to Saratoga. Meanwhile the American militia gathered in the woods on either side. Failing to break through south of

Surrender of Burgoyne at Saratoga, 1777

Saratoga, Burgoyne was then blockaded into surrender. This American victory had immensely important consequences. It tempted France and, a little later, Spain, who were both still smarting from their defeat in the Seven Years War, into renewed hostilities against Britain.

(3) Against southern colonies

The next year the British launched no major attack and abandoned Philadelphia. Then in 1779 they began their third main attempt to subdue the colonists. Leaving a large garrison in New York, General Clinton, the new commander-in-chief, attacked the southern colonies. In 1780 he took Charleston with its 5,000 defenders, and soon

Capture of Georgia and S. Carolina

most of Georgia and South Carolina was in British hands. Clinton then returned to New York, leaving the command in the south to General Cornwallis. The latter invaded North Carolina, but was troubled by guerilla warfare and risings in his rear. With great boldness he nevertheless decided in 1781 to march across North Carolina and

Cornwallis attacks Virginia

attack the rebels in Virginia. But though he had much success he was unable to crush all resistance, and soon Clinton ordered him to retire to a fortified base at Yorktown on Chesapeake Bay. Here Washington and the French now concentrated their forces against him.

British lose command of American waters, 1780

All might yet have been well for Cornwallis if at this critical moment the British Navy had not lost control of the American seas. Unfortunately the British fleet came off second best in a brush with the French under de Grasse, and it was the latter's fleet which now arrived outside

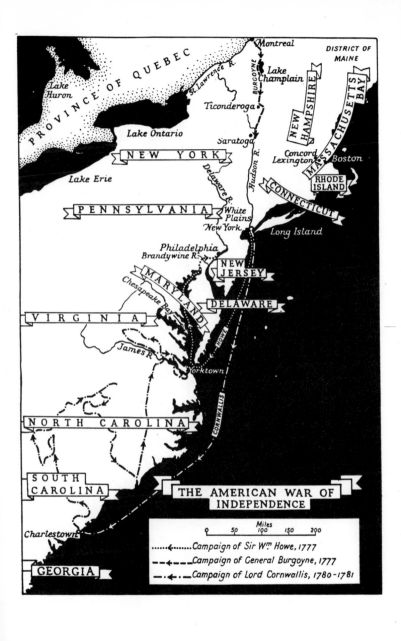

THE AMERICAN WAR OF
INDEPENDENCE

Miles
0   50   100   150   200

........◄........Campaign of Sir Wm. Howe, 1777
- - - -◄- - - -Campaign of General Burgoyne, 1777
-·-·-·◄-·-·-·-Campaign of Lord Cornwallis, 1780-1781

The Middle Deck of a Man-of-War (The *Hector*) in 1782

From an engraving by Rowlandson. The ship, of course, is in port—at Portsmouth.

Yorktown. Cornwallis was thus hemmed in by sea as well as land. There was no escape, and in October he was forced to lay down arms with his 7,000 men. At the surrender, Cornwallis has band, with some appropriateness, played 'The World turned upside down'—for Yorktown marked the triumph of the colonies over the mother country. After this, Britain made no further effort to restore the situation.

Cornwallis surrenders at Yorktown, 1781

Britain had been at war with France since 1778, with Spain since 1779, and with Holland—which objected to the British searching of neutral vessels—since 1780.[1] This was a powerful combination to face, and without allies Britain was unequal to the task. Against these continental powers the operations were mainly at sea or in the colonies, in the West Indies, West Africa, and in India. In Europe a French attack on Jersey failed, but a Spanish attack on Minorca succeeded. Gibraltar, however, was most gallantly defended by Sir George Eliott and repulsed every assault.

Other enemies— France, Spain, Holland

After Yorktown the king and his ministers were in despair. George III even talked of abdicating. The disaster was altogether too much for the corpulent Lord North, who had held the leading position since 1770, and who had allowed himself in effect to be guided by the king. Without the character to take prompt and firm decisions—a friend who visited him once spent all day doing nothing because North could not make up his mind which was the best place for a picnic—he nevertheless grew increasingly resentful of his position, and after his failure to subdue America he at length persuaded George to allow him to resign. His years of office had brought unparalleled disaster to Britain.

Resignation of North, 1782

The new ministers, who had bitterly opposed North in Parliament, and of whom the most important was soon Lord Shelburne, decided to recognize American independence. A treaty was finally signed at Versailles in 1783. By this Senegal and Tobago went to France, and Florida and

Peace of Versailles, 1783

[1] Other countries which objected to the British searching their vessels for contraband included Russia, Sweden, Denmark and Prussia. They did not enter the war, but formed an 'Armed Neutrality' ready to intervene if necessary.

Minorca to Spain; and—much more important—Britain recognized the independence of her revolted colonies. The

boundary between these and Canada was fixed along its present line except in the west, where nothing was as yet defined. Outside the thirteen colonies Britain thus surrendered comparatively little territory. This was due in

part to the sterling work of Warren Hastings in defending British interests in India, and in part to a brilliant naval

victory—the Battle of the Saints—won by Admiral Rodney in the West Indies (near Les Saintes) in 1782. In the course of this, Rodney captured de Grasse, and shattered at a blow the enemy's brief and fatal supremacy in American waters.

'The Liberty of the Subject' (Gillray, 1779)
The naval press gang (widely used during the American war) seizes a poor tailor against stout opposition from his females.

As for the newly-formed country known as the United States, this had a difficult time immediately after 1783, for many of the individual states regarded themselves as practically independent. It was not until the American Constitution was adopted in 1788 and George Washington became the first President in 1789 that a fairly strong central government was established.

Why did Britain lose the war? The most important reason is that she never had, after the entry of France and Spain, the same command of the seas as she had in the Seven Years War. Yet she had three years in which to win when the colonies were fighting alone and still she was unsuccessful. It can be argued that her generals were overcautious, and it is certain that the government was corrupt and highly inefficient, but even so this is not the whole explanation. In any circumstances the conquest of America would have been a difficult task. There were few vital objectives. The three largest towns, Boston, New York, Philadelphia, were occupied without decisive results. There was no regular American army to beat. The levies melted away, then reappeared when British forces were dangerously isolated. As long as a majority of Americans were really determined on independence, it would have been difficult for Britain to win without employing far greater forces than she could easily raise or even contemplate. As it was, she was driven to employ German mercenaries, which only inflamed the colonists still further. The twentieth century is much more efficient than the eighteenth in the art of ruling people against their will.

Causes of Britain's defeat: Loss of command of seas

Inefficient commanders and ministers

Distance and size of America: small professional forces engaged against a nation

Britain's failure dealt a harsh blow to George III's prestige. The ministers he had chosen were incompetent, they had backed the wrong policies, and some of their measures had seemed to many positively tyrannical. Wilkes and America alike could thus appear to many Englishmen as champions of liberty against an oppressive government. In the end, the king and his ministers had brought Britain to the verge of disaster and lost the thirteen American colonies. And since George III had used his patronage to suppress opposition in Parliament, during all this time the feeling had been steadily growing that the power of the Crown should be decreased—or among a few extremists that it should be abolished altogether—and that Parliament should be made much more representative of the nation. Not for the first time in history, defeat abroad begot the desire for revolutionary changes at home.

Effect on George III—

—and on public opinion

CHAPTER SIX

EIGHTEENTH CENTURY LIFE (I)
(*c.* 1720–1780)

1. *The Upper and Middle Classes*

Two
keynotes:
contrast—

CONTRAST and vigour were the keynotes of English life throughout the eighteenth century. Contrast was to be seen at every point, but especially in styles of living. The upper ranks of society lived amid a magnificence that we, in our more sombre days, find hard to comprehend. The poor existed in a squalor that those who have never travelled beyond Europe cannot imagine.

—and
vigour

It was partly because of these wide differences in fortune that the age was marked by such vigour. There were great possibilities of gaining wealth and a higher place in society —and, of course, even greater possibilities of losing them. Rivalry and competition were in the air, and in such an atmosphere few could rest idle. Even the peers and the gentry were for the most part busily at work. They were building their great palaces, supervising their estates and tenantry, introducing new methods of agriculture, acting as ministers of state or justices of the peace, and sometimes taking a hand in industrial developments—the Duke of Bridgewater, for instance, was the 'father' of English canals, and the Duke of Bedford had an important interest in the

All classes
busy

London docks. Meanwhile the merchants and seamen were ceaselessly trading and exploring across the distant oceans —Captain Cook, for instance, landed in New Zealand in 1769 and in New South Wales the following year. At the same time, too, new manufactures and a new class of manufacturers were arising in the Midlands and the North, especially from 1760 onwards, bringing prosperity to considerable numbers and drudgery to others. And needless to say, throughout the century working men found little rest.

A few made a fortune in the new industries but the great majority had to face long hours of toil—fourteen hours a day was quite usual—for very small rewards.[1]

The wealthiest of the noblemen lived in a style that was The great the envy of many continental princes. In the first half of nobility the century one of the most striking was the Duke of Chandos. He used the fortune he made as Paymaster Duke of General during Marlborough's wars to reconstruct on a Chandos lavish scale, and in the most up-to-date 'strictly Classical' style, his house of Canons near Stanmore in Middlesex. The walled garden alone covered eighty-three acres; and three great avenues—the longest nearly a mile long—led through the grounds to the nearest villages. He also contemplated building a private road to his town house in London, a dozen miles away. The grounds he stocked with exotic animals imported from all over the world—such creatures as Virginia deer, storks, flamingoes, eagles, macaws, and whistling ducks. A tiger was a present much appreciated by the Duke, and he took particular pride in growing pineapples.

Chandos's household in 1722 amounted to ninety-three persons. They ranged from the Master of the Musick, who received £100 a year—the Duke kept a private orchestra— to a stable hand who received only £2 a year. One musician patronized by the Duke was George Frederick Handel, the German-born composer, who lived for two years at Canons and there wrote one of his oratorios and the lovely pieces known as the Chandos Anthems. Among the Duke's nonmusical servants was a running footman who received an extra shilling every time he ran more than twenty miles. But even Chandos could not afford to live for long on so princely a scale, and after some serious losses during the South Sea Bubble he tried to economize. To raise more money he was willing to back almost any scheme, and impostors found him a gullible victim. At one time earth was being secretly scooped from land in Shropshire and sent in casks to a furnace at Canons where Chandos hoped

[1] For the social consequences of the agricultural and industrial revolutions, see pages 127–128, 144–148.

to extract gold from it. Of course the project was not a success, and when Chandos died his son had to sell Canons in order to pay off his father's debts. Within thirty years of its erection the whole vast mansion, the most costly in the country, was being pulled down and its materials sold to builders.

Other great noblemen

The Duke of Chandos was by no means alone in his magnificent ways. At Stowe Lord Cobham held court and there often entertained the elder Pitt, who came into politics as his client. At Wentworth Woodhouse Lord Stafford built the largest private house in England with a front 606 feet long. At Milton Abbas, in Dorset, Lord Dorchester completely demolished the medieval village in order that no buildings might mar the view from his fine new house abutting the Abbey. He flattened even the tombstones and 'landscaped' the surroundings into a lovely park. The local population he transferred to a brand-new village built in an adjoining valley, out of his sight and hearing.[1]

Coke of Holkham

Some of the gentry were nearly as prosperous as the nobility. Thomas Coke (pronounced Cook), who lived in splendour at Holkham in Norfolk, was for long known as the first commoner of England—he refused a peerage several times, but finally accepted one from Queen Victoria, and thus became Earl of Leicester of Holkham. Coke's early life was typical of his class. He was sent to Eton and then spent three years on the Continent doing the 'Grand Tour' of France, the Netherlands and Italy. In 1776 at the age of twenty-four he succeeded to his father's estate at Holkham. His father's uncle had begun the construction of

[1] The present-day fate of all these places is interesting. The site of Canons is occupied by the North London Collegiate School, whose modern building incorporates part of a much smaller eighteenth-century house built to replace Canons. Stowe, of course, is now a famous boys' school. The grounds of Wentworth Woodhouse have been much given over to open-cast mining, and the house is occupied by a college of physical training. Milton Abbey House, too, is now a school; and the village cottages (which received water and sanitation only in 1954) no longer form part of a great landlord's estate, but belong in the main to their occupants.

the great house and of the park after a long period in Italy studying classical art. Coke completed the work and made the house a great centre of entertainment. He had sixty servants, kept open house once a week, and at his annual sheep-shearing feast welcomed all those ready to discuss the new farming methods for which he was so famous. As a great 'improving' landlord his nearest rival was perhaps the Duke of Bedford, whose estates covered practically the whole of that county.

Holkham Hall

From a modern photograph. The residence of 'Coke of Holkham' and a great centre of entertainment for those interested in agriculture. The architect was William Kent.

The lesser gentry to whom the majority of the squires belonged merged gradually into the middle class, who were rapidly expanding with the growth of trade. Within this middle class there were many fine degrees of status. The small squire, though perhaps a working farmer, would consider himself the social superior of most members of the professions or of the rising industrialists in the North. The city merchant was of superior standing to the ordinary shopkeeper or craftsman skilled in the finer trades. Nevertheless, all these members of the middle class had many things in common. They frequently visited each other and

The middle class

married into each other's families, even if they remained conscious of their different social grades. And all lived a life of relative comfort and prosperity according to the standards of the day.

Upper- and middle-class feeding

Upper and middle classes alike were great eaters and drinkers. Parson Woodforde, who was rector of Weston in Norfolk during the last quarter of the century, had a habit of noting down his meals in his diary. On August 5th, 1783, he visited the local squire, and eight sat down to dinner. They were given 'fresh water fish, Perch and Trout, saddle of Mutton roasted, Beans and Bacon, a couple of Fowls boiled, Patties and some white soup. 2nd course: Pigeons roasted, a Duck roasted, Piggs Pettytoes—Sweetbreads—Raspberry Cream, Tarts and Pudding and Pippins.' Meals were usually served in this way—i.e., in two courses of many varying dishes, as with Chinese meals nowadays. The dishes were placed at different points round the table, and the guests usually helped each other and themselves.

These upper- and middle-class meals followed a different time-table from our own. Such people mostly rose an hour or so later than in the Stuart period—7 a.m. was now a usual time—and about 10 a.m., after three hours' work, many of them now took a light breakfast of bread and butter or toast with tea, coffee or chocolate. Ale as a breakfast drink was by this time uncommon except among farmers and labourers. The main meal, dinner, followed next. In the seventeenth century this had been taken at noon, but the hour gradually moved forward until, by 1760, 2 or 3 p.m. was usual in the country, and 5, 6 or even 7 p.m. in polite circles in London. As dinner went forward, so breakfasts became heavier. In the evening most people had a cold supper, about 9.30 or 10 p.m., and this meal became more important as the century wore on. Afternoon tea as a meal began only towards the end of the century in fashionable houses when the dining hour was late. Other households drank plenty of tea, but with breakfast or after dinner or supper.

Centres of upper society:

Although there was much entertaining in the country—as we learn from Parson Woodforde's diary—London and the new watering places like Bath and Tunbridge Wells, the earliest type of holiday resort, were the most important centres of upper- and middle-class society. In London, social as well as business life was much helped by the building of more bridges—for thus far there had been only one, London Bridge. In 1750 Westminster Bridge was opened to wheeled traffic, in 1769 Blackfriars Bridge. Round about the same time the residential quarters west of the City London began to extend fast. Grosvenor Gardens were built despite George III's desire to add the site to the grounds of Buckingham House (later Palace), which he had just acquired for the queen. Farther north, the districts round Oxford Street, Tottenham Court Road and Marylebone were being built up in this period.

Among the many London entertainments, masked balls London and the theatre perhaps held pride of place for polite entertain-society, but these were now also quite as popular with less-ments well-off citizens. The performances of David Garrick, Sarah Siddons and others could be applauded by all classes. Opera, light opera and public concerts were other favoured diversions, and for men the coffee-house continued to be one of the centres of London life, though less so than earlier in the century. Many coffee-houses had long been the resorts of people with particular interests, but some were now turning into 'clubs' open only to members. Such were White's and Brooks's, both in St. James's Street, where men of fashion gambled at cards and dice for high stakes. Of other coffee-houses, the Bedford at Covent Garden was now the hub of the artistic and literary world, while Lloyd's in the City became more than ever the centre for shipping news and insurance. Such places were greatly helped by the growth of newspapers and periodicals, which were provided for the benefit of the customers. The newspapers, which in the 1770s had won the right to publish details of Newspapers the debates in Parliament, mostly consisted of four pages, and lending and to their number was soon added *The Times*.[1] Reading libraries matter of a more extended kind was to be had from the

[1] *The Times* adopted its present title in 1788, three years after its beginning as *The Daily Universal Register*.

Lloyd's Coffee House, 1798

many booksellers and from the new 'circulating' libraries, the first of which opened in 1740.

The open air played its part in London's social life. Apart from holiday trips by middle-class citizens to villages nearby, such as Chelsea or Islington, people of quality walked in the parks in the morning and both the Mall and the Ring in Hyde Park were something of a fashion parade.

Pleasure-gardens 'Pleasure-gardens' were also laid out, and for evening entertainments those at Ranelagh and Vauxhall became especially famous. 'Polite society' flocked thither at first, but less so as the crowds grew thicker. At Vauxhall Gardens, very formal in their layout and lit by hundreds of oil lamps, concerts were given, and afterwards as many as three or four hundred sat down to supper at tables in alcoves. The 'dark' walks of the gardens were an added attraction to the adventurous and (of course) the amorous.

'Taking the waters' as a remedy for gout, indigestion and other ailments brought on by rich living, was already a fashionable habit by the end of the seventeenth century, though the spas visited were usually not farther from London than Epsom or Tunbridge Wells. They were soon supplanted in esteem by Bath, and to this day that city with its graceful crescents and Classical façades bears the stamp of the eighteenth century. Here, many a raw family, while taking the waters, learnt some of the customs of polite society. After bathing and water-drinking in the early morning—the bathing consisted of walking in the water dressed in canvas suits, with little floating trays for the ladies' vanity bags, etc.—in the evenings the visitors met at the Assembly Rooms. It was here that Beau Nash, who first established Bath's reputation for elegance, reigned supreme as Master of Ceremonies during the earlier part of the century.

The spas: Bath

'A Kick-up at a Hazard Table'

A gambler's quarrel, from an engraving by Rowlandson (1790).

Beau Nash   Though very ugly, Nash had some charm of manner, together with unlimited confidence and powers of flattery. He was educated at Oxford and studied at the Middle Temple, but throughout his early life he had had little money and on one occasion had won a bet of £50 by standing in the door of York Minister clad only in a blanket. When Nash arrived at Bath, he found it without any of the graces of a fashionable centre. There was bathing in the famous baths and drinking of medicinal waters, and, as special diversions, a band and dancing on the bowling-green. Displaying great resource, Nash had new and finer Assembly Rooms built where meals could be taken and balls held. Becoming prosperous from the profits, especially those made on the gambling tables, he adopted a flamboyant style of life. His coach was drawn by six greys and travelled with outriders and footmen equipped with French horns. He also built a playhouse and rebuilt the Pump Room. On all matters of etiquette at the Assembly Rooms his judgement was final. When a lady arrived one evening in an apron—by this time an old-fashioned garment reserved for morning wear—Nash removed it with his own hands, although its wearer was a duchess. The wearing of swords and top-boots by the men at these public gatherings was strictly forbidden, and so too was the use of strong language. From Bath—and London—higher standards of manners gradually spread throughout the country as a whole.

Upper-class fashions   It was often at spas like Bath and Cheltenham, Buxton and Tunbridge Wells, that new fashions in dress were first widely seen. At such places men could observe the latest form of adornment for the head, from the large wigs of the beginning of the 1700s, through the shorter wigs of the mid-century, to the powdered natural hair fashionable from then onwards. Ladies could follow the increase and decrease in the size of the hoops worn in their skirts, or the rapid rise and fall in popularity of huge head-dresses of horsehair powdered over and decorated with flowers, feathers and even model ships—head-dresses which took so long to build up that their wearers had to sleep in them for weeks at a time. And both sexes could watch the

'The Comforts of Bath'
I. Taking the Waters.

'The Comforts of Bath'
II. Dancing.
From a satirical series by Rowlandson issued in 1798

development of the umbrella from something entirely feminine in the first half of the century, to something which, by 1800, a gentleman could carry without attracting shouts of derision. From about 1760, however, the spas as centres of fashion began to be rivalled by seaside resorts. Sea-bathing first became popular after George III took to visiting Weymouth, and by 1780 Scarborough, Brighton, Margate and Lyme Regis were also favoured places of diversion for the wealthier classes.

Seaside holidays

George III's First Bathe at Weymouth, 1789

From a humorous print of the time showing the naked monarch escorted by bathing attendants and the town musicians.

2. *The Labouring Classes*

Working-class life

For ordinary working people there was none of this variety. Few during their lives travelled outside their own immediate district, though especially towards the end of the century men emigrated to the towns—London and the rising industrial centres of the Midlands and the North—where there was an increasing demand for labour and the wages were higher. On the whole the manual workers were fairly well off, by past standards, during the first half of the century; but with the growing movement to enclose the remaining open fields and divide them up into compact individual farms—a process which was at its height from 1750 onwards—many suffered a serious decline in their standard of life.[1] And all except those in a few favoured trades were badly hit by the big rise in prices which set in towards the end of the century, especially during the wars against revolutionary France.

For most of the eighteenth century, however, it was the comparative prosperity and independence of the working people that struck foreigners who came to England. They were surprised by the amount that English labourers ate. Unlike the upper and middle classes, they were not able to afford vast quantities of meat and poultry, but most of them shared in the general agricultural prosperity, at least to the extent of having a weekly joint, oddments in the way of rabbits and offal, and a plentiful supply of beer and bread—their staple food. Wheaten bread was by now normal in southern England, but in the North wheat, rye and oats were consumed in equal quantities and in Wales barley and rye were the main foods. Potatoes steadily grew in popularity, and in Ireland the population began to become dangerously dependent on them—dangerously because as a crop they were susceptible to blight and could easily fail. Tea, once an article of luxury, was regarded by the end of the century as an everyday necessity by all classes. Because of high duty—for long at five shillings a pound—it was dearer than either coffee or chocolate, but nothing could stop its ever-increasing popularity. In the middle years of the century a cheap tea on which duty had been paid cost twelve shillings a pound, and an expensive one thirty shillings a pound. But there was plenty of smuggled tea about—more in fact than unsmuggled; people in any case used only a very little to each pot; and the poor had a habit of using the same leaves three or four times over, or even of buying used leaves from the servants at better-off households.

For those members of the poorer classes who lost their *Poor-relief*

Working-class feeding

[1] See pages 127–128.

jobs through unemployment or sickness, life was often a terrible ordeal. Poor-relief was available to all and large sums of money were spent on it in the eighteenth century, but frequently little was achieved. Each parish was responsible for its own poor and an overseer was appointed for the purpose. The amount of help given varied. In one place, Cowden, when a family fell ill of the smallpox they received from the parish a nurse for five weeks, fuel, and a plentiful assortment of food. But often the overseer was concerned only to spend as little of the parish money as possible. He let out the poor-house to a contractor (who starved the inhabitants to make a profit), bound poor orphans apprentice to masters who treated them as slaves—in some cases they were even chained up at night to prevent their running away—and paid a pittance to the poor whom he did not remove from their homes to the poor-house.

Charity and philanthropy

These problems did not escape the people of the day. Charity was a social duty recognized by most of the better-off, and many individuals showed great generosity in the help they gave to the unfortunate. A good squire, and his wife and daughters, made a point of assisting any of the 'deserving' poor on his estate. In London the Foundling Hospital was set up by a benevolent retired sailor, Captain Coram, to take care of abandoned children; and during the century other benefactors founded many general and 'lying-in' hospitals (for childbirth) throughout the country. In 1772 a society was formed to relieve imprisoned debtors, and it secured the release of 12,000 in the first thirty years. Two philanthropists of especial fame were John Howard, who launched a campaign against the appalling state of the prisons, and Jonas Hanway, who as governor of the Foundling Hospital made the rescuing of pauper children his great task. The Church, of course, helped too, and in many churches boards of this time can still be seen listing the gifts made to the poor of the parish. Parson Woodforde naturally did his bit. He often records gifts of money to men or women in distress, and at Christmas it was his practice to give a dinner at his house to six or seven of the old and poor. Yet despite all the efforts of

The Foundling Hospital

Howard and Hanway

charity there was a very great deal of suffering that was not relieved. This was partly because the growth of towns tore up many people from their old roots in the country, but still more because, for all its veneer of elegance on the surface, the eighteenth century was an age immensely coarser and tougher than ours.

3. *Education, The Law, Medicine, Recreation*

Though peace reigned throughout the land during the whole century—with the brief interruptions of the '15 and the '45—violence and brutality were never far away. For over forty years out of the hundred, the country was at war with foreign powers; and although these eighteenth-century wars made no great demands on the national man-power, they did involve the use of that highly violent method of recruitment, the Press Gang. Moreover, there were several local risings by men infuriated by the high price of corn; and in 1780, after a motion in Parliament to relieve Roman Catholics of some of the laws against them, a mob led by Lord George Gordon, a crazy Protestant fanatic, approached Westminster, got out of hand, and for several days held London at its mercy. Roman Catholic chapels and houses were burned, the prisons broken open, the Bank of England and other public buildings attacked. *Violence and brutality:* *The Press Gang* *The Gordon Riots*

The same trend towards violence can be found in school life. There were three mutinies at Winchester within twenty-six years, and Keate, the headmaster of Eton, once flogged over eighty boys in one day. In general it can be said that the state of the two English universities and most of the public schools in this period was deplorable, and certainly much inferior to that in Elizabethan and early Stuart times. At Oxford few of the professors lectured, and those who did rarely had an audience. Single-word answers to two very elementary questions could suffice to get a degree. Many of the old-established grammar schools were in no better case, and perhaps the best schools were the Dissenting Academies. *Violence in schools* *The bad state of universities and schools*

In primary education, however, more energy was shown. *Primary education: the S.P.C.K.*

A great effort was made in the first part of the century by various voluntary bodies, particularly the Society for the Promotion of Christian Knowledge (started in 1698), to found schools for the instruction of children in reading and writing and the Christian faith. At the close of the eighteenth century a new system of education invented by Joseph Lancaster also gave at least a fillip to those who were trying to found schools. By this method, known as the monitorial system, information was imparted through question-and-answer, the older boys who had learned the lessons in turn passing them on to groups of a dozen or so younger boys. In this way Lancaster claimed that a thousand boys could be taught for the expense of one master. But under such a system the standard reached could not be high, and many lost such enthusiasm for learning as they possessed. Moreover, to the end of the century, many children never attended school of any sort, and thousands of the poorest classes in the towns remained sunk in the most brutal forms of ignorance.

The Lancastrian system

In a violent age, the spirit of violence naturally infected the law. In the absence of any effective police—the parish watchmen and constables were quite powerless in the towns, where they were most needed—very few criminals were caught. Those that were, were therefore punished in public and with great severity as a warning to others. Parson Woodforde, for instance, records for July 22nd, 1777: 'Robert Biggen for stealing potatoes was this afternoon whipped thro' the streets of Cary (Somerset) by the hangman at the end of a cart. He was whipped from the George Inn to the Angel, from thence back through the street to the Royal Oak in South Cary and so back to the George Inn.' Nowhere were such whippings more frequent than in the armed forces: a hundred or more lashes with the cat-o'-nine-tails was a not uncommon punishment for the slow or insubordinate seaman, and in the Army one soldier of George II is known to have received 30,000 lashes in sixteen years.

Crime and punishment

Flogging

As to executions, public hanging after a procession from the jail was a popular event and an excuse for a general holiday. In London such hangings took place at Tyburn

Hanging

The Rake's Progress
Scene VIII: The Madhouse

The last scene in Hogarth's famous series shows the Rake insane, and in Bedlam. A faithful female still attends him, while a gaoler slips irons round his legs. Others here have been driven mad by love, melancholy, music, study, dreams of grandeur and religion. Two ladies visit the asylum for amusement.

until 1783, when they were transferred to Newgate. The following year James Boswell, Dr. Johnson's biographer, saw fifteen men hanged there at one time. Not one of them was a murderer and most were thieves—for with the growth of crime in the eighteenth century more and more offences (200 in all) became punishable by death, and by this time the death penalty could be inflicted for stealing anything to the value of five shillings from a shop or one shilling from a person. Another frequent sentence was transportation to America or, later, to Australia. Imprisonment was a punishment little less severe, for prisoners were

Transportation

Imprisonment

ill treated by gaolers anxious to wring money out of them, and the overcrowding and filthy conditions were so bad that few survived a long term. 'Gaol-fever'—a form of typhus—was constantly breaking out, and in 1750 at the famous Black Sessions at the Old Bailey four out of the six judges and forty of the other officials died from the fever they caught from the prisoners at Newgate.

In such an age people were used to witnessing suffering, and were often callous except where they themselves or their near ones were concerned. Suffering from disease and ill-health was of course ever present, and dentistry in particular was still very primitive. 'My tooth pained me all night', records Parson Woodforde. '. . . got up a little after 5 this morning and sent for one Reeves, a man who draws teeth in the parish, and about 7 he came and drew my tooth, but shockingly bad indeed. Gave the old man

Dentistry

Transplanting Teeth, 1787

From an engraving by Rowlandson. The poor sell their teeth—the woman look ruefully at the coin in her hand—and these are transplanted into the jaws of th better-off.

The Dissecting Room, 1790
From an engraving by Rowlandson.

that drew it, however, 2/6*d*. He is too old, I think, to draw teeth, can't see very well.' Normally teeth remained in the mouth until they gave so much pain that they had to be extracted, for stopping was almost unknown. False teeth, however, could now be supplied; they were either made from bone or were real teeth taken from corpses, and they were fastened in by wire.

In medicine, though the general level was far from high, Medicine there were real improvements. Hospitals were built all over the country—Guy's, Westminster, St. George's, London Hospitals and Middlesex hospitals were all founded in London between 1720 and 1745—and surgeons became distinct from barbers. Operations of course remained dangerous and there were no anaesthetics: normally the patient was given brandy and people stood by to hold him down. Ordinary doctors were indeed still old-fashioned, and most people made do with a traditional remedy prescribed by

D*

Rustic Amusements

From a painted screen in the Victoria and Albert Museum. *Top, l. to r.,* hunting, cockfighting, shooting and fishing. *Bottom, l. to r.,* cards, bowls, racing, dice, bathing

the woman of the house, the apothecary, the midwife, or the village blacksmith. Nevertheless, such men as John Hunter, the surgeon, were responsible for an immense improvement in medical knowledge. And in its closing years the century saw the great scourge of smallpox at last checked when Edward Jenner, against intense opposition, introduced vaccination. Hunter and Jenner

It was partly owing to this improvement in medical science, and partly owing to practical improvements in some of the towns, such as the paving and lighting of streets and the covering-in of drains, that from 1730 onwards the death-rate began to fall sharply. Better supplies of food and goods, including china and earthenware crockery and washable cotton clothes, also helped. So great was the decline, especially in infant mortality, that the population of England and Wales, estimated at 5½ million in 1700, was 9 million when the first census was taken in 1801. During the same period the population of Ireland rose even more steeply—from about 1½ million to 4 million. Decline in death-rate Increase in population

In a tough age many of the sports favoured by high and low alike were tough or even cruel. Cock-fighting was the most popular: the fights lasted as long as an hour, for the birds were specially bred, and rarely stopped until one was dead. At a main—a meeting at which a large number of fights were arranged—a competition might be held on 'knock-out' lines, lasting three or four days, at the end of which only one cock out of sixty or so would still be alive. Heavy betting took place at these meetings, as it did at the great prize-fights which were another popular entertainment. The champions fought without gloves and the fight continued over perhaps fifty rounds until a knock-out. Bear-baiting and bull-baiting also remained popular, and in some places (such as Stamford) bulls were baited throughout the length of the town. Sports and pastimes Cock-fighting Boxing

In the country, hunting the fox was gaining favour over the older sports of deer-hunting and hare-hunting, and the middle years of the century saw the birth of several of the great Hunts, such as the Belvoir, the Cottesmore and the Pytchley. Shooting with the shotgun was replacing hawking, Hunting Shooting

A Prize Fight, 1810

From an engraving by Rowlandson. Ten thousand people, it was reckoned,
gathered to see this match for 200 guineas between Dutch Sam (*l.*) and Medley (*r.*)
on Moulsey Hurst, near Hampton. Sam won, 'after a severe and bloody contest
of 49 rounds'.

netting and liming, and poaching was becoming more
difficult as game laws and gamekeepers multiplied. Of
indoor pastimes in town and country alike, dancing and
drinking retained their immemorial appeal, and cards
were becoming ever more popular. From about 1770
smoking ceased to be a habit of polite circles, who confined
themselves to snuff-taking: but those beneath the gentry
continued to puff their pipes. Of the open-air games, bowls,
skittles and fives were still favourites, and football still a
village rough-and-tumble. And it is pleasant to think that
among our many debts to this fruitful and vigorous age, is

Cricket   modern cricket. From a rustic game played with a curved
bat and two stumps, into the space between which the
ball had to be popped while the batsman was running, it
became a sport in which squire joined with servant, county
clashed with county, and a third stump and a straight bat
brought untold possibilities of skilful play—to those with
the necessary skill.

CHAPTER SEVEN

EIGHTEENTH CENTURY LIFE (II)
(c. 1720–1780)

1. Wales, Scotland, and Ireland

MANY of the changes in English society during this period also affected Wales; but perhaps the most distinctive development in Welsh life was the educational revival which set in under the first two Georges.

Up to this point, as the upper classes had modelled themselves on their counterpart in England and the lower classes were illiterate, Wales was steadily losing her separate identity. Charity schools and Sunday schools were now started and run by voluntary subscription and help, the main purpose being to teach the uneducated masses to read the Bible. In most areas it was the Welsh Bible they were given. At the same time a number of great preachers arose who put Christianity vividly before the Welsh people in their own language. The religious movement they set on foot gradually united with Methodism and eventually took the great majority of Welshmen outside the Church of England. In these two developments may be found the seeds of the great revival of Welsh national feeling and culture during the nineteenth and twentieth centuries.

In Scotland the most striking fact during the first half of the eighteenth century was the continued poverty of the country. Gentry elected to Parliament found it difficult to afford the journey to Westminster; and ordinary men lived little above the starvation level. The main cause of this, apart from the low fertility of the Highland soil, was to be found in a bad system of land tenure and primitive methods of agriculture. No attempt was made to drain the valleys, and there were few trees to shelter crops and cattle, a fact which led Dr. Johnson to observe that 'a tree in Scotland

Wales

Popular education begins

Welsh language and culture

Scotland: The general poverty

Swansea at the End of the Eighteenth Century

From an engraving by Rowlandson.

is as rare as a horse in Venice'. The cattle remained poor and low in yield of milk, and most agricultural workers existed largely on oatmeal. The houses of these workers were no more than huts (which they sometimes shared at night with their cattle), and their clothes were of an extremely coarse home-spun. In some areas no shoes were worn except on Sunday, and then—so uncomfortable were they to walk in—they were often put on only at the church door.

Improvement after 1750

After 1750 there was a steady improvement in living conditions. New methods of agriculture brought in from England gradually increased the yield of the land and with it the wealth of the people. In some cases the desire for increased returns tempted lairds and chiefs to evict their tenants, but the great migration from the Highlands that began in the 1770s was also due to reports of opportunities in America sent back by the Highlanders who had served there in the armed forces.

Migration from Highlands

The Scottish towns had always enjoyed a higher standard of life than the countryside, and during the second half of

the eighteenth century Edinburgh and Glasgow boasted
many of the foremost scholars and thinkers of the day. They
included Adam Smith, the great economist and author of
The Wealth of Nations—a plea for freer trade and less
official regulation of industry—David Hume, the philosopher and historian, and Dr. Black, the famous chemist.
By 1801 Glasgow, which was growing wealthy on the
American and West Indian trade, was larger than Edinburgh. But the latter, too, expanded in the second half of
the century. In particular, building started in the Princes
Street area, and people of quality gradually left the old
city to live in these newly developed districts.

In the Scottish capital the day's work started early at the
beginning of the century. The shops were open by seven.
The shopkeepers took breakfast at eight, leaving their wives
to tend the shops, and dinner at one. Shops reopened at two
and closed at four. At that hour started the four hours
observed all over Scotland when the ladies entertained in
their houses. Until 1720 they offered—and drank—ale and
claret, but after that tea became the more polite beverage
for this time of the day. At eight o'clock followed supper.

All was different on the Sabbath, both in Edinburgh and
throughout Scotland. In the earlier part of the century
everyone had to attend two services on a Sunday, both
lasting over two hours. Practically no other activity was
allowed. It was an offence to fetch a pail of water, cut kail,
or go for a walk. The ecclesiastical authorities even banned
Sunday smuggling. But as Scotland gradually became less
isolated, so the strictest severity of the Sabbath was relaxed,
and by 1800 people were free, at least in Edinburgh, to go
out for a walk on Sunday. They could too, without undue
risk, cut the services. Nevertheless, the conception of a strict
Sabbath continued to be generally upheld throughout Scotland—as indeed in many quarters it still is.

In Ireland too, as in Scotland, the gentry were often
poor, but for a very different reason. They were notorious
for their extravagance, and often ruined themselves by the
grand scale on which they entertained. Lord Chesterfield,
a Viceroy of Ireland in the 1740s, wrote: 'Drinking is a

most beastly vice in every country, but it is really a ruinous one to Ireland. Nine gentlemen in ten in Ireland are impoverished by the great quantity of claret which from mistaken notions of hospitality and dignity they think it necessary should be drunk in their houses.' One gentleman of the period is reported to have kept a brace of loaded pistols on his dinner table: one he used for tapping the

Making Linen Thread in County Down, *c.* 1790

From a contemporary engraving. The processes shown are spinning (two women are engaged in this), reeling with the clock reel, and boiling the yarn.

cask of claret after dinner, the other to challenge anyone who failed to do justice to the wine. The other great occupation of the Irish gentry was equally expensive—hunting. 'My dearest life will be surprised', wrote an Irish gentleman to his wife in 1726, 'and I fear be angry, when I tell you that I went to bed last night at one of the clock, was on horseback this morning at four, rode eight miles before daybreak, hunted a fox afterwards, came back afterwards here to dinner and rode a-coursing this afternoon till nightfall—and I thank God I cannot say I am much the worse for it.'

Throughout the eighteenth century Dublin remained the second-largest city of the British Isles. Its intellectual life was vigorous, its social life gay; but both were the preserve of the Anglo-Irish Protestant minority, not the Irish Roman Catholic majority. Among the other Irish towns, Cork with its port and Belfast with its great linen trade rose to second and third place. Outside the towns the lot of the Irish peasant remained, as ever, miserable. Towards the end of the century it did improve, only to become dangerously dependent on a single crop—the potato.

Irish towns

The Irish peasant

2. *The Church and John Wesley*

Though Christianity remained a great and powerful force throughout Britain, under the first three Georges the pulse of religious life beat much more slowly than under the Stuarts. This was especially apparent in the Church of England, to which the great majority of the population still belonged. The strife of the previous century and of Anne's reign had left men suspicious of any form of religious enthusiasm, and inclined to place more emphasis on decent Christian living than on any particular Christian beliefs.

Decline of religious enthusiasm

This had the great advantage that the Church of England became more tolerant and no longer tried to force everyone to worship God within its walls. But it also had a disadvantage—that, as the extremes of religious zeal were discouraged, so slackness crept in. Some—though by no means all—of the higher clergy paid insufficient attention to their spiritual duties. Most of the bishops, for instance, while extremely intelligent and at least moderately pious, were appointed because they were Whig in sympathy, and were not persecutors of Nonconformists. They owed their positions to the favour of men like Walpole and Newcastle, and were therefore expected to live much of the year in London so that they could attend the House of Lords and support the ministry.

The Church more tolerant but slacker

Moreover, many of the higher clergy drew a good income by holding several posts at once and employing curates to carry out their duties for them. This was tolerated because church livings were regarded as property, to be received gratefully from a patron and enjoyed thereafter as the holder—and the patron—thought fit. Between the higher clergy and such curates there was of course the immense gap that we find in every sphere in the eighteenth century. The Bishop of Durham—one of the richer sees—had an annual income of £6,000; a curate commonly earned no more than £50. Parish livings also varied greatly in value, but in general they were becoming worth more and more as agriculture prospered and the proceeds from tithe or the glebe farm increased. This made them an increasingly desirable form of property. It was in the eighteenth century that the squire began to make a regular practice of appointing one of his younger sons to a living within his gift.

Together, all these things—absentee clerics, concern for property, and dislike of fanaticism—brought about a somewhat lukewarm atmosphere in the Church. While many clergy were conscientious and pious, many others were idle and worldly. It is therefore neither surprising that the great religious revival that took place in the later half of the century should have been the work of a priest of the Church of England—John Wesley—nor surprising that when it came the Church authorities disliked it and finally forced it outside the Church.

Wesley's father, the rector of Epworth in Lincolnshire, was a serious Christian, but still more devout was his mother. Intensely strict, she ruled her family of ten children (nine others had died) with a rod of iron, her motto being 'break the child's will'. When her children were whipped —which was frequently—she insisted that they should cry no more than 'softly', on pain of further whipping. Her strength of character was fully inherited by John, who already displayed it in remarkable fashion at the age of five. There was a fire at the rectory and John was asleep in the attic. He awoke to find the rafters and staircase in flames. He calmly dragged a chest over to the window, and clambered on to it so that those below could see him, with the result that two men climbed up and rescued him just before the roof crashed in. This coolness in danger was to stand him in good stead in later life.

Wesley's schooldays at Charterhouse were fairly normal, and it was not until he went up to Oxford that the full strength of his character emerged. When he arrived there in 1720, the atmosphere was very easy-going. There were few lectures or examinations and the majority of both fellows and undergraduates gave their attention to social pursuits. Wesley, however, though fond of light reading and good company, began to defy fashion and to work harder and harder. After five years he was ordained; then he adopted an even stricter mode of living, soon establishing the habit of rising every morning at four. In 1729, while a don, he took over the leadership of a small group of undergraduates who had gathered round his younger brother, Charles. Among the other members was George Whitefield, whose later talents as a preacher rivalled even Wesley's. The object of the group was to lead a more Christian life and help their fellows amidst the general slackness of Oxford. They prayed incessantly, attended communion once a week instead of the normal three times a year, fasted, preached in gaols, relieved the poor, and even practised such austerities as lying for hours in the snow to humble the body. Most of the University thought them a joke, if an uncomfortable one, and nicknamed them 'The Holy Club' or the 'Methodists' (because they strove to live by a certain method or rule of life). Wesley in the end accepted the latter term, which was a revival of a nickname earlier given to certain Puritans. He gave it a very simple definition: 'A Methodist is one who lives according to the method laid down in the Bible.'

Wesley at Oxford

The 'Holy Club', or 'Methodists'

John Wesley, however, was not yet certain that he was a true follower of Christ and that his soul had been saved. Leaving Oxford, he went with Charles on a mission to the newly founded colony of Georgia. His enthusiasm, individual ways and magnetic personality caused many storms among the colonists and the mission proved

Wesley's mission to Georgia

unsuccessful. But on his travels he had met, and been impressed by, a group of German Christians, and after his return he underwent a profound experience during one of their meetings at Aldersgate. It convinced him that he had found the true way to Christ and that he was in a deep, close and personal relationship with God. *His* sins had been forgiven, *his* soul had been saved. He now determined to bring the same comfort to all whom he could reach.

His
campaign
in Britain,
1739-91

In 1739, at the age of thirty-five, he started his great campaign. In the next fifty-two years he travelled nearly a quarter of a million miles and preached over forty thousand sermons, an average of roughly fifteen a week. To Ireland alone he went twenty-one times. What a familiar figure throughout the country he must have been! His clothes were simple, neat and black. His hat, black too, had no braid or lace. He never wore a wig. His figure was small

His
endurance

and wiry, yet graceful, He was inexhaustible and never wasted a moment. Until his last years he rode everywhere on horseback in all weathers, and while he rode he read, though this meant slackening the reins and resulted in several falls. After a year or so he preached practically

Open-air
preaching

always in the open, for most of the clergy greatly disapproved of the emotional scenes which his sermons produced, and the doors of the churches were soon shut against him. He began at Bristol, to which he had been called by Whitefield (who had started a mission to the miners of Kingswood), and his audiences often ran into thousands. His manner was quiet, simple and grave, but he gripped his hearers irresistibly by speaking straight to their hearts, and it was with ordinary working people, especially around Bristol and in the North, that he had his greatest successes. He had indeed an extraordinary magnetism which compelled attention. When he spoke of death —an ever-present reality in the eighteenth century—and the dangers of hell-fire, he made his message so vivid and so personal to each of his hearers that men as well as women frequently collapsed, weeping, crying out hysterically, and resolving to be born anew in a true Christian life.

Methodist
societies

When Wesley left a place he did not abandon those he

had converted. Methodist societies were set up all over the country—societies composed of local groups who prayed, confessed and consulted together. Over them all, and their finances, Wesley kept the strictest control—so much so that his critics dubbed him 'Pope John'. These societies were

John Wesley Preaching, 1766

Wesley preaching in the open air, from a painting by
Nathaniel Hone.

intended by Wesley to supplement attendance at the parish church, not supplant it. But soon Methodists were building their own chapels, partly because in many places there was no church, and partly because it was useful to' have a building in which a Methodist preacher was sure of a welcome. Moreover, in some churches Methodists were refused communion. From this, Methodism gradually became another branch of Nonconformity—though Wesley would never acknowledge the fact. The decisive moment came in 1784 when Wesley needed priests to administer communion to the growing numbers of Methodists in America—and no bishop would ordain any. So Wesley took it upon himself to ordain priests—first for America (where one soon called himself a bishop), then for Scotland and England. This was so great a violation of Church tradition that from this time onwards Methodism was, in effect— **Separation from Church of England** except in Wesley's own eyes—a movement separate from and outside the Church of England.

Charles Wesley In spreading Methodism one of Wesley's chief helpers was his brother Charles, a man of perhaps greater originality and wisdom, though much less driving-force. He was the great hymn-writer of the movement and was partly responsible for the increased importance of hymns in church services from the eighteenth century onwards—for before then congregational singing was mainly confined to psalms. **George Whitefield** Another great helper at first, George Whitefield, later left the movement, though he and Wesley continued to work in the same field. In some ways he was an even more forceful speaker than Wesley. Once he was comparing a sinner to a blind man tottering towards the edge of a precipice. The audience was held so spellbound that at the critical point, when the blind man was on the brink, a nobleman who was present leapt from his chair and exclaimed, 'By God, he's over!'

Mob violence The Methodists had no easy success. They were often savagely attacked by mobs who were sometimes egged on by the local squire or parson—for Wesley and his followers seemed a challenge to the established order of the country. At other times sheer delight in riot and disorder impelled the crowd, as so often in the eighteenth century; and many simple folk must also have been infuriated when members of their household who had become Methodists adopted saintly and uncomfortable ways. At all events, mob violence put Wesley himself on several occasions in danger of his life.

George Whitefield Preaching in Moorfields, 1750
From an engraving by R. Prancker.

He met every attack, however, with wonderful calm and assurance. In 1749 he only just escaped with his life from Falmouth. He returned two years before his death, and thus recorded his visit in his Journal (which he kept unflaggingly for half a century): 'The last time I was here, above forty years ago, I was taken prisoner by an immense mob gaping and roaring like lions. But how is the tide turned!—high and low now lined the street from one end of the town to the other, out of stark love and kindness, gaping and staring as if the King were going by. In the evening I preached on the smooth top of the hill to the largest congregation I have ever seen in Cornwall, except in or near Redruth.'

In many ways Wesley was an extremely unenlightened man, and in some ways his influence was positively harmful. He was immensely autocratic, and blind to the need for any political reform. He was highly intolerant of Roman _{Wesley's faults}

Catholics and Jews, believed firmly in devils and witches, and took grave decisions by opening the Bible at random and acting according to some text discovered on that page. In a medicine book that he published he recommended swallowing three ounces of quicksilver slowly as a cure for a twisted gut. Children, he maintained—following his mother —should have their will broken early; and, above all, they must never for a moment be allowed to play, but must always work—for as the hymn puts it, 'Satan finds some mischief still, for idle hands to do.'

His
achieve-
ment

Yet for all these opinions, as unattractive to most of us now as the architecture of his chapels, Wesley's was indeed a great work. For Wesley, conversion was all-important, but it was only the starting point: what must then follow was a life which expressed this Christian grace within—a life of thrift, sobriety, ceaseless toil and ceaseless charity. The result of his teaching was seen in a generally more serious approach to religion, and in the decline of that savagery which had been so strong a part of eighteenth century life. It was a great tragedy that his movement, against all his own wishes, was forced outside the Church of England. Nevertheless, few people in English history, and none in the eighteenth century, did more to make Christianity a prime influence in the life of the people.

CHAPTER EIGHT

SCIENCE AND DISCOVERY IN THE EIGHTEENTH CENTURY

1. *Science and the Steam-Engine*

ONE of the most important developments in Britain during the later seventeenth century had been the growth of experimental science associated with the newly formed Royal Society. In 1714, at the beginning of our period, there was still living one of the early members of this Society and the most famous scientist that Britain has yet produced—Sir Isaac Newton. He did not die until 1727, though his most important work was done in the seventeenth century. Before 1700 he had set out laws on such fundamental matters as the motion of earthly and heavenly bodies—laws which have been superseded only in the last fifty years. In mathematics and astronomy, optics and mechanics, he had broken entirely fresh ground; and to the eighteenth century his work was truly summed up in Pope's famous epigram:

> Nature and Nature's laws lay hid in night:
> God said, *Let Newton be!* and all was light.[1]

Though the eighteenth century produced no scientist quite so eminent as Newton, much important work was done. In physics much was discovered about heat and some of the first important experiments with electricity were carried out. It had long been known that amber and certain other substances will attract light objects when rubbed—hence the term 'electricity', which was first used

Sir Isaac Newton (margin note)

Electricity (margin note)

---

[1] A modern poet, J. C. Squire, has added a sequel:
>   It did not last: the Devil, howling 'Ho!
>   Let Einstein be!' restored the status quo.

in the 1640s, and which comes from the ancient Greek 'elektron', meaning amber. Beyond this, however, little more knowledge was gained until the eighteenth century. In 1729 an Englishman, Stephen Gray, discovered the principle of the conduction of electricity, and soon went on to find out which were the best conductors. About sixteen years later a Dutch professor discovered how to store the electrical charges produced from friction in an apparatus called the Leyden jar, and giving electrical shocks became a popular game. Louis XV of France, for instance, saw an electric shock administered to a line of monks a mile long and roared with laughter when they all jumped. In these early investigations into electricity two men of British stock took a leading part—Benjamin Franklin and Henry Cavendish.

Benjamin Franklin

Franklin (1706-90) was born in America, lived most of his life in Philadelphia, and after winning fame as a journalist, philosopher and reformer became one of the leaders of the American revolution. In this last capacity he spent some years in Europe—first negotiating with the British in an effort to avoid the conflict, and then negotiating with the French to secure their alliance. One of his many interests was electricity—he was responsible for the 'positive' and 'negative' classification—and he produced a theory that lightning was due to electricity and not to exploding gases as was then generally thought. He decided to test this theory. He made a kite with a pointed wire projection and at promising moments waited patiently in a shed for a thunderstorm. Eventually one came. He launched his kite and attached a metal door-key to the string. Before long, sparks were seen at the key—obviously the string was heavily charged with electricity. His theory had been

Lightning conductors

proved right, and it led to his lightning conductor—an invention which George III ordered for Buckingham Palace. Perhaps the most remarkable fact about the experiment was that Franklin did not electrocute himself.

Henry Cavendish

Cavendish (1731-1810), too, carried out extensive experiments with electricity. He tried to measure the relative conductive powers of different solids and liquids, but left

Franklin Drawing Lightning from
a Thundercloud

The scene reconstructed imaginatively by a modern
artist, A. R. Thompson.

unpublished most of the results, which were not known until after his death. The grandson of the second Duke of Devonshire, he was a complete recluse and had no interest except science. He lived by himself in a large house on Clapham Common, ordering all his meals by notes left on the hall table. His female servants were forbidden to come within his sight, he inherited a great sum of money and spent very little, and when he died he left over a million pounds.

Cavendish also played an important part in investigating the nature of matter and the change of substances from solids into liquids and from liquids into gases. This was the most important advance in eighteenth-century science and it laid the foundations of modern chemistry. Besides Cavendish, there were two other well-known British scientists engaged on these problems, the Unitarian minister Joseph

Priestley and Black

Priestley and Joseph Black, the Professor of Medicine and Chemistry at Glasgow. By the

Henry Cavendish

From a contemporary study.

end of the century the researches of these three and of the Swede, Karl Wilhelm Scheele, brilliantly supplemented and interpreted by the famous French chemist, Antoine Lavoisier, had utterly discredited the traditional theory derived from the Middle Ages that matter consisted of four elements only—earth, air, fire, and water. They discovered that there were different kinds of air or gas—Black for instance, discovered what we now call carbon dioxide, Cavendish hydrogen, Scheele and Priestley (independently) oxygen—and that the atmospheric air, instead of being the only one, was not a basic element and could be split up into component gases. Their researches—though the Englishmen failed to recognize it and Lavoisier did—pointed to the fact that 'phlogiston', the 'fiery matter' which apparently issued from anything when it was burnt, was a myth; combustion occurred not because the substance 'lost' its phlogiston but

End of 'Four elements' theory

A Newcomen Pumping Engine, 1705

[Al]ternate admission of [ste]am into the cylinder [fro]m the boiler beneath, [an]d condensation of the [ste]am to create a partial [va]cuum, caused the [pis]ton in the cylinder to [ris]e and fall. This [roc]ked the connected [ligh]tly balanced beam [up] and down. By means [of] rods at the far end of [the] beam, a pumping [ac]tion was produced in [the] mine below.

The ENGINE for Raising Water (with a power made) by Fire

A Watt Steam-Engine for Rotative Motion, 1787

Steam enters the cylinder (left) successively at each end, so driving the piston both up and down. A separate condenser (in cold water beneath), kept vacuous by an air pump, obviates any need to chill the cylinder. 'Sun' and 'planet' cog-wheels — the former fastened to the fly-wheel, the latter to the connecting rod — convert the rocking of the beam into the rotary motion of the flywheel.

because it gained oxygen from the air. By the end of the century the exact nature of air, water, respiration and com-
Modern chemistry bustion was at last clear. The modern study of chemistry had begun.

While the investigation of electricity had for a long time little direct effect on national life, the research into gases and the heat required to convert a liquid into a gas soon had immense practical consequences. For it led to the rapid improvement of the steam-engine—an event which more than any other single factor brought about the Industrial Revolution.

Steam engines The earliest steam-engines in England owed little to science. The first to be used commercially was produced
Newcomen's engine about 1705 by Thomas Newcomen, a Devonport black-smith. By 1750 several hundred of these engines were at work, mainly in mines, in Cornwall, the Midlands and the North. They were used for little except pumping, as they produced only an up-and-down motion. They were atmospheric engines as much as steam-engines, i.e. the steam drove the piston up, but the weight of the atmosphere was used to drive it down. The cylinder was filled with steam and this forced the piston up. Cold water was then injected, which caused the steam to condense; and this created a partial vacuum so that the pressure of the atmosphere drove the piston down. This meant that little power could be developed, especially as really accurate metal-working was impossible at this time and leaks were frequent. The engines were immensely wasteful of fuel and could only be used where coal was very cheap or the mineral being mined was very dear. They were also extremely cumbersome. An improved version designed by Smeaton in 1774 had a cylinder 6 feet in diameter and $6\frac{1}{2}$ tons in weight. The piston stroke was $9\frac{1}{2}$ feet. Even so, it developed no more power than the engine of a modern lorry.

It was James Watt who brought about a radical improvement in the design. He was born in 1736 at Port Greenock, near Glasgow. He went to London to learn instrument-making and returned to Glasgow to follow this trade, setting up his shop inside the University buildings. One day he was asked to repair a model of Newcomen's pump that belonged to the University. He made it work but was amazed at its inefficiency. This set him thinking, and he discussed the whole question of steam with students and with Professor Black. He soon realized one of the main causes of waste in the Newcomen engine. Every time the cold water was injected into the cylinder the temperature of the latter was reduced to 100° Fahrenheit. Every time a fresh charge of steam was let in, the cylinder had to be reheated to 212° and four-fifths of the steam was spent on this reheating. Until the cylinder reached that temperature the steam condensed and was simply wasted from the point of view of creating power.

After two years Watt in 1765 found a solution to the problem. He fitted a separate condenser outside the cylinder and linked to it by valves. The condenser was surrounded by cold water. At the right moment the valve was opened, and the steam entered the condenser and condensed there. No cold water was injected into the cylinder, the temperature of which was not greatly reduced. This was a much more economical principle, and purchasers of Watt's engines paid for them on the basis of the coal they saved. *Watt's first engine* *The condenser*

Watt later made two other important improvements, which were included in the new patent he took out in 1782. He made the engine double-acting—i.e. steam was let in on both sides of the piston alternately—and he adopted a device for turning the up-and-down movement into a rotary motion. This meant that the engine could be used in mills for driving machinery. Some of Watt's earliest engines can still be seen in the Science Museum, and though by modern standards they are hopelessly inefficient they were an enormous improvement on their predecessors. His double-acting engines were, of course, pure steam-engines—i.e. worked by steam only—though at low pressure. The high-pressure steam-engine was still something for the future, for metals of sufficient strength and workmanship of sufficient accuracy did not yet exist. *Watt's later engines* *Rotary motion*

2. *Measurement and Maritime Discovery*

Measurement

The eighteenth century also saw many improvements in the accuracy with which measurements could be made—a basic need of modern science. The Fahrenheit scale for temperature was drawn up, and before the end of the century was widely accepted. Among other improvements in measurement in England was the abandonment of the old and inaccurate calendar, the Julian Calendar (so called from Julius Caesar), which was behind time as its year was in fact slightly longer than the actual time taken for the earth to revolve round the sun.

Gregorian calendar introduced, 1752

During the sixteenth century a revised calendar—the Gregorian (from Pope Gregory XIII)—had been drawn up, with its system of leap-years, and it had been gradually adopted by most countries in Western Europe. Now at last in 1752 Britain followed suit. The day after Wednesday, September 2nd, was called September 14th, thus cancelling the eleven-day error that had accumulated over the years. The alteration caused some outcry: 'Give us back our eleven days!' ran the slogan of those who thought that the government had cheated them out of several days of their life—and summer days too. At the same time as this major change the new year was henceforth, in accordance with the normal use on the Continent, taken to begin on January 1st, instead of on March 25th as previously.[1]

Another most important improvement during the eighteenth century was in the measurement of time at sea. An accurate chronometer was at last invented, and this solved the mariners' greatest problem—that of fixing their longitude. Sailors had long known how to discover their latitude by finding the angle between the horizon and the sun or some star. They were enabled to do this with

Longitude and the chronometer

[1] In the old style of dates, any event in January–March thus belonged to a year previous to the one we should count it in. Thus the execution of Charles I took place, according to the contemporary English reckoning, in (January) 1648, but by our reckoning in 1649. In Scotland, the change to a new year beginning on January 1st had been introduced in 1600.

greater accuracy after the invention of the sextant in the eighteenth century. Longitude was theoretically easy enough to discover if the time of sunrise could be compared with a clock set to some standard time. But clocks of the sixteenth and seventeenth centuries when taken to sea lost or gained as much as fifteen minutes a day and were hopeless for navigation—an inaccuracy of fifteen minutes is equivalent to nearly four degrees of longitude. In 1707 an English fleet met disaster on the Scilly Isles, the admiral being drowned, owing to a mistake in the reckoning of longitude. In 1714, partly as a result, the government set up a 'Board of Longitude' which was to give £20,000 to the first man to discover an accurate method of determining longitude. At length, in 1762, Harrison, a London watch-maker, produced a chronometer which after a voyage of 147 days had an error of only 1 minute 54½ seconds. The problem of longitude was solved, and George III forced the reluctant Board to pay Harrison the full reward. Harrison's chrono-meter, 1762

During the same period navigation was also much aided by the establishment of lighthouses. One example will suffice. Thirteen miles south of Plymouth lie the dangerous Eddystone Rocks. Here in 1759 the engineer Smeaton succeeded in building a stone lighthouse after two previous wooden lighthouses had been destroyed. It lasted until 1882, and was abandoned then only because the rock on which it was built was crumbling. Lighthouses

Such developments as these lightened the task of the British sailor. Among these sailors was the greatest of all British maritime explorers, and one who himself added much to scientific knowledge, James Cook. Captain Cook

Born in 1728, Cook first went to sea in a Whitby collier. Later he joined the Navy and played a major part in the difficult task of navigating the fleet during Wolfe's expedition to Quebec. At the age of forty Cook's great chance came and he seized it with both hands. The Royal Society decided to send a party to the South Pacific to observe the transit of Venus across the face of the sun, and the Navy provided a vessel. Cook was appointed by the Admiralty as commander, and the *Endeavour*, a Whitby collier of

360 tons, was chosen as the ship. Cook was ordered to take the scientists to Tahiti, recently discovered, and then to investigate the coast-line of the great southern continent which was marked in many maps of the time. According to some of these—presumably compiled from a mixture of legend and hearsay—this coast-line stretched from Staten Land (now Staten Island) south of Cape Horn in a vague line to the north point of New Zealand. With an even greater vagueness this vast continent was called Terra Australis Incognita. From this great land-mass the continent later called Australia was already known to be separate—a fact established by the Dutch explorer Tasman in the seventeenth century.

Cook's voyage of 1768-71

Cook's first voyage lasted from 1768 to 1771. He reached Tahiti successfully by 'running down the latitude', for he had no exact idea of the longitude of either Tahiti or his own ship. He did not carry one of Harrison's chronometers till his second voyage. After observing the transit of Venus, Cook sailed south and then west to investigate the supposed southern continent. He met no land until he came to New Zealand. It was at Young Nick's Head (called after the boy

Survey of New Zealand

who sighted it) that Cook made his landfall. He surveyed the entire coast, discovering the strait which separates the North and South Islands and which bears his name. More important still, he sailed round South Island, thus proving it was no part of a southern continent. From New Zealand

Survey of east coast of Australia

he sailed west and eventually struck the east coast of Australia, which he claimed for Britain. He decided to sail north along it, a voyage till then not attempted. Along the coast of New South Wales all was well, but farther north the Great Barrier Reef closes with the coast and Cook was in great difficulties. *Endeavour* struck a reef. It was twenty-four hours before Cook got her off, and then it was touch and go whether she would sink. He managed to beach her on the Queensland coast and effect repairs. He then passed through Endeavour Strait and so proved that Australia and New Guinea were separate—a fact previously discovered by the Spaniards, but by now either forgotten or denied. After refitting in Batavia he sailed back to England.

John Smeaton
From a painting by Romney.

James Cook
From a painting by John Webber.

Cook's second voyage lasted from 1772 to 1775. The southern continent was still his main objective. It proved very elusive. Twice he crossed the Antarctic Circle, a feat never before recorded in history, but in the southern latitudes he could find no continent—only individual islands like South Georgia. He also discovered many of the small islands farther north in the Pacific. Perhaps the most remarkable thing in this voyage was that he lost only one man from sickness. This was because he insisted on rigorous cleanliness and always took fruit juice among his stores, so largely eliminating scurvy.

Voyage of 1772–5

Search for southern continent

South Georgia

In 1776 Cook sailed on his third voyage. He had now cleared up the geography of the extreme south, and this time his object was to discover whether there was a passage out of the Pacific north of America into Hudson's Bay— 'the North-West passage' so often sought from the Atlantic side in the past. After discovering the Sandwich Islands in the Pacific, he sailed north through the Bering Strait, but was there met by a solid wall of ice which prevented further progress. Returning, he explored Hawaii. On his first arrival there he was treated as a god, but quarrels over pilfering soon arose, and in 1779, while trying to take a hostage, he was set upon by the natives and clubbed to death. Thus ended the life of a man who had pursued geographical exploration in a truly scientific spirit, and who in so doing had laid bare most of the last great secrets of the seas.

Voyage of 1776–9

Sandwich Islands

Hawaii

Death

CHAPTER NINE

THE AGRICULTURAL REVOLUTION

THE term Agricultural (or Agrarian) Revolution is generally applied to the extremely important changes that took place in British agriculture during the eighteenth century. These changes may be summed up as the development of better crops and livestock, and intensification of the enclosure movement.

The introduction of the new farming methods owed little to scientific study. Rather was it due in the main to the practical good sense of a number of gentlemen farmers. The first of these was Jethro Tull (died 1741), who after an education at Eton and Oxford decided to run a farm in Berkshire which he had inherited. He was an enterprising man and tried out many new ideas. The most fruitful was a new method of sowing. Up to this time seed had been scattered broadcast from the hand of the sower. Tull, from observation, found out that seed grew best at definite depths and intervals which differed according to the crops. Accuracy could not be obtained from broadcast sowing, and Tull solved the problem by inventing a horse-drawn drill which sowed the seed in rows and at the right depth. This had another advantage—it made hoeing possible, and Tull invented a horse-drawn hoe which could be used between the rows. This not only kept down the weeds but ventilated the soil and so improved the growth of crops. Tull achieved startling results, getting crops twice as heavy as normal from fields where he had sown only a third of the normal quantity of seed.

An even more important improvement in farming was the introduction of the Norfolk rotation. This consisted of a four-year sequence of crops—clover, wheat, turnips, barley —which could be started again at the end of the fourth year. By this system land could be kept under crop every year, for the clover and the turnips broke up the soil and allowed it to recover its nitrogen. The common practice of letting land lie fallow every third year, or even in some places every other year, thus became unnecessary, with immensely beneficial results to the national food supply. _{Fallow avoided}

Two Agricultural Labourers

om drawings by a Swiss artist, S. H. Grimm, who worked in England from 1768 to 1794.

In this change Lord Townshend, who put all his energy into farming after he retired from politics in 1730, was the most important figure, although he did not invent the system. The idea came from Holland, where Townshend had been ambassador, and other farmers had experimented on the same lines. It was called the Norfolk rotation because Townshend's estates were there and he was enough of an enthusiast to have earned the nickname of 'Turnip'. Apart from introducing the new rotation, Townshend also greatly increased the fertility of his estates by marling, a practice in which he was followed by another famous Norfolk farmer, Coke of Holkham, forty years later. This consisted of digging up the marl—a compound of clay and lime that lay beneath the surface—and mixing it with the light sandy top soil.

Tull's and Townshend's methods led to better cultivation, and their ideas gradually spread. It has been reckoned that between 1750 and 1800 the yield of wheat per acre in Britain increased by a third. But the widespread introduction of turnips—which had previously only been grown experimentally or as a garden vegetable—had another result almost as important, for it provided livestock food for the winter, and so rendered unnecessary the annual autumn slaughter of cattle which had gone on from time immemorial. And with herds being kept throughout the winter, there was soon an improvement in the quality of livestock quite as striking as the improvement in cultivation.

Winter food for cattle: no autumn slaughter

Robert Bakewell and stock-breeding

The leader in the new methods of improved stock-breeding was Robert Bakewell (died 1795), a tenant farmer in Derbyshire. By intense inbreeding for the points he required he produced larger and better-quality sheep and cattle. The result is shown by the figures that still exist for the sales of cattle at Smithfield in this period. Between 1710 and 1795 the average weight of oxen increased from 370 lb. to 800 lb. and that of sheep from 38 lb. to 80 lb. These figures must be treated with some caution, as it seems that in the case of cattle and oxen it was not the practice at the beginning of the century to send the largest animals to London. No one, however, can reasonably doubt that there was a large increase in size owing to Bakewell's methods and the better supplies of fodder.

Potatoes

Apart from turnips, another root crop, the potato, was also now increasing in favour. By 1750 it was important in Ireland, in Scotland and Wales, and in the north-west of England. It could be found too in the market gardens round London, but it was not yet a staple article of diet throughout the British Isles.

Enclosure

While the improvements were spreading among those who already enjoyed compact farms, at the same time there was a growing movement to enclose those areas where the open-field system still existed. The pace of enclosure, which had been going on since Tudor times—the lord of the manor's demesne land was of course the first to be enclosed—increased very rapidly after 1750, and by 1850 the open

Tees-Water old or unimproved breed.

Tees-Water improved breed.

Old Style Sheep—and New

Note the great increase in weight of eatable flesh.

fields had practically disappeared from the English land-scape. In some areas, notably the Midland plain and the eastern counties, over half the land was enclosed during this period. So complete was the process that the only places where open arable fields can be seen today are small patches at Braunton (North Devon), Laxton (Nottinghamshire) and Haxey and Epworth (Isle of Axholme).

How was the land enclosed? The process was usually started by the larger local landowners, who were aware that the old system of commons and open fields was inefficient. In particular, they had come to realize that a great deal of time was wasted in travelling between the scattered strips; that new methods of cultivation could not be applied in open fields where everyone grew the same crop; and that the commons yielded very little, and encouraged the spread of disease among the cattle which mingled freely there. They therefore wanted the land enclosed in compact fields, each belonging to an individual. Before 1750 this rearrangement was often made by local agreement, but after 1750 it was practically always ratified or enforced by Parliament. The local landowners presented a Bill to Parliament; and provided that the lord of the manor, the tithe-holders, and the owners of four-fifths of the strips were agreeable, the Bill was passed and became an Act. Under the Act, Commissioners were appointed to redistribute the land. They descended on the area, marked out the new fields and allotted them in solid blocks to the various landowners in proportion to land and common rights they had previously held. The new owners were obliged to fence their fields within twelve months. This was a very expensive process, for a bank or ditch had to be made, and a paling put up until the hawthorn or quickset hedges, which we can still see stretching for hundreds of miles in the Midlands, had become effective barriers.

Method of enclosure

What were the effects of enclosure? It greatly changed the pattern of the English countryside in that broad belt across the Midlands where the open-field system had been most widely established and where most of the enclosures were made. Gone were the old fields open to sky and wind

Effects of enclosure

Changed pattern of countryside

A Lord of the Manor receiving Rents

From a satirical drawing by Rowlandson. The bloated and gout-ridden figure of the landlord is in sharp contrast to the lean frames and worn faces of the tenants.

with their dozens of strips, their green balks and their winding paths. Gone, too, was the old common land, lying beyond the open fields. This also was divided up into fields surrounded by hedges, and gradually farmhouses were built out in the middle of the fields so that the farmer could be on the spot. In Leicestershire many were built at this time, as their names indicate—names such as Quebec, Belle Isle, Hanover, Bunker's Hill and New York.

In general the Commissioners seem to have been very conscientious in allocating land, even to the humblest free-holder or commoner; but there was one class very badly hit by the new measures—the cottager who was not a com-moner. Though he had no legal right to do so, he had often fed his animals on the common land for generations, and often too his dwelling was on the common land—again with no legal right. As a result of enclosure a 'squatter' of Hardship to 'squatters' on commons this type might find himself deprived of his hut and his use of the common. Sometimes the Commissioners compensated him for the latter even where he had no legal title, but there were many squatters who would have echoed the famous complaint of one villager: 'Parliament may be tender of property: all I know is that I had a cow, and an Act of Parliament has taken it from me.' According to law the Commissioners were right; according to justice they were often wrong.

Expense for smallholders   Another class who may well have suffered were those who received a plot of land but lacked the means to clear it and to hedge and ditch it. Many of these sold up to larger landowners and either became landless labourers or went off to try their fortune in the towns.

It cannot, however, be denied that in general the enclosure movement was greatly for the good of the country. In combination with the new farming methods it enabled Increased food supply   the land to produce much more food. Without this an increasing population could not have been sustained and the situation during the Napoleonic wars would have been still more difficult than it was. Old common or waste land—and the two are difficult to distinguish—was far more Commons in cultivation   profitably used when it was enclosed, and it is reckoned that between 1750 and 1850 another two million acres were brought under cultivation as a result of enclosure. Also, as we have seen, the narrow strips of the old fields discouraged efficient agriculture and prevented proper drainage. They would have created an impossible problem later when agricultural machinery began to be used on a large scale.

Nor did enclosure bring any general depopulation of the countryside. Until after 1815 the villages continued to grow at a rate not much less than the towns. Hoeing, hedging, ditching, all created new demands for labour. Even the number of smallholders, both freeholders and tenants, seems to have increased until 1815, and their decline after then was mainly due not to any direct result of enclosure but to the post-war slump in prices and the inefficiency of this type of holding as compared with the larger farm. Only in the Highlands of Scotland was there direct and wholesale eviction. Here the landowners introduced sheep-farming on a big scale and, like their counterparts in Tudor England, turned out their tenants in the glens to provide more winter feeding for the sheep. All told, however, in relation to the size of the change and the benefits achieved, the amount of hardship involved in the enclosure movement of eighteenth-century Britain was small. Certainly it was insignificant compared, for instance, with the immense human suffering caused by the great agricultural changes in Russia during the 1930s.

Hardship small in relation to benefits

CHAPTER TEN

THE INDUSTRIAL REVOLUTION

1. *Coal, Iron, and Engineering*

ROM Tudor times onwards, the industries of Britain had been steadily expanding and multiplying. In the latter half of the eighteenth century the speed of this growth was so quickened, and its nature so extended, that the term 'industrial revolution' has been applied to the changes which then began.

The industrial developments which Britain first saw during these years were so sweeping that it is impossible to describe them in a few words. The most fundamental, however, was the introduction of man-made power. In earlier times, unless he could harness the wind or a river, man had been forced to use either his own muscles or those of a domestic animal for every task. The Industrial Revolution began to alter all this.

The new ideas and practices introduced during the eighteenth century by no means affected all industries. They transformed, however, three great industries—the coal, iron, and textile—and created a fourth—engineering. The textile industry apart, the great centre of these changes was the West Midlands, in what was soon, unfortunately, to be accurately described as the 'Black Country'. Here large industrial towns, such as Birmingham and Wolverhampton, quickly grew up. Birmingham, for instance, in the course of the eighteenth century grew from a small country town to a major industrial centre with a population of over 70,000.[1] During the same period, Warwickshire and Staffordshire doubled their number of inhabitants.

It was not in the heart but on the western fringes of this district, on the wooded banks of the Severn, that the first

The Industrial Revolution

The fundamental: machine-power

The industries first affected

The West Midlands

Birmingham

The Severn Valley

---

[1] Today it is the second largest city in England.

Darby's Ironworks at Coalbrookdale
One of the first great enterprises of the Industrial Revolution.

great discovery of the Industrial Revolution was made. Round about 1709, at Coalbrookdale in Shropshire, the Quaker ironmaster Abraham Darby discovered how to *Darby and* smelt iron ore with coal that had been coked. The process *coke-smelting,* was much improved by his son between 1730 and 1740; *c. 1709* and it completely overcame the great difficulty attending all efforts to smelt iron with untreated coal—that the gases released from the coal affected the iron and made it too brittle.

As the practice of smelting by coke spread, it completely altered the site and scale of the iron industry. Iron ore can be found in many different parts of Britain, and in earlier days the centres of the trade had been in Sussex and the Forest of Dean. Here there were ample supplies of wood which was turned into charcoal and then used for smelting the ore. In the eighteenth century both these areas and especially Sussex were running short of timber; and for this reason ironmasters had been attracted to Shropshire, where there were still large woodland areas. It was pure chance that Shropshire had coal which, when coked, proved particularly suitable for smelting. Once, however,

Changes in centres of iron industry

coke was substituted for charcoal the sites of the industry were shifted to those areas where coal and iron could be found near together. Such districts became great new industrial centres—among them not only the West Midlands, but also South Wales, Tees-side, Tyneside, and the Scottish Lowlands.

Growth in iron output

The use of coal made the smelting of iron ore very much cheaper and easier. An immense expansion of output followed. From an annual production of less than 3,000 tons of pig-iron in the early years of the century, the Shropshire industry developed until by 1788 it was producing nearly 25,000 tons a year, more than a third of England's total output. By 1830 Shropshire alone was producing 70,000 tons, but by then had been overtaken by other districts. The Shropshire industry was concentrated in a narrow district around Coalbrookdale and the Severn valley, where there were soon more blast-furnaces than in any other comparable area in Britain. By 1785 the Darby works at Coalbrookdale comprised ten blast-furnaces, nine forges and sixteen 'fire engines' (steam-engines). Twenty miles of iron railway connected their various installations.

John Wilkinson

By this time the most famous man in the iron industry was John Wilkinson. His father had been an ironmaster in north Lancashire, but the family had moved south to Wrexham, where they owned a furnace. John Wilkinson was attracted from here to the Severn valley, and in 1757 he made his headquarters at Broseley, on the opposite side of the river from Coalbrookdale. He soon became the owner of a furnace and foundry nearby at Willey. He also set up another works at Bradley, nearer Birmingham.

Uses for iron:

pots and pans—

What was all the iron used for? It was here that John Wilkinson and his rivals showed their ingenuity. The first Darby had used his iron for casting pots and pans, but Wilkinson and the Shropshire ironmasters were by now

Ironbridge, Shropshire

The first iron bridge, from an eighteenth-century engraving.

much more ambitious. In co-operation with the third Abraham Darby, Wilkinson constructed the first iron bridge near Coalbrookdale. It stands to this day, and so bridges-- novel was the idea that the small town nearby is now called Ironbridge. William Reynolds, a member of the Darby family, played an important part in constructing the Shropshire Canal, which enabled the goods of the iron- masters to be exported northwards. He also helped Telford in constructing the great cast-iron aqueduct of the Ellesmere aqueducts— Canal. Wilkinson became famous for the quality of the cannon he produced. The French were so troubled by the cannon— bursting of their guns during action that they sent an agent over to inspect Wilkinson's works. He persuaded John's brother, William, to go over to France, where he built a state ironworks near Nantes.

Another entirely new purpose to which John Wilkinson put iron was for building the first iron boat. He also secured boats— a contract for supplying forty miles of iron piping to the water-pipes

Wilkinson's Cannon Factory and Boring Mill

Paris waterworks. A cast-iron pulpit which he made for a Birmingham chapel is still in use. And true to his principles to the last, he had himself buried at his lonely mansion on the north Lancashire coast in a cast-iron coffin under a cast-iron obelisk, both made at his works at Bradley. Indeed, so unusual was his personality that many of his workers believed that his ghost, riding his grey horse, would revisit his blast-furnaces on the seventh anniversary of his death. Several hundreds gathered near Bradley on July 14th, 1815, to see this spectacle. Unfortunately they were disappointed.

Wilkinson and the manufacture of the steam engine

A very important part of Wilkinson's work was connected with Watt's steam-engine. We have seen in a previous chapter how Watt improved the steam-engine. These technical improvements were useless unless the engines could be put on the market. This was an extremely expensive process which Watt could not have attempted unaided. His first partner was John Roebuck, the owner

Roebuck and Watt

of the Carron Iron Works near Falkirk, which produced a gun famous all over Europe as the Carronade. But the steam-engine had serious 'teething troubles', and Roebuck, in financial straits, in 1773 sold his share of the partnership to Matthew Boulton of Birmingham—whither Watt migrated.

Boulton and Watt

Matthew Boulton (died 1809) was the owner of a hardware factory at Soho, just north of Birmingham, where he produced buttons, buckles, ornaments and clocks. He was faced with constant difficulty from lack of power, for though his factory had a water-wheel there was often not enough water to turn it. This prompted his interest in the steam-engine of Watt, for whom he made an admirable partner. He had the necessary money—though the engine brought him difficulties, as it was fourteen years before it began to show a profit—and, almost equally important, his optimism and confidence inspired Watt, who was always prone to melancholy.

Boulton

After sucessful experiments Boulton and Watt decided to manufacture the engine. They had, however, no means

Boulton's Factory at Soho, near Birmingham

of casting and boring the cylinder, so this job they entrusted to Wilkinson. Wilkinson, too, took over the proto-
type engine, which was erected at Broseley and used to blow
the bellows of the blast-furnace. For twenty years Boulton
and Watt insisted that their customers should have their
cylinders made by Wilkinson; but in 1795 they quarrelled
with him, and as a result built a new foundry at Soho
where they could make all parts of the engine. Most of the
early engines went to the Cornish mines, where Watt spent
much of his time. Once the rotary movement had been
invented, new uses quickly developed. Steam-engines began
to appear in iron-forges (for working the hammers), in
flour-mills, and after 1785 in cotton-mills. Later they were
introduced into the wool industry.

The results were revolutionary. As Boulton remarked to
Boswell, the biographer of Dr. Johnson, 'I sell here, Sir,
what all the world desires to have—power.' Power removed
industry from the rivers. In the Black Country, for instance,
the combination of the steam-engine and the canal led to
the rapid extension of the Birmingham district. At the same
time the Severn valley began to decline, for the river, though
navigable, was liable to serious floods and droughts, and
in 1777 to transport a cylinder from Broseley to Newcastle
took the whole year. Today the tide of the Industrial
Revolution has passed from this area, which still preserves
much of the atmosphere of its early days.

The expansion of the Midland iron industry was boosted
by the discovery which Henry Cort patented in 1783. Up
to this time the only type of iron that could be produced
by coke-smelting was cast iron. To make wrought iron,
which is softer and more malleable, the 'pigs' of cast iron
had to be reheated with charcoal in the forges and beaten
to expel some of the impurities. Cort invented the process
of 'puddling', by which the impure 'pigs' were mixed with
iron oxides in a vessel heated by a special furnace. The hot
metal was then 'puddled', or stirred, with long hooks, so
helping the excess carbon in the pigs to combine with the
oxygen in the oxides and come off in the form of gas. This
left the iron much less brittle; and the lumps were then

pressed between rollers, also invented by Cort, to reduce them to bars. Thus an abundant supply of wrought as well as cast iron was secured for the metal and hardware industries of Birmingham, now rapidly growing. During the Napoleonic wars Birmingham produced over three million gun-barrels and nearly as many gun-locks. By 1835 there were over 150 steam-engines at work in Birmingham's factories.

The steam-engine, though much the greatest, was far from being the only product of the new engineering industry. Perhaps none of the early engineers was more fertile in ideas than Joseph Bramah, who from a cabinet-maker developed into a great inventor. Between 1778 and his death in 1814 he invented among other things an improved water-closet, a hydraulic press, the public-house beer-engine (with pull-over handle), a planing machine, and a numerical printing machine for bank-notes, besides suggesting the principle of screw-propulsion for steamships. He also invented a lock that was not picked till 1851 —and then an expert took sixteen days to do it. *The new engineering: Joseph Bramah*

The expansion of the iron and engineering industries was a 'snowball' process. The steam-engines required iron, and were then employed in manufacturing more iron. Both needed coal, and so at the same time there was an enormous growth in the Midlands coal industry. There was a splendid coal seam, known as the thick or ten-yard seam, that stretched seven miles from Bilston to Stourbridge. This made mining easy, so that as soon as the canals came, coal from this area could be sent all over the Midlands. By 1798 the west Midlands (including the Shropshire field) were producing over 1,000,000 tons of coal annually, compared with about 50,000 in the previous century. In that year another use was found for coal when William Murdock, Boulton and Watt's foreman, succeeded in lighting the Soho works by coal-gas—a product of the conversion of coal into coke. In 1802 the whole Soho foundry was illuminated by gas to celebrate peace with France; and five years later gas was used to light a London thoroughfare— Pall Mall. By 1814 gas lighting was general in the main *Murdock and gas lighting* streets of Westminster, and from then on its use spread quickly.

Developments in south Yorkshire

The expansion in the metal industries was by no means limited to the Midlands area. In south Yorkshire Samuel Walker started the Rotherham Iron Works in 1748. Nearby

Huntsman

at Doncaster a Quaker clock-maker—Benjamin Huntsman —discovered a new method of making steel, which is tougher than wrought iron and more flexible than cast iron. The process proved particularly suitable for watch springs and knives and was partly responsible for the expansion of the cutlery trade in Sheffield. Nevertheless, the manufacture of steel remained difficult, and it was not mass-produced until the introduction of new processes in the second half of the nineteenth century.

The main centres of iron and steel production

By 1800 the largest iron-producing district was South Wales. Here, too, coal and iron were found close together, and during the later part of the eighteenth century Anthony Bacon built up a great business around Merthyr Tydfil. Later Crawshay and Guest set up important concerns in this area. The iron trade also expanded very greatly in Lancashire, in the Tyne valley, and in the valleys of the Forth and Clyde. In 1802 the blast-furnaces of Britain produced less than 200,000 tons of pig-iron. By 1850 their

Increase in iron output

output had grown more than tenfold to 2,000,000 tons.

Coal-mining

Though all these districts now produced coal, the biggest coal-mining centre was still the Tyne valley. This and the other mining areas saw the invention or application of many new ideas in the years under discussion. The great problem of flooding, of which Newcomen's steam pump had touched barely the fringes, was virtually solved with the introduction of Watt's steam-engine. Ventilation was immensely

The steam-engine

improved by the exhaust-fan invented by the engineer and

Exhaust fan

coal-owner John Buddle; and another major advance towards greater safety came with the famous miners' lamp

Safety-lamp

of Sir Humphry Davy (1815).

Steam-haulage

Nor were these the only inventions. Wooden pit-props began to replace unhewn pillars of coal, and steam-haulage (Watt's engine again!) to replace the carrying of the coal in baskets up ladders—an appallingly laborious

A Welsh Coal Mine, *c.* 1785

From a water-colour by Paul Sandby. Note the use of horses and a revolving gin
to supply power.

task performed by women and girls. Until wire ropes were
invented about 1840, however, steam-haulage was confined
to shallow workings. Only then did really deep working
become possible. Transport along the ground, both above
and below the surface, was revolutionized much earlier.
The use of wooden, and later iron-plated rails, along which
trucks were drawn by horses, had become common in
collieries during the eighteenth century; and now, in 1804,
Richard Trevithick added new possibilities of power and Locomotives
speed by constructing 'Uncle Dick's Puffer'—the first
steam locomotive.

Together, these and other inventions did for coal what
those of the Darbys and Cort had done for iron. Great
Britain, which had produced about six million tons of coal
in 1770, by 1840 was producing nearly forty million tons.

Increase in
coal output
On this great increase in output depended the speed, the
scope and the success of the Industrial Revolution.

2. *Textiles and the Factory System*

In the eighteenth century the two most important textile
industries were wool and cotton. The manufacture of
woollen cloth had been England's greatest industry for
centuries, but after 1700 the manufacture of cotton steadily
increased, especially in south Lancashire. The basic
processes of the textile industry are spinning and weaving.
Both of these were transformed after 1760 by a number of
important inventions which were at first applied only to
the cotton industry.

The cotton
industry

Spinning
inventions:
1. Har-
greaves'
spinning
jenny

Between 1764 and 1767 James Hargreaves, a weaver and
carpenter of Blackburn, made a machine called—after his
wife—the spinning jenny. By means of this a woman could

Hargreave's Spinning Jenny

From a model in the Science Museum, South Kensington. The type of
jenny is that in use about 1764.

Sir Richard Arkwright

From the portrait by Joseph Wright. A remarkable study of the self-made man whose inventions and enterprises helped to revolutionise the textile industry.

spin eight threads at once instead of one, which was all that could be done on the old-fashioned spinning-wheels. Larger models, with up to eighty spindles, soon followed: but the yarn spun on all these various machines was weak and suitable only for the weft, or cross-threads, of the fabric.

A machine, was soon invented capable of producing a thread tough enough for the warp. This was the water-frame, invented in 1768 by Richard Arkwright, a barber and wig-maker of Preston. Unlike the jenny, the frame required greater power than human muscles could produce, and so had to be installed in a mill with water power.

2. Arkwright's water-frame

To combine and crown these inventions came another. About 1785 Samuel Crompton, a Bolton weaver, introduced a device called 'the mule' because it was regarded as a cross between the jenny and the frame. It produced a fine but strong yarn, suitable for both warp and weft; and it was so good a machine that mules are still in use today for fine-quality spinning. The later models of the mule were driven by water power. From this time onwards, too, Watt's steam-engine was also used to drive spinning-machines.

3. Crompton's mule

Before these inventions, spinning had been a very much slower process than weaving. On the very efficient hand-loom, a man could weave in an hour the yarn that had been produced by five hours' work with the spinning-wheel. Now spinning leapt ahead, with the result that yarn piled up and there was a pressing demand for the services of weavers. As yet the inventions had not touched weaving,[1] so the

[1] Apart from Kay's 'flying shuttle' of 1733, which had enabled broadcloth to be woven at the loom by one man instead of two.

1780s saw the golden age of the cottage weaver, and loom-houses were thrown up beside cottages all over the country-side. But the hand-loom weavers' prosperity was short. Already in 1784 Edmund Cartwright, a clergyman, had devised a power-loom. It was not much used until after 1800, when further improvements were made, but from 1820 it was steadily adopted, and from then on the days of the hand-loom weavers in the cotton trade were numbered. The demand for their services fell off, their wages correspondingly slumped, and by 1850 they were earning no more than five shillings a week and were on the way to extinction.

Weaving invention—Cartwright's power-loom

Inventions in spinning and weaving were applied much more slowly to the woollen industry. As late as 1850 some wool was spun by hand, and cottagers who worked looms in their own home continued to produce much of the cloth. To this day they still survive in the Western Isles and Ireland.

The woollen industry

The effect of the inventions of Arkwright and Crompton was to revolutionize the cotton-spinning industry. Though Arkwright's home was in Lancashire, which was already the centre of the cotton industry, he, like Hargreaves, migrated to Nottingham where the hosiers were in need of cotton. So it was in this area that the first cotton mills or factories of the new era were built. Steam power was not yet available, so the factories had to be on a river. In 1776 Arkwright built a factory at Cromford on the Derwent, not far from the silk factory that Defoe had visited. More factories for cotton spinning soon followed, at Belper, at Chorley—the first water-driven factory in Lancashire—and in many other valleys of the north Midlands.

Cotton factories

Water power

These factories were the death-knell of the old domestic manufacture, and the factory system soon spread into other industries. Already in 1769 Josiah Wedgwood had opened his great new china factory at Etruria in the potteries, and there were the large-scale works at Coalbrookdale and Soho. It was, however, in the cotton-spinning industry that the factory system gained its most rapid hold. With the coming of steam there was a great increase in the number of mills in the towns, and in 1802 Manchester had fifty-two,

Factories in other industries

Josiah Wedgwood

The great potter, depicted in a medallion (blue and white jasper) designed by William Hackwood and produced in Wedgwood's own firm.

whereas twenty years earlier it had had only two. These factories were still comparatively small, employing men by hundreds rather than thousands, but by 1815 the great cotton factory run by Robert Owen at New Lanark employed 1,600 people. After 1806, with the development of the power-loom, the factory also Weaving factories invaded the cotton-weaving industry. There followed a concentration of the cotton industry in the towns of Lancashire, which grew at mushroom speed, and in the neighbourhood of Glasgow. During the first thirty years of the nineteenth century the populations of Man- Growth of Manchester, etc. chester, Bolton, Oldham and Blackburn all increased between two- and three-fold.

The coming of the factory was indeed an industrial Effects of factory system revolution—and a revolution in more than one respect. Instead of working in his own home or his master's house with a dozen or fewer workmates the ordinary working man was drawn into these vast barracks, where he worked with hundreds of others in the soulless monotony of a large concern. But at the same time the factory enormously increased the scale of production, particularly in the cotton industry. In 1764 Britain had imported 4,000,000 lb. of raw cotton; in 1833 she imported more than 300,000,000 lb. In 1835 it was reckoned that Britain was responsible for sixty per cent of all the world's cotton production. She exported great quantities of cotton cloth to America and India, and cotton had replaced wool as Britain's chief textile export. Asia's age-old position as the world's greatest cotton manufacturer was shattered. So the Industrial Revolution simultaneously created for the people of Britain new opportunities of wealth, and new and difficult social problems which have never been fully solved.

3. *The Social Effects of the Industrial Revolution*

Increase in population (not primarily due to Industrial Revolution) In the past it was often wrongly said that the Industrial Revolution was responsible for the immense increase in population which occurred in Great Britain at this time. When the first census was taken in 1801 the population of Britain was 10½ million. By 1851 the figure had risen to 21 million. The main reason for this increase was in fact the decline in the death-rate after 1750, brought about by better sanitation and the growth of medical knowledge. Nevertheless, the Industrial and Agrarian Revolutions, though not the prime cause of the rise in population, did help to make it possible by the increased production of clothes and food. This rise in population is the more remarkable as an ever-greater proportion of the people shifted to the towns, where life had always been more unhealthy. The increase is a basic fact which must be weighed against all the accounts of the horrors of life in the early industrial towns.

Growth of towns If the Industrial Revolution was not primarily responsible for the rise in population, it certainly caused the movement of the population from the country to the towns, where most of the new factories lay. This was the most revolutionary and lasting of its effects on our social life. In 1801 London's population was 1 million; in 1851, over 2½ million. In the new industrial towns, there was a still more spectacular growth. In the same period Liverpool and Glasgow increased four-fold and the population of Bradford, one of the centres of the Yorkshire woollen industry, rose from 13,000 to 104,000. By 1831 there were probably as many town-dwellers as country-dwellers. Since then the towns have continued to grow; and today, whether we like it or not, we are one of the most urban countries in the world. In fact, the great majority of the British population has now even reached the point of ceasing to think of the countryside as a source of food, and regards it in the main as a place for holidays, picnics and excursions.

The Industrial Revolution brought prosperity to many. Not only did it bring princely fortunes to some of its leaders like Arkwright and Wedgwood, but it also gradually increased the proportion of the middle classes to the manual working class. The new industrial methods required more and more engineers and technicians, and the great export and import businesses built up on them needed thousands of office workers and salesmen. As steam power and machinery developed, so the number of better-paid jobs increased. In a recent survey more people in this island claimed to belong to the middle than to the manual working class. *Increase in middle class*

Some of the fortunate ones rose from very humble circumstances. Samuel Walker of Rotherham started business on a very small scale with his brother Aaron. He records the event thus in his diary in 1741: 'In or about October or November of the same year Samuel and Aaron Walker built an air furnace in the old nailer's smithy on the backside of Samuel Walker's cottage at Grenoside, making some small additions there-to and another little hutt or two: and after rebuilding the chimney or stacks once and the furnace once or more began to proceed a little, Samuel Walker teaching the school at Grenoside and Aaron Walker making nails and mowing and shearing part of his time.' By 1745 there was so much business that Samuel had to give up his school. They allowed themselves only ten shillings a week for personal expenditure and used all their profits to enlarge the business. By 1812 the assets of their firm were reckoned to be worth £300,000. Similarly the Welsh iron magnate William Crawshay, who had started his career on the road to London 'with all his fortune in his stout arm and his active brain', died worth £1½ million. *Some industrial manufacturers: Walker* *Crawshay*

But however much the Industrial Revolution brought fortunes to some and in the long run raised the general standard of life, it was far from bringing prosperity to *Ill effects on certain workers* everyone at the time. To those who tried to earn their living in the old ways it brought hardship and suffering. The hand-loom weavers (as we have seen) and the frame-work knitters who competed against the factory fought a long and losing battle far into the nineteenth century. It

The Luddite riots was among these that violence flared up into the Luddite riots of 1811 and 1812—the riots so called after a real or mythical leader, Ned Ludd. In Nottingham, enraged workers destroyed the new wide knitting frames which were taking away their livelihood by producing a cheaper and inferior type of stocking. In Lancashire after 1815 they tried to destroy the new power-looms.

Grim conditions in factories Those who went into the factories were often attracted from the countryside by the higher wages that were offered. But once there they must have found the conditions grim. At Tyldesley, near Manchester, the spinners had to work in a temperature of 80°. This is how the conditions were described there in a pamphlet issued during a strike: 'At Tyldesley they work fourteen hours per day including the nominal hour for dinner: the door is locked in working hours, except half an hour at tea time; the work people are not allowed to send for water to drink in the hot factory; and even the rain water is locked up by the master's order, otherwise they would be happy to drink even that.' There was also a severe system of fines. Here are a few examples:

Any spinner found with his window open	1/-
Any spinner spinning with gaslight too long in the morning	2/-
Any spinner heard whistling	1/-
Any spinner being sick and cannot find another spinner to give satisfaction must pay for steam per day	6/-

Tyldesley was by no means unique in its fourteen-hour day. In this period this was not unusual, for many of those who worked in their home or the fields were used to equally long, if not longer, hours. In the factory, however, they had

Lack of freedom no freedom. In domestic industry it had often been the practice for the worker to take two or three days off, then work furiously for perhaps fifteen or sixteen hours a day near the time when the goods were due. A domestic worker, as long as he finished his goods on time, could always knock off and enjoy a pipe when he felt like it, or go and do some gardening. All such freedom disappeared with the factory system. Uniformity and punctuality became essential, and everyone had to be at his or her place when the machinery started up. At Etruria a great bell was rung at 5.45 from Lady Day to Michaelmas to make sure the workers were standing ready by 6 a.m. When the Duke of Bridgewater complained to his men that they had not returned punctually to their work at 1 p.m., they told him they had not heard the clock strike one. He immediately had it changed so that it struck thirteen! This insistence on regularity and discipline in the interests of commercial working was immensely burdensome. As one report put it: 'Whilst the engine runs the people must work—men, women, and children are yoked together with iron and steam. The animal machine—breakable even in the best case, and subject to a thousand sources of suffering—is chained fast to the iron machine which knows no suffering and no weariness.'

If some of the mill-owners were cruel and greedy, others like the first Sir Robert Peel (father of the Prime Minister) and Henry Fielden were humane and enlightened men. It was they, more than anyone else, who began the efforts to regulate the factory system. Sir Robert Peel concentrated on trying to remedy the very worst evil of the factory system—the employment of young children down to the tender age of five or even four. Most of these children had been made over to the employers by the overseers of the poor, who were glad to be rid of paupers or orphans. Others had been forced into the mill by the need or wishes of their parents—for the employment of children was old-established and widespread in the domestic industry. But neither group can have been used to so rigorous a life as they were subjected to in the factories, where long hours, fines, floggings and a hot and unhealthy atmosphere became their daily lot. It was Peel who secured the passage

Factory reform

The first Sir Robert Peel

Factory
Act for
children,
1802

of the first Factory Act, in 1802, limiting the working hours of the young 'pauper apprentices' in cotton factories to twelve and forbidding them to work at night. The new law was not much observed, for there were no paid inspectors to enforce it, but at least it was the start of a long fight for decent factory conditions.

Many of the towns in which so much of Britain's population was now concentrating were ugly and squalid. In old-established towns like London, conditions actually improved during the period of the Industrial Revolution, and it is

Conditions
in towns

also doubtful whether conditions in the big new towns like Manchester and Birmingham were ever as bad as in the London of 1700. This, however, was not much comfort to the new inhabitants who came in from the countryside where there was plenty of room and fresh air. In the new towns all the traditional evils of the old were repeated. The rivers were used as drains; the smell of the Irwell at Manchester was particularly notorious. There was terrible overcrowding, and the houses were jerry-built—many of those in Birmingham in the 1820s cost only £60 apiece.

One of the worst cases of bad town conditions arose at Nottingham, where during this period 11,000 houses were constructed in a confined space. Many of them were built in cramped courts and alleys opening off narrow streets, and were entered through tunnels. Of the 11,000 houses, some 7,000 were built side to side and back to back. And in Liverpool and Manchester people were soon living in cellars. It was not that living conditions in large towns deteriorated during the Industrial Revolution, but that old evils which had been largely confined to London became more widespread as new towns were born and others expanded. This was one of the more unfortunate legacies of the Industrial Revolution, and one which endured all too long.

CHAPTER ELEVEN

CANALS AND ROADS IN THE EARLY INDUSTRIAL ERA

1. *Canals*

THE Industrial Revolution could not have developed as it did without the help of new methods of transport. Despite some improvements which we shall look at later, eighteenth-century roads remained utterly inadequate for the transport of such heavy and bulky goods as coal and iron. These could go only by water. We have already seen that many of the British rivers had been made navigable,[1] but rivers served very limited areas and were subject to all the troubles of flood and drought. Something different was required, and the answer proved to be artificial waterways, or canals, which became the arteries of the Industrial Revolution.

The idea of canals was old. They had been in use for many years on the Continent, but in Britain only one—the Exeter Canal—had been built for transport (as opposed to drainage) before the eighteenth century. It was not until after 1760 that Britain began to build transport canals on a large scale. From then onwards they were constructed systematically, but at first mainly in Lancashire and the Midlands, the two earliest centres of the Industrial Revolution. ^{Canals}

To the Duke of Bridgewater must be given the chief credit for the development of the canal. He had an estate containing collieries at Worsley, a few miles north of Manchester, but the only means of moving away the coal was by pack-horse. In 1759 he therefore secured an Act of Parliament allowing him to make a canal from Worsley to Manchester; and in the same year he took into his employment James Brindley, who was to become the greatest of ^{Brindley} ^{Duke of Bridgewater}

[1] Page 5.

the canal engineers. Brindley, the son of a poor Derbyshire crofter, was a millwright by trade, but his mechanical ingenuity and his industry had become widely known in the North, and these he now applied to the problem of building the canal.

The Aqueduct at Barton

The Bridgewater Canal crosses the River Irwell—from Aiken's *Description of Country Roads Round Manchester*, 1795.

The result was a triumph. Among other difficulties the Irwell had to be crossed, and this was done by building an aqueduct over the river at Barton. When it was about to be filled Brindley had a fit of nerves and fled to his inn. All was well, however, and by 1761 coal was arriving in Manchester by barge direct from Worsley. The Duke then had tunnels bored from the canal into his mines so that the barges could be loaded in the collieries. The result of all this was to halve the price of coal in Manchester, where it could now be obtained at the Duke's wharf for 3½d. a

The Bridge-water Canal (Worsley–Manchester), 1761

Price of coal halved in Manchester

hundredweight. This not only increased the Duke's sales, but also proved a great benefit to the people of Manchester generally.

So successful was the Worsley–Manchester canal (thenceforth known as the Bridgewater Canal) that its promoter immediately undertook to finance the construction of an extension from the Manchester section to Runcorn on the Mersey estuary. This extension, also built by Brindley, became known as the Duke's Canal. It made communication by water between Liverpool and Manchester much easier, and so placed a good port at the service of the growing cotton trade. The Duke's Canal (Manchester–Runcorn)

Soon afterwards there was born the ambitious plan of linking up all the great river systems by canals. The first through waterway to be planned was the Grand Trunk Canal, from the Mersey to the Trent. Josiah Wedgwood was one of the main promoters of this, since it would serve the Potteries and he badly needed a smooth means of conveyance for his more delicate wares. Bridgewater, too, was concerned, as the Mersey end of the project ran into the Duke's Canal and made use of the same flight of locks down to Runcorn. All told, the Grand Trunk stretched for ninety-three miles; and its construction involved making a tunnel through Harecastle Hill more than one and a half miles long. Once again Brindley was the engineer, though he died before the work was completed in 1777. Since the Trent and the Humber already formed one water system, this new canal linked Merseyside and Lancashire not only with the Midlands but also with the North-East and the port of Hull. The Grand Trunk (Mersey–Trent), 1777

Brindley also constructed a link between the Grand Trunk and the Severn. This was called the Staffordshire and Worcestershire Canal. Starting from Stourport on the Severn—a town created by the canals, for there was only one house on the spot before—it joined the Grand Trunk at Haywood in Staffordshire. In turn it was soon connected by a tributary canal to Birmingham. This tributary passed over the famous ten-yard seam, with the result that the price of coal in Birmingham fell from thirteen shillings to Other Midland canals: Birmingham–Fazeley seven shillings a ton. Before long the whole Birmingham district with its mines and ironworks became a network of canals.

Links with the Thames

The movement next spread south to take in the Thames. This was connected with the Trent by the Coventry and Oxford Canals, with the Avon near Bristol by the Kennet and Avon Canal, and with the Severn by the Thames and Severn Canal running through Stroud. Later the Midlands were connected with London and the Thames in a more direct route by the Grand Junction Canal. Opened in 1805, this ran to the Paddington Basin. In turn it was connected with the London docks at Limehouse by the Regent's Canal.

Grand Junction (Trent–London), 1805

Apart from these trunk routes most of the English canals (and practically all the successful ones) were built in the industrial districts. In addition, to connect the manufacturing areas of Lancashire and Yorkshire, three canals were cut over the Pennines, each a very considerable engineering feat. One of them, the Huddersfield Canal, had the longest tunnel (over three miles) of any canal, and by means of scores of locks reached the highest level (637 feet).

Canals in Lancashire and Yorkshire

Canals were also built in Scotland, including three important ones which ran from coast to coast. The best known is the Caledonian Canal down the Great Glen from Inverness to Loch Linnhe. Built by the government, this cost over £1 million. It was intended to serve defensive as well as commercial purposes, as warships could use it to sail from one coast to the other without rounding the north of Scotland. With the coming of steam, however, the voyage round the north became much less formidable, and the canal has never been as much used as was anticipated. The most successful of the Scottish canals in fact proved to be the Forth and Clyde, with its various branches. This was completed in 1790 after a government loan, and on its waters the first British steam-boat sailed. Wales, too, shared in the great canal movement. The big Welsh iron and coal industry was made possible by the construction of canals down the long South Wales valleys to the sea.

Scotland: Caledonian Canal, 1822

Forth–Clyde, 1790

Welsh canals

Finance

The building of a canal was a complicated process. First

the money had to be found, and in the early days this was often no easy task. In the great majority of cases it came from private individuals—often local industrialists or gentry —who formed a canal company. Later, when canals 'caught on', the story was different; people hastened to invest, and the demand for shares reached a point where it could be described as 'canal mania'. There was a sharp 'Canal attack of this in 1792 in the Bristol district, where large mania' numbers subscribed money to various unsound schemes. A meeting to launch one of these was to be held at Devizes, and the news leaked out in Bristol only the day before. Hundreds of Bristolians thereupon hired or bought any horse they could find and rode to Devizes along the muddy roads throughout a long winter's night in order to buy the shares next morning.

After the capital was raised an engineer had to be Construc-engaged to plan and supervise the construction. Apart from tion Brindley, the most famous was Thomas Telford, the great Telford road-maker and the son of a Scottish shepherd. He built among others the Caledonian Canal and the Ellesmere, linking Shrewsbury with the Dee and so with Chester. The actual work was carried out by contractors whose gangs of navigators or 'navvies' (canals were called 'inland naviga-tions') often caused chaos in the countryside. The main technical problem, apart from shifting earth, was to make the canal watertight over porous ground. This was done by puddling, i.e. applying several layers of well-tempered clay and sand to the bottom and sides of the canal. Other prob-lems were to find the skilled workmen needed for the making of the locks, and to prevent the unskilled Irish navvies going off on their all-too-frequent drinking bouts.

Once the canal was completed most companies arranged Canal only to take tolls and maintain their canals, leaving the traffic actual running of the traffic to other firms, such as Pick-ford's. Most of the barges were towed along the canals by horses, though sometimes this work was done by gangs of men. In the tunnels, before they were equipped with tow-paths, the boatmen lay on their backs on special boards fitted to the boats and 'legged' the barges through by pushing on the sides or roof of the tunnel. Though a steam paddle-boat was tried out on the Forth and Clyde as early as 1789, steam barges and tugs were not much used on the canals till after 1850.

It was in the districts where there was traffic in coal and iron and other heavy goods that the canals were most prosperous. They were, however, also employed for *Passenger-carrying*. In 1806 the Grand Junction Canal was used for the movement of troops from Paddington to Liverpool. Relays of horses were specially ordered and the journey took only seven days instead of the fourteen it would have taken to march. Similarly, passenger services were run regularly on a number of canals by special fly- or swift-boats, which could average ten miles an hour. On the Duke's Canal, as early as the 1770s, there were special passenger barges, 'each provided with a coffee-house'. In 1831 sleepers were fitted to the boats between Edinburgh and Glasgow—for the journey lasted eleven and a half hours. There were accidents too. One Sunday a party of drunken men at Bury, in Lancashire, insisted on rocking a boat which was setting out on a trip to Bolton. It capsized, and many lives were lost.

The canals (like the Wiltshire or the Leominster) that served agricultural areas were failures, and most of the shareholders got little return on the money they had risked. The trunk routes and the canals serving industrial areas often paid very well, and the cheap transport they provided made the rapid advance of the Industrial Revolution possible. Even these, however, quickly felt the force of *Decline with advent of railways* competition when the railways came along, and in the years after 1840 many were closed. Nevertheless, some are still used to this day—though to an ever-declining extent.

2. Roads and Coaches

Meanwhile an effort had been made to improve the roads. These were supposed to be kept in repair by the parishes *The roads* through which they passed. As most parishes had neglected to do so, and as no new hard roads had been constructed

A Stage Coach on the Dover Road, 1775

rom a picture by P. de Loutherbourg. Note the ruts and the discomfort of outside travel.

since the days of the Roman occupation, by the beginning of the eighteenth century British roads were notoriously bad. In the course of that century, however, a different method of financing and maintaining roads became widely adopted. This was through bodies known as Turnpike Trusts. A group of individuals formed a company or trust, and in return for improving or building a stretch of road they were allowed to charge tolls.

Turnpike Trusts

This enabled the standard of road construction to be much improved. The technical changes were brought about in the main by three men—John Metcalfe, Thomas Telford and John McAdam. It was with a new turnpike road between Harrogate and Boroughbridge constructed in 1765 that Metcalfe, a native of Knaresborough, made his name. He had been blind since the age of six, when a violent

Metcalfe

attack of smallpox robbed him of his sight, but his stone-laid roads and his bridges proved such a success that he became widely employed in Lancashire and Yorkshire.

McAdam
and
Telford

McAdam and Telford, who were born about forty years later than Metcalfe, both produced a surface much smoother and harder than ever before. They laid small broken stones to a considerable depth on a foundation only slightly cambered (so that traffic would not hug the centre of the road) and then crushed them down. McAdam, a wealthy Scottish gentleman for whom road-building was a lifelong passion, gave his name to this process, which became known as macadamizing. He contended that any subsoil, if properly drained, would do for the foundation, as long as an adequate layer of stones was put on top. His rival, Telford, preferred to lay a hard foundation first, and to cover the broken stones on the top with gravel. He did his most outstanding work in Scotland, where he built nearly a thousand miles of good road, and on the important post road from London to Holyhead, in the section beyond Shrewsbury. His improvements to this last road included

The Menai
Suspension
Bridge

the greatest of his engineering feats—the suspension bridge over the Menai Straits, completed in 1825. The distance between the main piers of this bridge was nearly 600 feet. Between the piers the chains, made in Shropshire of special wrought iron, were suspended, and from them hung bars which held the bridge beneath. The hanging of the first chain was a very tricky job. When it was done, three daring workmen celebrated the event by scrambling along the whole length of the chain—the width of which was only nine inches.

Traffic on
roads

Progress in road-building soon led to faster traffic. In 1754 it took four and a half days to travel from London to Manchester; by 1788 the time had been reduced to twenty-eight hours. Some years later the Lord Chancellor of the day wrote of a journey from London to Edinburgh that he had accomplished it 'with a marvellous velocity taking only three nights and two days for the whole distance. But this speed was thought to be highly dangerous to the head, independently of all the perils of an overturn, and stories were told of men and women who having reached London with such celerity died suddenly of an affectation of the brain.'

A Contest for Precedence

ver the Downs between Stockbridge and Salisbury. Disputes between drivers ere known long before the age of the motor car. From an engraving by Rowlandson made in 1782.

Such was the progress in road-building that in 1784 an enterprising theatre-manager of Bristol, John Palmer, was able to persuade the government to let him organize a mail service by coach between Bath and London. Before that date the post had been carried by post-boys on horseback. The new practice spread, and by 1800 some four hundred towns were getting a daily delivery by coaches which travelled at an average speed of six miles an hour. With further improvements, by 1830 the average speed had reached nine miles an hour. Long-distance travelling by coach nevertheless remained dear and uncomfortable, and it could not long survive the superior speed, comfort and cheapness of the railways when these gradually spread over the countryside during the 1830s and 1840s. All the same, the improvements in the roads during the period 1760–1830, and the development of regular coach and mail services, had done much to open up the countryside and to establish fairly easy and regular communication between towns far apart. Like the canals, the new roads and coaches of the later eighteenth century, though they carried people and not heavy goods, played a vital part in the great movement of the Industrial Revolution.

Mail services by coach, 1784

Coach services decline with railways

CHAPTER TWELVE

THE YOUNGER PITT AND THE YEARS OF RECOVERY

1. *Pitt and Fox*

WILLIAM PITT the Younger and Charles James Fox stand out as the two great men in the politics of the last twenty years of the eighteenth century. Alike in this, they resembled each other in very little else, and least of all in character.

William Pitt   Pitt, the younger son of Chatham, was brought up by his father to carry on his political work. Though a sickly child, he soon became a prodigy of learning. Chatham did not send him to school but entrusted his education to a tutor and often took a hand himself. His methods were such that by fourteen his son was almost grown up. He could read all Latin authors with ease, could translate most Greek at sight, and his conversation deeply impressed adults. At this age he went up to Cambridge, after which he took up the profession of a barrister. In 1781, when he was twenty-one, he entered the House of Commons as the representative of a 'pocket' borough controlled by a family friend. Grave, and with a wonderful command of language, he at once made a deep impression. Within eighteen months, in 1782, he had been offered, and accepted, the post of Chancellor of the Exchequer under Lord Shelburne. A year later he was Prime Minister.

Prime Minister at twenty-four

This was an unheard-of record, and many were the gibes directed at Pitt's youth. As Byron put it:

> A sight to make surrounding nations stare:
> A Kingdom trusted to a schoolboy's care.

But youth was not his only difficulty, for in the first months of his ministry he could not command a majority in the Commons. Yet he overcame all obstacles and remained Prime Minister for no less than seventeen years.

William Pitt

From a sketch by Gillray made when Pitt was about thirty.

A slim, solitary figure with a chilling manner, Pitt nevertheless had something of his father's greatness, and he proved himself to be as successful a minister in peace as his father had been in war. Like Chatham, he had great singleness of purpose—political power was the aim to which he subordinated all else. Like Chatham, he loathed corruption. Like Chatham, he had supreme self-confidence—though he declared his in milder terms: 'I place much dependence upon my new colleagues; I place still more dependence on myself.' After his maiden speech in the Commons, Edmund Burke, the great political thinker, pronounced him to be 'not a chip of the old block, but the old block itself'.

Charles James Fox
From a portrait by K. A. Hickel.

Charles
James Fox   Where Pitt was stiff and cold, Fox was gay and warm. He was born in 1749, the third son of Henry Fox, later Lord Holland, who had made a fortune out of the office of Paymaster General during the Seven Years War. Embittered by later disappointments in politics, Henry Fox had decided that at least in his family there should be happiness. This he thought could best be obtained by granting his children's every wish. 'Young people', he declared, 'are always in the right, and old people in the wrong.' To his children he used to say: 'Never do today what you can put off till tomorrow, or ever do yourself what you can get anyone else to do for you.' Luckily Charles had an avid desire for knowledge which he was given every opportunity to gratify, and this survived a period at Eton, which he decided to attend at the age of nine. At fourteen he was taken away from school for four months. These he spent at a fashionable resort on the Continent, where his father gave him five guineas a night and instruction in the art of gambling—a taste for which he never lost. A year later he went to Oxford, where he continued to show a great zest for every form of knowledge. His physical energy equalled his mental, for on one hot summer's day he walked from Oxford to Holland House in Kensington—a distance of fifty-six miles.

At nineteen Charles Fox was elected M.P. for Midhurst. Fox's early He was still eighteen months beneath the legal age, but the career Commons had heard so much about him that they let him take his seat. He started as a supporter of North and George III. He soon made a great name for himself inside Parliament by his speeches and outside by his extravagant mode of living. He quickly became the centre of life at Almack's (later Brooks's), the most select of the clubs and little more than a casino. Here he lost thousands of pounds and inspired a famous entry in the club betting book: 'Lord Clermont has given Mr. Crawford 10 guineas upon the condition of receiving £500 from him whenever Mr. Charles Fox shall be worth £100,000 clear of debts.' It was a safe bet, for Fox's debts grew faster and faster. In 1773, when Charles was twenty-four, his father had to find no less than £140,000 to meet the obligations of Charles and his brothers—a heavy price to pay for mistaken educational methods.

Fox had plenty of energy left over for politics. On one occasion he played at Almack's for twenty-two consecutive hours and lost £11,000, but the next day spoke and voted in Parliament as usual. All that night he sat up drinking at White's, and the following day gambled again, winning back £6,000 before leaving for the races at Newmarket. In

He opposes
North over
America

politics he displayed the same rashness. He soon quarrelled with George III and North over their American policy. After North's fall he took office under Lord Rockingham, but on Rockingham's death resigned rather than serve under Lord Shelburne. In 1783 he then joined forces with

The Fox–
North
coalition,
1783

North (whom he had so recently been denouncing), to overthrow Shelburne. For the moment the king had to accept a Fox–North coalition; but the manoeuvre greatly discredited Fox, and George III quickly found an opportunity to be rid of the new allies.

The Mask

From a caricature by James Sayers satirising the Fox-North coalition of 1783. Fox on the left, North on the right, together made up a face not to be trusted.

Pitt, Prime
Minister

It was at this stage that the king asked the youthful Pitt to form a ministry. For three months Pitt carried on the government with a majority of the House of Commons led by Fox against him. In 1784 George dissolved Parliament, elections were held, and in the new assembly Pitt had a He gains a majority, 1784 majority of over two hundred. The electorate had confirmed the king's choice. But though many of Fox's supporters were rejected, Fox himself secured a personal triumph in a close fight for the Westminster constituency, where all householders were entitled to vote. In the closing stages— the poll lasted more than six weeks—the most beautiful woman in England, the Duchess of Devonshire, came to his aid and used her charms and even her kisses to secure votes for him.

2. *Pitt's Peacetime Ministry, 1783–1793*

In 1784 party divisions, which had been obscured since the The new Whig and Tory parties beginning of George III's reign by the large number of small groups centring round various noblemen, were still far from clear. Not until 1790, when differing views were taken about the French Revolution, did two main bodies re-emerge with sharply contrasting ideas, the Tories (and Whigs who came round to the Tory point of view) under Pitt (who continued to call himself a Whig!) and the more 'advanced' Whigs under Fox. Meanwhile the greatest difference between Pitt and Fox, apart from purely personal issues, lay in the former's emphasis on the efficient running of government, as against the latter's emphasis on liberty and the need to protect the subject from tyranny.

As well as being First Lord of the Treasury—the official Pitt's financial reforms position which the Prime Minister holds—Pitt was his own Chancellor of the Exchequer. His programme consisted mainly of financial reforms, and by these he successfully restored national prosperity. On taking office he was faced by a serious deficit in the Budget, for during the American war the finances had been badly handled. He raised a loan to overcome the immediate problem and then imposed extra taxes on an assorted series of objects ranging from Extra taxes racehorses and servants to candles and windows. To cope with the National Debt, which had been vastly increased by the war, he soon set up, like Walpole, a sinking-fund. Sinking-fund This paid off £10 million before the French Revolutionary

Wars came along to send the Debt once more on the upward path.

Pitt also immensely simplified the complicated system by which Customs and Excise were collected. Some duties he lowered, notably the tea duty, which had been over 100 per cent and which he brought down to $12\frac{1}{2}$ per cent for the ordinary type of tea. This made the smuggling of tea hardly worth while—and although the new system produced little more revenue at first, it soon did so as trade improved. In addition he made other attempts to lower Customs, for he had been converted to the idea of freer trade by Adam Smith's great book *The Wealth of Nations*. He failed in an attempt to establish free trade with Ireland, but he had better luck with France, making a trade treaty in 1786 in which both countries reduced almost all their tariffs.

Reduction of duties, e.g. tea

Influenced by Adam Smith

Trade treaty with France

In the field of political reform Pitt was not so active. We have seen that reform of the parliamentary system was in the air after the Wilkes episode and the disastrous events in America. In 1782 a Bill introduced by Burke and known as the Economical Reforms Bill was passed by Parliament and forced upon the king. It considerably diminished the number of sinecures, or official positions with little or no work attached to them, and so greatly limited the patronage at the king's disposal. In addition it debarred revenue officers from voting, thus making it impossible for the king or his ministers to count on the support of these officials at elections. Several members of Parliament, including Pitt, wanted to go further than this. In 1785 he therefore produced a Bill to buy out the owners of thirty-six 'pocket' and 'rotten' boroughs and give the seventy-two members to the counties and London and Westminster. But even so mild a measure as this provoked great opposition among the majority of M.P.s, who had been elected on the old system and wanted to stick to it. Defeated on this Bill, Pitt gave up any attempt to reform Parliament; and it was not until 1832, a full generation later, that the agitation for parliamentary reform was at last successful.

Political reform

Burke's Economical Reforms Bill, 1782

Pitt proposes Parliamentary reform, 1785

There was another proposed reform which in these early days of his political career enjoyed Pitt's sympathy. In 1787

William Wilberforce

A portrait of the great 'emancipator', painted by Lawrence in 1828.

William Wilberforce started his great campaign for the abolition of the slave-trade. Pitt, who was his close friend, gave him support, and in 1792 in a moving speech he pleaded for the immediate end of the trade. The motion failed to pass the Commons, however, partly because of the chaos that had broken out in the French West Indies after the slaves there had all been given freedom. *Pitt supports movement to abolish slave-trade—unsuccessfully*

Another long-overdue reform Pitt did succeed in passing through Parliament. In 1791 an Act at last allowed Roman Catholics official religious toleration—though it did not relieve them from the various restrictions on their political activity. *Toleration for Roman Catholics, 1791*

Pitt and the Empire

Pitt's India Act, 1784

In imperial matters Pitt's interest was less than his father's. His most important measure was his India Act of 1784. This gave the government much greater control over the East India Company, which was the ruling power in the parts of India controlled by the British. The Company's territory had been extended after the Seven Years War, especially in the Ganges valley, only to be threatened with disaster during the American war, when the French succeeded in creating a strong anti-British alliance. This alliance, however, was crushed by the energy of the Company's Governor-General, Warren Hastings. Never-

The trial of Warren Hastings

theless, after Hastings returned to England in 1785 he was bitterly attacked by the Whigs and his impeachment on charges of corruption and tyranny lasted seven years. The combined effect of Pitt's Act and this long political trial—

Greater control over East India Company

though Hastings was rightly acquitted—was to secure a type of rule in British India much more responsible to the government at home and more restricted in its methods.

Pitt's Canada Act, 1791

The other big imperial measure with which Pitt was associated was his Canada Act of 1791. Many of the British supporters in the American War of Independence—the 'United Empire Loyalists'—had left the United States for Canada and New Brunswick, and Pitt was confronted with the problem of finding a form of government suitable both for the original French population of Canada and the new British immigrants. Most of the British who went into Canada had gone to the Ontario district; so Pitt decided virtually to divide the country into two—an Upper Canada (modern Ontario) predominantly British, and a Lower Canada (modern Quebec) predominantly French. Each part had its own elected assembly, which enjoyed, however, only very limited powers. The solution carried Canada forward for some years but began to break down about 1830.

The settlement in Australia

Outside Canada and India, Pitt's most eventful action for the Empire was to send an expedition of convicts, soldiers and officials to make a settlement in Australia. The settlement was duly established, in 1788, at Sydney; and from it flowed far greater consequences than Pitt ever imagined—for he himself was thinking only of finding an outlet for convicts, and had no grand plan of imperial development.

In 1792 Pitt was in a strong position. His administration was efficient and he had cut out wasteful expenditure and methods. This, combined with increasing trade, had brought back national prosperity. If his methods provoked serious opposition, he withdrew them—for he was no crusader and was anxious to avoid stirring up trouble. His most difficult moment had been in 1788, when George III went mad for the second time, and the Prince of Wales (who was a close friend of Fox and, like all the Hanoverians, heartily disliked his own father) claimed the full royal authority as Regent. But the prince's desire was frustrated, and George III more or less recovered the following year. With his mind in decline the king thenceforth took a less active part in politics, with the result that the Prime Minister became more powerful. *Restoration of national prosperity*

The Regency crisis

Pitt's authority established

It was at this very moment of his greatest power that Pitt now found himself confronted with problems graver than any he had yet faced—the ever-widening effects of the recent revolution in France, and the imminence of war once more between France and Britain. *New problems from France*

3. *The Impact of the French Revolution*

Of all the political events on the Continent during the eighteenth century by far the most important was the French Revolution. The great changes it brought and the ideas it threw up affected not only France but most of Europe, and not only the men and women of the time but generations far into the future.

In the beginning the revolution was aimed at the dictatorial and inefficient arrangements (usually referred to as the *ancien régime* or the 'old order') by which France had been governed for many years. Under this method of government all political power was vested in the king. Louis XIV at the end of the seventeenth century had remarked with truth 'L'état—c'est moi!' ('The State? It is myself!'); and his descendant Louis XVI, when told that *The ancien régime*

Absolute royal power

one of his decisions was illegal, replied, 'The thing is legal because I wish it.' The nearest thing to Parliament in France, the States General, had not been called together since 1614, and during the eighteenth century no organized body existed which could effectively check the power of the monarch.

The three Estates

Under the *ancien régime*, French society beneath the monarchy was divided into three Estates or orders. The First Estate consisted of the clergy, the Second Estate of the nobles, and the Third Estate of everyone else. The nobles

Privileges of upper clergy and nobles

and the bishops and abbots (who controlled the clergy) had a highly privileged position and were, of course, the chief supporters of the monarchy. They held most of the land, drew large pensions from the king, and were exempt from certain taxes. By contrast the Third Estate, consisting of almost ninety-nine per cent of the population, were heavily loaded with taxes. These they had to pay not only to the king but to the Church and their local lord as well; and in addition many of the peasants were also liable to forced labour (*corvée*). It was a fantastic system. Those who had wealth escaped heavy taxation, and those who had little bore the full brunt.

This was not the only grievance of the people of France. The king and clergy maintained a strict and narrow

No freedom of speech

control over French life. There was no freedom of person or of speech. All were liable to arrest and imprisonment without trial by the issue of a *lettre de cachet* (a writ bearing the king's seal)—an action frequently taken against writers who dared to criticize Church or monarch. Savage punishments were inflicted on those who took an independent line. Men were still broken on the wheel in the country that liked to consider itself the most civilized in the world. Their offence might be only that they were Protestants.

Critics of the *ancien régime*

No man of intelligence could support such a system, and all the great French writers of the eighteenth century— among them Voltaire, Diderot and Rousseau—denounced it in one way or another. Fortunately the *ancien régime* was also very inefficient, so their books were never effectively banned. The great tide of dissatisfaction came to a head in 1789 when Louis XVI, finding himself in a hopeless financial position, largely due to the debts that France had piled up during the War of American Independence, called together the States General for the first time for 175 years. This body quickly ignored the king's instructions, formed itself—on the insistence of the Third Estate representatives —into a single National Assembly (instead of three separate assemblies of clergy, nobles, and others) and demanded reforms. When the king demurred and dismissed the minister who had advised him to call the States General, the Paris mob rose and stormed the Bastille, the great royal prison in Paris and a symbol of oppression. There they found only seven prisoners—and those not political ones. They released them and massacred the garrison—not a very auspicious start to a revolution whose declared aim would soon be to bring a golden age to France.

Louis XVI calls States General, May 1789

The Bastille stormed, July 14th, 1789

The example of Paris was followed throughout the land. The castles of the nobles were attacked, and records of labour and money dues destroyed. Before long the royal authority was little more than a shadow. In the spirit of the hour the Assembly proclaimed its ideas in a notable document called The Declaration of the Rights of Man— ideas intended to free France and indeed all mankind from its oppressors. This document declared that all men were by nature equal, that liberty of person and speech were the sacred privileges of all mankind, and that government (in which the people must participate) must express the will of the people as a whole and not only that of the king. More-over, the Assembly abolished the feudal privileges of the nobles, nationalized much of the vast property of the Church, and wrote out a new constitution for France. At this stage the revolutionaries were still prepared to live under a monarchy, provided the king had little power.

The nobles lose privileges

Declaration of the Rights of Man

Much Church property nationalized

The news of these great events was at first greeted with general joy by the British, who had long hated the despotism of the French kings. Fox, for instance, wrote of the fall of the Bastille, 'How much the greatest event it is that ever happened in the world! and how much the best.' Words-worth later recalled his own feeling:

First reaction in Britain—a warm welcome

Fox

> Bliss was it in that dawn to be alive,
> But to be young was very heaven!

The Non-
conformists Especially enthusiastic were the Nonconformists, for in France complete religious equality was granted in the early stages of the Revolution, whereas in England the Nonconformists (like the Roman Catholics) were still suffering from various political restrictions. Their most noted minister, Dr. Richard Price, delivered in 1789 a famous

Pitt sermon in praise of the Revolution. Even Pitt spoke of the movement with qualified approval during its early days.

Popular
societies And everywhere there sprang up in Britain societies of men who, fired by the ideas of the French Revolution, wished to reform the British constitution and make Parliament more truly representative of the people.

The attack
Burke Slowly this enthusiasm waned. The first to attack the Revolution was Edmund Burke, who published his *Reflections on the Revolution in France* in 1790. Burke, an Irishman, had entered Parliament twenty-five years earlier under the protection of the Marquis of Rockingham, and became the spokesman of the group of Whigs which that nobleman led. He had attacked with great force and eloquence the government's American policy, and had supported the stand of the colonists. He had served with Fox in the Fox–North coalition, and had gone into opposition with him after his dismissal. Acting as a self-appointed champion of the Indian masses against unscrupulous and dictatorial rule, he had then taken a leading part in the prosecution of Warren Hastings. A man of Burke's record thus far might have been expected to welcome the French Revolution; but Burke was cautious. Unlike the gay and carefree Fox, he would give no opinion until he had thoroughly studied a subject. And the more he looked into the French Revolution, the more hostile he became.

Burke's
Reflections In the *Reflections*, Burke launched a full-scale attack on the recent developments in France. He argued that the constitution and laws of a state were the result of the long experience of many generations, and that they must be worked by experienced statesmen. The new French constitution, he said, was an artificial paper creation, thought up

in a few months by theorists, and in the National Assembly there were few politicians of experience. On these two points he could hardly be contradicted. He concluded that the new French constitution would never last, and that in place of the liberty it promised it would bring anarchy. He prophesied that extremists would gain control, that the new paper currency would become worthless, that Christianity would be abolished as the official religion, that terror would become the order of the day, and that finally the resulting chaos would be ended only by some popular general seizing power and establishing a military dictatorship. *Burke's prophecies*

Burke's book had a large sale, but next year (1791) a reply was published that did even better. This was *The Rights of Man*, by Thomas Paine—an ex-revenue officer returned to his native England after fighting for the Americans during the War of Independence. In it Paine championed the right of each generation to set up its own style of government, and proclaimed that the only true form of government was a democracy. A year later he published a second part of the book, advocating not only a democracy but a republic. Meanwhile, already in 1791 feeling on both sides was growing strong. In particular there was trouble in Birmingham when admirers of the Revolution, mainly Nonconformists, organized a dinner to commemorate the second anniversary of the fall of the Bastille. In response an anti-French mob filled the streets and burned down the chapels and houses of dissenters, including that of the famous Unitarian scientist Dr. Joseph Priestley. *A reply to Burke: Paine's Rights of Man* *The Birmingham riots, 1791*

It was in 1792 and 1793 that British feeling veered decisively against the Revolution. Events in France began to justify Burke's prophecies to the hilt. In April 1792 Louis XVI was forced by his new ministers and the Assembly to declare war on Austria, which was threatening to support him against his own people. The war went badly for France, and in August the extremists in Paris, among whom the group known as the Jacobins became the most powerful, seized power by an insurrection.[1] Convinced *Britain swings over to Burke's view, 1792–3* *France at war, 1792* *The Jacobins to the fore*

[1] They were called Jacobins from their first meeting-place in Paris— the disused convent of St. Jacques.

Louis XVI
suspended
that Louis XVI—who had earlier tried to flee abroad and been ignominiously brought back—was in league with the enemy, they deposed him and soon proclaimed France a republic. The panic grew worse as Prussia joined Austria,

The
September
massacres,
1792
and there followed the hideous September massacres, in which more than two thousand priests and royalists held in the prisons of Paris were killed by the extremists in an attempt to eliminate their enemies. So indiscriminate was the slaughter that many of those who lost their lives were thieves, debtors, and even boys and girls at a reformatory, of far from noble blood and quite unconnected with politics.

Execution
of Louis
XVI, 1793
Early in 1793 the dominant Jacobins sent Louis XVI to his death by the new revolutionary 'humane-killer'—the guillotine—and later in the year his Austrian wife, Marie

War
between
France and
Britain
Antoinette, met the same fate. Britain and Spain became numbered among France's enemies, and in Paris the 'Reign

The 'Reign
of Terror',
1793-4
of Terror' set in with a vengeance. It reached its peak in 1794, when thousands were sent to execution and the daily offerings to 'Madame Guillotine' became the main public entertainment. Force and terror stalked the land, and when the revolutionaries had finished butchering the royalists they fell to quarrelling among themselves and butchered each other instead.

It was under the Jacobin Robespierre that savagery reached its highest pitch. When Lyons revolted against his government, a decree was passed that Lyons should be destroyed and on its ruins a column set up with the inscription 'Lyons made war on Liberty: Lyons no longer exists.' At the same time no one was louder than the Jacobins in proclaiming the great revolutionary gospel of *Liberté, Égalité, Fraternité* (Liberty, Equality, Fraternity). The astonishing contrast between the faith they preached and their actual deeds would be impossible to believe if it were not true. The only shred of excuse that may be advanced on their behalf is that France was at war, and there was always the possibility that their opponents at home would act in league with their opponents abroad.

CHAPTER THIRTEEN

BRITAIN AND THE REVOLUTIONARY WAR

1. Crisis and Repression

Most people in Britain judged the French revolutionary leaders by what they did rather than by what they said—the only sensible test in politics—so that the first outrages quickly killed the earlier British sympathy with the Revolution. Moreover, the Revolution soon became a direct threat. During 1792 the Austrian and Prussian invasion of France had been beaten back, and the French went over to the offensive. Their proclaimed intention was now to spread the principles of the Revolution far and wide throughout Europe. 'Peace to the peoples, war on the tyrants', was the official French watchword. *France repels Austrian and Prussian attack, 1792*

At this stage Pitt, who had reduced expenditure on armaments as late as 1792, still stood aloof from the conflict; but when the French counter-offensive carried them into the Austrian Netherlands (the modern Belgium) and they annexed this territory to France, he began to see the need for intervention. Relations rapidly grew worse between the two countries, especially after the execution of the king, and early in 1793 the French declared war on Britain. So Britain became engaged in another—and mercifully the last—great contest with France. With only one short interval, it was to last for twenty-two years. *French annex Austrian Netherlands (Belgium)* *France declares war on Britain, 1793*

The various British societies and clubs which had been formed in support of the Revolution, and which were especially strong among the middle and lower classes in the industrial areas, now came under suspicion. The members of these clubs, most of them early believers in democratic government, were usually known at the time as radicals, since they aimed to reform government radically, or from *Pitt attacks the British reforming societies*

Pitt Addressing the Commons in 1793

From the painting by K. A. Hickel. This is one of the best pictures of the old House of Commons in St. Stephen's Chapel. In the Chair may be seen Addington, the Speaker; and in the corner on the right, front row, Charles James Fox.

the root (Latin *radix* = root). Once Britain was at war with France, they became possible supporters of the enemy, the more so because they were in direct touch with similar organizations in the enemy country. No government would have tolerated this in wartime, and Pitt stopped the radicals' contacts with France and arrested many of their leaders. Most of them had been simply campaigning for a general right to vote, but they were suspected of demanding the vote in order to establish a republic. Among those who escaped Pitt's net was Paine, who fled to France—where he was later thrown into prison for opposing the execution of Louis XVI and only just escaped the guillotine.

With the advent of war, the prosecutions came fast and thick. Political societies were forced to close down, public meetings without a licence were forbidden, and the Habeas Corpus Act (by which the government is bound to justify in court the arrest of any offender) was suspended. Most of the prosecutions for treason, in fact, ended in acquittal—a remarkable tribute to British justice—but Pitt was not deterred by this, and simply kept considerable numbers in prison without trial. In Scotland the prosecutions met with more direct success. Here the Scottish judge, Lord Braxfield, conducted the cases with the fierce prejudice against the accused that we see today in the 'People's Courts' of Eastern Europe.

Suspension of Habeas Corpus Act: imprisonment without trial

Braxfield in Scotland

Despite the arrests of the radicals and the sharply rising cost of living brought about by the war, there was only one serious disturbance in England during this period. This took the form of mutinies by the Fleet in 1797. The first outbreak occurred at Spithead in the Channel Fleet, and was caused not by political motives but by the appalling conditions aboard the ships—conditions particularly intolerable to men who had been press-ganged into service. This mutiny was settled when the government, frightened of its spreading elsewhere, agreed to increase the sailors' pay (which was usually about two years in arrears!), supply better provisions in port, and dismiss a number of especially brutal officers.

The mutinies in the Fleet, 1797 Spithead (the Channel Fleet)

Meanwhile, however, the infection had spread, and the

government found itself faced by a mutiny at the Nore and at other ports sheltering the North Sea Fleet. This soon turned into an affair of the utmost gravity, for some of the mutineers, and particularly their leader, 'President' Parker, an ex-midshipman and schoolmaster who had suffered greatly on his own ship, were much wilder than those at Spithead, and the government was determined to make no further concessions. It refused to relieve the Nore Fleet of unpopular officers or to make a fairer distribution of prize money, and it cut off the mutineers' supplies of food and water. At this the mutineers blockaded the mouth of the Thames and threatened to take the Fleet over to French, Dutch or Irish ports—a manoeuvre frustrated by a naval captain who removed all the buoys and lights marking the shallows of the Thames. Eventually, disliking Parker's violence and fearing government vengeance, the sailors gradually surrendered their ships under a promise of pardon to all except ringleaders. Twenty-nine of these were executed, including Parker, who was hanged from the yard-arm of his own ship.

Order having been once more restored to the Navy, further repressive Acts were then passed—for the government, without much evidence, considered that the mutiny was caused by Jacobin influence. Laws were aimed against
the existence of any society that proposed even parliamentary reform, let alone revolution, and in 1799 the Combina-
tion Acts forbade workmen to act together (i.e. in trade unions) to secure higher wages, shorter hours, etc. These measures went through quietly, for by now most people in Britain had been thoroughly disillusioned by events in France and would have agreed with the poet Cowper, who wrote in 1793: 'I will tell you what the French have done. They have made me weep for a king of France, which I never thought to do, and they have made me sick of the
very name of liberty, which I never thought to be.'

In 1789 Fox and his Whigs had come forward in Parliament as the champions of the French Revolution. Then came Burke's book. This and the subsequent events in France turned most of the Whigs against the Revolution,

French Liberty—British Slavery

From a satirical print by Gillray in 1792. The Frenchman, with a map of French conquests above the fireplace, is extolling the blessings of liberty and the end of taxation and slavery. He nevertheless starves on vegetables. The Englishman curses the Ministry's heavy taxation which is producing, he thinks, starvation and slavery. He is nevertheless able to help himself liberally to beef, wine and beer, and seems almost bursting with plenty.

but Fox remained unmoved. It is difficult to explain his attitude. It was due partly to stubbornness, partly to his determination to oppose Pitt in whatever he did, partly to a taste for theory rather than fact. Soon Burke and Fox, old friends, found themselves at a parting of the ways. By 1791 their friendship was broken for ever; and when some years later Burke lay dying, and Fox sent a note to ask if he could see him, Burke refused. As for the rest of the Whigs, they had to choose between the two. Most of them followed Burke; and Pitt, who was anxious to widen his government, soon gave office to some of these. On the other side, a few stayed with Fox, mainly out of personal loyalty or affection. After some years of this fruitless opposition to Pitt and the war, in 1797 Fox withdrew from Parliament.

His quarrel with Burke

Pitt as a war minister

Subsidies to allies

Expeditions to Continent and enemy colonies

French defeat Holland— which joins France

Prussia and Spain retire

Bonaparte's first Italian campaign, 1796

Austria retires, 1797

Spain joins France, 1796

1797— Britain's black year

Britain's successes 1794–7

Pitt was not so successful a minister in war as he had been in peace. He tended to pursue too many objects at once. British subsidies were used to build up a big coalition, the main members of which were Prussia and Austria; but not all the money supplied was used by these allies for military purposes. In addition, British troops were sent to the Netherlands to support the forces of the coalition, to Toulon and La Vendée to help the French Royalists, and to the West Indies to conquer the French sugar islands. Everywhere the British troops at first met disaster—in the West Indies mainly through disease. They were badly led (and in the West Indies unsuitably equipped) and the money allocated to them was shamelessly misused, commissions even being given to children. (In 1795 the Duke of York, the Commander-in-Chief, ordered a return of all captains under twelve years of age and all lieutenant-colonels under twenty.) On the other hand, the French troops they met, though poorly clothed, were enthusiastic and sure of the rightness of their cause. In turn the French occupied the Austrian Netherlands, defeated Holland (which became, with its fleet, a French satellite), and frightened Prussia and Spain into withdrawing from the war. Then in 1796 a young Revolutionary general, Napoleon Bonaparte, threw the Austrians out of their northern Italian possessions in a single campaign, whereupon the Austrians, too, made peace with France, ceding to her Belgium and Lombardy. Britain was left alone to face the enemy, allied since 1796 with Spain as well as Holland.

1797 was Britain's darkest hour. Her last ally on the Continent was gone, and in India her possessions faced possible attack by the French-inspired Tipu Sahib, the 'Tiger of Mysore'. Fortunately she had managed so far to maintain the command of the seas that were her main defence, and had kept much of the French fleet blockaded in its ports. In 1794, at the battle of 'The Glorious First of June', Admiral Howe had won a victory over the French off Brittany, and early in 1797 Admirals Jervis and Nelson defeated the Spanish off Cape St. Vincent. Also, despite the great losses of men, a number of colonies had been captured from France and Spain in the West Indies, as well as Ceylon and the Cape of Good Hope from the Dutch. Nearer home, however, the danger was acute. In December 1796 a force of 15,000 men sailed from Brest under General Hoche to invade Ireland. Mercifully a gale dispersed the fleet soon after it arrived in Bantry Bay, and no troops got ashore. In February 1797 a small French force actually landed in Wales, but soon surrendered—frightened, it is said, by the red cloaks and beaver hats of some Welsh-women. Then the mutinies at Spithead and the Nore paralysed the British Navy. Admiral Duncan's fleet, charged with blockading the Dutch fleet in the Texel, sailed back to England to join the mutineers at the Nore; and only Duncan with his flagship and one other ship stayed behind and bravely hoodwinked the enemy by making signals to a fleet that did not exist. On top of all this, there was a financial crisis at home, and the government was forced to start a paper currency and suspend payments in gold.

During all this time the situation in Ireland remained tense. The political temperature there had for some years been steadily rising. In the crisis of the American war Henry Grattan, a Protestant but a patriotic Irishman, had organized the United Volunteers to protect Ireland from French invasion. He had used them to secure concessions from the British government, which renounced its centuries-old practice of controlling the measures of the Irish Parliament. But after the failure of Pitt's attempt to give Ireland free trade in 1785, feeling against England grew. Now that she was in peril once more, it seemed to many Irishmen an ideal moment to strike. Moreover, the French revolutionaries had promised to aid all peoples against their kings.

In 1791 Wolfe Tone, a young Belfast lawyer, had formed the 'Society of United Irishmen', whose aim was originally to free Ireland from English control and establish religious equality. Gradually, however, it had become a predominantly Roman Catholic group intent on overthrowing English rule with the help of the French revolutionaries. Tone, who was in France in 1796, stirred the French into sending an expedition at the end of that year, but—as we

Marginal notes:
French attempt to invade Ireland, Dec. 1796

French landing in Wales, 1797

The mutinies, 1797

Financial crisis: paper money, 1797

Ireland

Britain's concessions

Tone's 'United Irishmen' 1791

have seen—it met with disaster in Bantry Bay. Repressive measures by the government followed. Several of the chief leaders of the movement were seized, and in 1798 a desperate effort at rebellion by the main body of their followers was easily crushed at Vinegar Hill, not far from Wexford. French troops, with Wolfe Tone, were on the way but arrived too late; when they landed they were eventually overwhelmed after a gallant resistance. Tone himself was captured in a French man-of-war and committed suicide to escape execution.

Britain thus survived the danger in Ireland—thanks in large part to the re-establishment of order in the fleet during 1797 and the great victory over the Dutch won by Duncan at Camperdown as soon as the mutinies were over. The various other perils of 1797 were surmounted too. Even the storm of the financial crisis was weathered—partly by Pitt's introduction of a form of Income Tax. But though the country came through its perils, the distress among its poorer classes was now acute. The war had already sent food prices soaring, even before the introduction of the paper currency; but wages made no corresponding advance, especially in country districts in the south, and for many starvation loomed ahead. This problem had to be faced by the local magistrates responsible under the Poor Law for the relief of distress. In May 1795 the magistrates of Berkshire met at Speenhamland, near Newbury, to fix a minimum wage which by ancient law they could compel all employers to pay. Unfortunately they decided not to do this but instead to supplement existing wages by an extra payment from the parish rates. A scale was drawn up that linked the amount to be paid with the cost of bread and the number of children of the applicant. This Speenhamland system was then gradually adopted by the magistrates of many other southern counties. It proved to have disastrous consequences; for though introduced with good intentions, its results were that the employer no longer had to pay a living wage, that the labourer had to get help from the Poor Rates to save himself from starvation, and that the ratepayer had to meet much of the employer's

United Irishmen rebel. Vinegar Hill, 1798

The perils of 1797 overcome

Camperdown

Income Tax

Distress in the country

The Speenhamland decision, 1795

labour bill. It was a remedy which soon greatly worsened the disease—of poverty—which it was intended to cure.

Summarizing the main effects of the French Revolution on Britain to this point, we may see that they were thus to involve Britain in a lengthy war; to end any hopes of reform; and to depress very sharply the standard of living of the great mass of the British people. From this we must not, however, conclude that the Revolution was in itself evil. In point of fact it accomplished a large number of necessary reforms, and it inspired men all over the world with ideals of lasting worth. But unfortunately the violence into which it degenerated, and the warfare it brought about, completely overlaid the finer side of the revolutionary movement. In Britain, as in most other countries, any early enthusiasm soon wore off before the harsh realities of bloodshed and a rising cost of living. Only when the dust of conflict had settled, and historians of a later generation could see matters—from their comfortable studies—in a wider perspective, could the permanent value of the revolutionary ideas and achievements be properly assessed.

Summary: effects of French Revolution on Britain

2. *The Rise of Napoleon Bonaparte*

While the French Revolutionary armies were battling in Europe, the government in Paris had undergone a number of changes. During 1794 the Jacobin leader Robespierre, a sincere 'democrat' ruthlessly prepared to butcher all those of contrary views, alarmed so many of the other Jacobins by his threats that they combined to 'down' him. Organizing a successful movement against him in the Convention (the successor of the National Assembly), they were able to send him and his friends to the guillotine which he had kept so constantly employed. After this fresh batch of executions the Terror was soon brought to a halt by the new leaders, and in 1795 the Republican government took on a fresh form.

Fall of Robespierre, 1794

By the new constitution the vote was restricted to property-holders—a reaction against extreme democracy —and power was vested in five Directors, aided by an

The Directory, 1795

Assembly of two Houses. When these arrangements were challenged by a mob in Paris, forty guns under a young artillery general, Napoleon Bonaparte, crushed the attack almost before it had begun. As a reward the Directors gave Bonaparte the command of the army that was to invade Italy. There, as we have seen, he carried all before him in 1796 and 1797. Returning to France, he was next put in command of the 'Army of England', with which the Directors hoped to invade Britain. This project he soon saw was unlikely to succeed. He therefore suggested that greater damage might be done to Britain if France seized Egypt, and so placed herself in a position to control the trade of the eastern Mediterranean and the land gateway to India. He was immediately given command of an expedition to this end.

The character of this man, who was soon to become the virtual dictator of France and most of Europe, is something of an enigma, although all the facts about his life are well known. He was a native of Corsica, a French citizen but of Italian stock—for Corsica had only recently passed beneath French rule. He had joined the old royalist army in 1785, and received rapid promotion when many officers threw up their commissions after the Revolution. He was only twenty-seven when he was given command of the army in Italy, yet within a year he was recognized as France's greatest general. His appearance was no great asset. Black of hair and sallow of complexion, he was very short, and became all too stout as the years went by. His eyes, however, had a force about them that brought many beneath his spell.

Bonaparte's mental qualities were truly remarkable. He was both a dreamer and a man of action. In his early life he was solitary in his habits, and spent much of his time reading books, especially on history and mathematics. The power of imagination was always strong with him, and when he embarked on his Egyptian expedition he saw himself as the founder of another eastern empire like that of Alexander the Great. This imaginative approach he combined with great ability in practical affairs. He was a man

Bonaparte

Bonaparte's Italian campaign, 1796-7

The Egyptian expedition

Personality of Bonaparte

of restless energy who never relaxed. 'I am always working,' he said, 'even when I am at dinner or at the theatre and in the middle of the night.' Eight minutes for lunch and twelve minutes for dinner were often all he allowed himself. So immense a capacity for work eventually gave him a great mastery over detail. As a general he was distinguished by his belief in attack, by his use of artillery, and by his capacity to size-up ground and possibilities of movement so quickly that he was able to out-manoeuvre opponents and defeat their forces in detail before they had time to concentrate. His ambition was unlimited and had at this time no fixed objective. Perhaps, as Cromwell said, 'No one goes as far as he who knows not whither he goes.'

Bonaparte's Egyptian expedition of 1798 was one of the most hazardous he ever undertook, for he was risking himself over a sea which the French fleet did not command. In fact, the British government had sent a squadron under Rear-Admiral Nelson to blockade Toulon, where the expedition was assembling. But Bonaparte was able to slip by while Nelson's fleet was still disabled by a storm, take Malta from the Knights of St. John, and then proceed to Egypt. Nelson was soon in hot pursuit. He had guessed that the French destination was Alexandria. Unfortunately he overtook the French vessels at night and did not see them— as could easily happen before recent scientific inventions. At Alexandria he found no French, so he sailed away. A few hours after his ships had disappeared over the north-eastern horizon, watchers from the Pharos, the famous lighthouse at Alexandria, saw the French expedition appear in the north-west. The troops landed and soon conquered northern Egypt from its masters, the Turks. *Voyage of the Egyptian expedition, 1798*

Bonaparte, however, had not heard the last of Nelson. As soon as the British admiral had definite news, he returned to Egypt. At noon on August 1st, 1798, he sighted the French fleet at anchor in Aboukir Bay, near Alexandria. The French were in a line parallel with the shore and close to it, and the bay was full of shoals, but with superb daring Nelson at once decided to attack. Some of the British ships even placed themselves between the enemy and the shore, *Battle of Aboukir Bay, 1798*

a side on which the French had not even cleared their gun ports. The result was an outstanding victory. Eleven of the thirteen French ships of the line were either captured or destroyed, and Bonaparte and his army were cut off from France.

Nelson

The British admiral was, as admirals go, young. He was thirty-nine, but had been at sea since he was twelve, when he left his home in a Norfolk rectory to become a midshipman in the Navy. He was of medium height, slight in build but active, and not particularly handsome. By the time of the Battle of the Nile his hair was white and he had lost both an arm and an eye in action. His courage was superb, and in quickness of decision and resoluteness in action he has few equals in history. He also inspired extraordinary devotion among both officers and men at a time when there was much bad feeling in the Navy. Soon after Cape St. Vincent, when he had been promoted an admiral and was flying his flag in the *Theseus*, he received a note which read: 'Success attend Admiral Nelson! God bless Captain Miller! We thank them for the officers they have placed over us. We are happy and comfortable and will shed every drop of blood in our veins, and the name of the *Theseus* shall be immortalized as high as the *Captain*'s' (Nelson's ship at the battle of Cape St. Vincent). The message was signed 'Ship's Company'.

The loss of Bonaparte's fleet at Aboukir Bay had no immediate effect on the French general, for his army was independent of supplies from France and remained in control of northern Egypt. It was even able to advance overland into Syria, before being held up at Acre by combined Turkish and British resistance. Nelson's victory turned the tide, however, against the French in Europe.

Second coalition, 1799

Early in 1799 Pitt succeeded in forming another coalition with Austria, Russia and Turkey, and before the end of the year the French armies had to abandon Italy. Farther

French defeats

north, France's newly won Rhine frontier, too, was threatened. This reverse of fortune made the Directory very unpopular in France. Bonaparte, hearing of the situation, accordingly decided to try his luck. Leaving his troops

Fighting for the Dunghill

From a patriotic cartoon by Gillray produced in 1798 after the Battle of the Nile.
On Jack Tar's hat is the legend 'Britannia Rules the Waves'; in Bonaparte's
stomach is a gaping wound marked 'Nelson'.

in Egypt, where they were later defeated by a British
expedition and surrendered, he managed to evade the
British frigates watching off Egypt and reached Toulon Bonaparte
in October. He received a tremendous welcome. After the France
defeats of the summer a successful general was just what the
French wanted, and the fact that his Egyptian expedition
was cut off from its sea communication and doomed to
disaster was quite forgotten in the enthusiasm of the
moment. Here was the man, they thought, who would
surely save France from the enemies encircling her.

This time Bonaparte was not content with a military
command. So long as the Directory was in existence, his
wishes could be thwarted. He wanted supreme control, and He seizes
early in November with the help of some confederates he becomes
seized power. Yet another constitution was produced, and First Consul

this time the main authority lay in the hands of three Consuls. The First Consul was much the most important of the three, and he of course was Napoleon Bonaparte. These arrangements were confirmed by a plebiscite. Burke's prophecy that the Revolution would end in military dictatorship had thus come true, and from this time onward Bonaparte was the real ruler of France.

Once installed in power, he quickly infused new vigour into the conduct of the war—the course of which was already swinging back somewhat in France's favour. He took the field in 1800, recaptured Italy and drove the defeated Austrians to conclude peace. Russia had already withdrawn from the war on the decision of her erratic Tsar Paul, and soon Britain remained France's only opponent.

Bonaparte next decided to direct his energies against British commerce, for this, as he rightly saw, was vital to —in his scornful phrase—'a nation of shopkeepers'. He closed as many ports to British imports as he could, and encouraged the Tsar to form the 'Armed Neutrality of the North'. This alliance of Russia, Sweden, Prussia and Denmark was intended to prevent Britain from searching the shipping of these powers—for Britain in her blockade of France had claimed and exercised the right of searching all neutral shipping to stop them carrying 'contraband of war' (i.e goods of various kinds as decided by Britain) to French ports.

The threat was grave, for the Baltic powers, and especially Denmark, possessed a considerable fleet. But the British government took swift preventive action. Early in 1801 it sent a fleet to the Baltic under Sir Hyde Parker, with Nelson as second-in-command. An ultimatum was first presented to the Danes demanding their withdrawal from the Armed Neutrality. They rejected it. Sir Hyde Parker then had qualms about the great risks involved in an immediate move against the Danish fleet and forts in front of Copenhagen, but Nelson pressed for such an attack and in the end was allowed to lead it. The Danish position was extremely strong and the channel through which the British approached was narrow and shallow. Three British ships ran

Defeat of Austria, 1800

Retirement of Russia

Bonaparte's campaign against British commerce

The 'armed neutrality'

Britain's reply: attack on Danish fleet

aground—whereupon Parker, who was some distance away, thought further progress impossible and hoisted the signal for 'Discontinue Action'. When this was reported to Nelson (who had discretion from Parker to ignore it) he remarked: 'Leave off action! Now damn me if I do!' Putting his spy-glass to his blind eye, he then announced, 'I really do not see the signal.' In the end Nelson overcame the Danes' fierce resistance, and they were forced to withdraw from the alliance. Sweden hastened to follow suit: and Nelson was about to deal with Russia when it was learned that Tsar Paul had been strangled in a palace revolution. His successor, Alexander I, was anti-French. So the Baltic coalition against Britain collapsed, and a serious danger to Britain's conduct of the war at sea was removed.

Nelson's victory at Copenhagen, 1801

Alexander I of Russia Break-up of armed neutrality

Meanwhile in March, before the battle of Copenhagen had been won, Pitt had resigned office. The problem of Ireland brought this about. The rising of 1798 had shown clearly the state of unrest in that country; and since the concessions to Grattan the Irish Parliament had independence in law-making and might pass measures completely contrary to the British interest. Pitt accordingly decided that the situation demanded an Act of Union to unite the Irish and British Parliaments—just as the Act of Union in 1707 had united the English and Scottish Parliaments. Pitt saw that this Act would not allay unrest unless at the same time Roman Catholics could be 'emancipated', or freed from their remaining restrictions, and particularly those which forbade them to vote for or sit in Parliament, or hold any government office.

Pitt and Ireland

He decides for parliamentary union and Roman Catholic emancipation

There was of course strong opposition to Pitt's proposals among the Protestant minority which ran the Irish Parliament and government. To appease this, Pitt decided not to include Catholic emancipation in the Act of Union, but to grant it afterwards. Even so, the Irish Parliament rejected the Bill in 1799 and only passed it in 1800 after large-scale bribery. It soon passed the British Parliament and became law. By it Great Britain and Ireland were to have a common king, parliament, army and flag. Twenty-eight elected Irish peers and four bishops were to sit in the

The Act of Union, 1800

House of Lords and one hundred Irish M.P.s in the House of Commons. There was to be free trade between the two countries.

It was now time to carry out Pitt's promise of concessions to the Irish Roman Catholics—a promise which had won
their support for the Union. But at this stage George III put a spoke in the wheel. He said that he could not consent to Catholic emancipation, since to do so would violate his coronation oath to maintain the privileges of the Church of England. From this dilemma Pitt could see no way out but to yield to the king, drop Catholic emancipation and resign office as an honourable gesture. He later even promised, when the king complained that the Catholic emancipation proposal had brought on his last fit of insanity, not to raise the subject again. Whatever chance Pitt had of solving the Irish problem was thus wrecked by the obstinacy—or conscientious scruples—of George III.

George III rejects Catholic emancipation

Resignation of Pitt, 1801

With the resignation of Pitt and his chief colleagues another Prime Minister had to be found. George asked the Speaker of the House of Commons, Henry Addington, a very dull man, to form a ministry, and he did so. Canning, one of Pitt's junior ministers, soon composed a jingle which expressed what was in everybody's mind:

Ministry of Addington, 1801–4

> Pitt is to Addington
> What London is to Paddington.

The one achievement of Addington's ministry was to make peace with France. This policy was supported by Pitt himself, for at this stage, with Britain in control of the sea and Bonaparte of the land, there seemed no possible end to the war. Peace was obtained by the Treaty of Amiens, finally signed in 1802. By this treaty Britain was to give back all her conquests except Ceylon and Trinidad, while France kept most of hers, undertaking to withdraw only from Egypt—where the French troops had already been defeated—and from the Papal States in Italy. Above all, she kept the Austrian Netherlands (Belgium)—her occupation of which in 1792 had been one of the main causes of the conflict.

Peace of Amiens, 1802

France keeps most conquests, including Austrian Netherlands

CHAPTER FOURTEEN

THE FIGHT AGAINST NAPOLEON

1. *From the Renewal of the War to the Treaty of Tilsit*

THE conclusion of the Peace of Amiens was greeted with great joy in Britain, and when Bonaparte's first representative arrived in London his carriage was drawn through the streets by cheering crowds. True to form, Britain began to disarm rapidly—only to find that the peace rested on very shaky foundations. From the start, Bonaparte showed no sign of living peacefully within the enlarged boundaries of France. He interfered in Switzerland and Italy and, what was far more serious to Britain, sent French expeditions to both the East and West Indies. He also sent French officers to Egypt. Moreover, British merchants soon found that French ports were still closed to their imports. Faced with these hostile actions, the British for their part deferred their departure from Malta, which they had seized after Bonaparte's Egyptian expedition and promised in the peace-treaty to evacuate. The First Consul—now First Consul for life—complained of this and of the bitter attacks on him in the British press. After he had had a stormy interview with the British ambassador in Paris, diplomatic relations were broken off. Regarding renewed hostilities as inevitable, Britain then declared war. The peace had lasted just over thirteen months.

The Peace of Amiens breaks down

War renewed, 1803

Britain was now once more threatened by invasion. It became known that Bonaparte was assembling a great army along the coast of France, Belgium and Holland. At the same time a fleet of flat-bottomed barges was collected to convey the army across the Channel. The British government prepared to meet this danger. It concentrated troops on the south and east coasts, and appointed Sir John

Bonaparte's invasion threat, 1803–5

British preparations

Moore with a specially picked Light Brigade to the command of Shorncliffe Camp, directly in the probable path of the invasion. Martello towers, round with flat roofs, and so-called after a similar tower at Cape Mortella in Corsica, were built as observation and defence points along the coasts. Later the Royal Military Canal was built behind Dungeness to aid the defences. In addition, volunteers for home defence were enrolled in large numbers: indeed, the response was so good that the government stopped recruiting, for they could arm many of the volunteers with nothing but pikes. A system of beacons was also established to give warning of the approaching invasion force. If the French came during the day, damp hay was to be used instead of wood, for smoke could be seen more clearly than flames.

Needless to say, these beacons were sometimes lit on false alarms. On one occasion a butler in a great house near the Scottish border is reported to have opened the drawing-room door and announced in his normally unruffled tones: 'Supper is on the table—and the beacons are lighted on the hills.' In the nursery, babies were hushed with songs like this:

> Baby, baby, naughty baby,
> Hush, you squalling thing, I say;
> Hush your squalling, or it may be
> Bonaparte may pass this way.

The Emperor Napoleon, 1804

The invasion plan

But Bonaparte, who in 1804 had taken the title of Napoleon, Emperor of the French, never came. In truth, like Hitler's at a later date, his plans for crossing the Channel were always a little hazy. He had 100,000 men and 1,500 flat-bottomed barges, which, except in complete calm, were very unseaworthy: 'The Channel', he remarked scornfully, 'is a ditch which it needs but a little courage to cross.' All the same, he could not quite hit on the right way of doing it. His first idea was to cross in the calm following a storm which would have dispersed the British ships. Then he hoped for a three-day fog—but the weather did not oblige. In the end, turning to more orthodox plans, he decided to use his fleet to gain a temporary naval superiority in the

Channel—a superiority which would last long enough for the invasion fleet to cross.

Napoleon had at his disposal not only the French fleet but the Spanish fleet as well, for Spain had renewed her alliance with France. His first object was to break the British blockade of ports where the French and Spanish warships lay. This done, his squadrons would be sent out across the Atlantic in the hope that in chasing them the British would become scattered or follow false trails. Then his ships would double back, enter the Channel in overwhelming force and escort the invasion fleet across. *The British fleets to be lured from the path*

Let us see what in fact happened. The two main French squadrons lay at Brest and Toulon. These were ordered across the Atlantic to the West Indies. In March 1805 the French admiral at Toulon, Villeneuve, gave Nelson the slip, successfully picked up a Spanish squadron at Cadiz, and reached Martinique. Thither Nelson, after first vainly seeking him in the Mediterranean, pursued him. When he heard of Nelson's arrival in the West Indies Villeneuve hastily left and steered for Europe without having linked up with the Brest squadron, which was still bottled up in port unable to elude the British blockade—a serious blow to the French plans. As soon as Nelson suspected Villeneuve's move he sent a fast sloop to give warning at home of the French admiral's approach. On its passage across the Atlantic the sloop saw Villeneuve's fleet and was able to report the enemy's position and numbers accurately to the Admiralty. A British squadron under Sir Robert Calder was then sent to intercept Villeneuve, and did so. The battle, fought off Cape Finisterre, resulted in the capture of only two Spanish ships, but at the end of it Villeneuve turned south for Spain. The danger of a large Franco-Spanish fleet in the Channel was at an end. *Villeneuve leaves Toulon, 1805* *He picks up the Spanish at Cadiz* *The French Atlantic fleet still blockaded* *Nelson guesses Villeneuve's plan* *Villeneuve intercepted and driven back to Spain*

Having put in to Cadiz, Villeneuve then attempted, on Napoleon's direct orders, to re-enter the Mediterranean and intercept a British convoy, despite the fact that by now Nelson was lying in wait for him. It was while he was trying to do this that the decisive sea battle of the Napoleonic war occurred. On October 21st, 1805, Nelson caught Villeneuve's combined

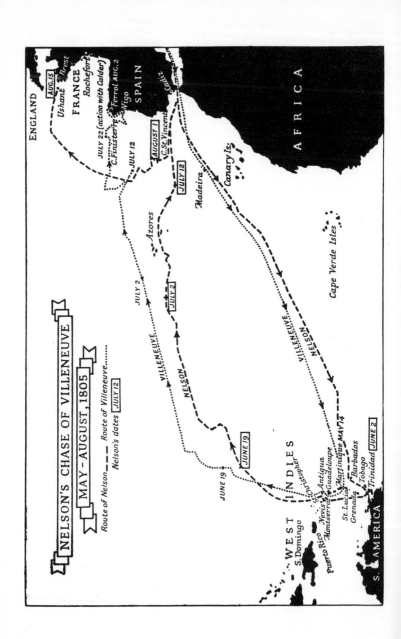

NELSON'S CHASE OF VILLENEUVE
MAY–AUGUST, 1805

Route of Nelson ———— Route of Villeneuve ········
Nelson's dates JULY 12

fleet off Cape Trafalgar. Ever eager for action, Nelson de- Trafalgar, 1805
cided to attack the long and straggling line of French and
Spanish ships in two divisions. He had twenty-seven ships of
the line against the thirty-three of the enemy. Battle was
joined about noon, when his two divisions concentrated on
their different parts of the enemy line. Shortly before, Nelson
had made his famous (and last) signal: 'England expects
that every man will do his duty.' By evening Britain had
won her greatest naval victory, but Nelson was dead, Death of Nelson
having been mortally wounded by a musket-ball. As many
as two-thirds of the enemy ships were destroyed, scuttled or
captured, while not a single British ship had been lost. Yet
joy for the victory was tempered with grief for Nelson's death.
The depth of this feeling may be judged by this letter from
an ordinary seaman in the fleet to his father: 'I never set eyes
on him [Nelson] for which I am both sorry and glad; for to
be sure I should like to have seen him, but then, all the men
in our ship who have seen him are such soft toads, that they
have done nothing but Blast their eyes and cry ever since he
was killed. God bless you! chaps that fought like the Devil,
sit down and cry like a wench.'

Trafalgar confirmed Britain in her mastery of the seas
for the rest of the Napoleonic wars, and, indeed, for much
of the nineteenth century. But other news that reached
London at the close of 1805 called a halt to any rejoicing.
Pitt, who had agreed to take office again as Prime Minister Pitt, Prime Minister again, 1804.
in 1804, had succeeded in 1805 in creating another coalition
on the continent to fight Napoleon. The two main allies Third Coalition, 1805
were Austria and Russia, but they were soon defeated.
Even before the final naval clash at Trafalgar, Napoleon
had left Boulogne with his army and was marching across
Europe. After capturing one Austrian army at Ulm, in Napoleon's victories at Ulm and Austerlitz, 1805
Bavaria, at Austerlitz he utterly defeated the combined
Austrian and Russian forces, with the result that Austria
soon withdrew from the war. The news of Austerlitz was
a terrible blow to Pitt, whose hopes of quick success were
now all shattered. Entering his home and seeing a map of
Europe, he remarked bitterly: 'Roll up that map; it will
not be wanted these ten years.' Early the following year,

worn out by his long years of immense responsibility and exertion, he died at the age of forty-six.

Death of Pitt, 1806
Ministry of All the Talents, 1806

Pitt's death led to the formation of the so-called 'Ministry of All the Talents', a coalition which had members from several groups, including Fox and his followers—for even Fox had now lost his enthusiasm for developments in France. In office again for the first time since 1783, Fox was able in 1806 to secure one important reform: resolutions were passed, embodied the next year in an Act of Parliament, making it illegal for the British to take part in the slave-trade. But before 1806 was out, Fox, too, was dead. On his death the Ministry of All the Talents collapsed, and for the remainder of the war the Tories (and Whigs turned Tory) were in office.

Slave-trade illegal for Britons (as from 1808)
Death of Fox, 1806

Napoleon defeats Prussia and Russia, 1806–7

Meanwhile, Napoleon's grip on the Continent tightened. Prussia belatedly entered the coalition against him, only to have her famous army overthrown in a single day on the battlefield of Jena. Defeated again at Friedland, the Russians, too, retired from the conflict, the Tsar Alexander making peace with Napoleon at Tilsit. Having completely shattered the Third Coalition, Napoleon then decided once more to concentrate on the defeat of Britain, the only country which still retained the power and the will to resist him. Unable to attack Britain by sea, he now staked everything on measures directed against her trade. By the Berlin Decrees, passed after the defeat of Prussia, and by other measures before and after, he forbade all lands controlled by France to import British goods. He hoped in this way to strike a vital blow at British industry, and at the same time cause a currency crisis, as imports into Britain would have to be paid for in gold instead of by exports. And at Tilsit, Alexander of Russia, too, agreed to enforce the Berlin Decrees in his territory, so that nearly every port from the Baltic to the Straits of Gibraltar was closed to British ships. These measures Britain did not, of course, take lying down. By way of retaliation she issued from 1807 onwards Orders in Council which declared that she would prevent ships of any other country entering ports from which British ships were excluded.

Treaty of Tilsit, 1807

His attack on British trade
Berlin Decrees, 1806

British Orders in Council, 1807 onwards

To enforce his policy against British trade—his 'Continental System', as it is often called, since he intended it to apply to the whole European continent—Napoleon had to block all loopholes. He would have a difficult task, for at this time British-manufactured goods, thanks to the Industrial Revolution, were more plentiful and cheaper than those of other countries, and therefore much in demand. In 1807 he was about to force the Danes into applying the System and using their fleet at his direction when he was balked by a swift and high-handed action on the part of Britain: though not at war with Denmark, she sent an expedition to Copenhagen and bombarded it until the Danes agreed to hand over their fleet to Britain's keeping. This kept the Baltic open to British shipping and dealt Napoleon's scheme a grave blow at the northern end of Europe. *Implications of Napoleon's 'Continental System'* *Danish fleet seized by Britain, 1807*

At the southern end of Europe Napoleon had similar plans to stop the important British trade with Portugal. In his determination to do this, before the end of 1807 he sent an expedition into that country and occupied Lisbon. The next year he took advantage of a quarrel between the King of Spain and his heir to secure an even more subservient government in Spain. He ousted the ruling family and, instead, conferred the throne on his brother Joseph Bonaparte. A large French army poured into Spain and the Spaniards were promised all the blessings of the French Revolution. These promises, however, though they had at first aroused enthusiasm among the peoples of Germany and Italy—until they found out the disadvantages of French control—in Spain fell on stony ground from the start. The Spanish peasantry were devoted not to democratic principles but to their independence and to the Roman Catholic Church. After a short interval they revolted against Joseph, and Napoleon for the first time found himself fighting on land not the professional forces of despotic monarchs but a whole people inspired by a proud and fierce patriotism. *The French in Portugal— —and Spain, 1808 Joseph Bonaparte, King of Spain The Spaniards revolt against Joseph*

Apart from involving Napoleon in constant trouble with his allies, his Continental System entirely failed to break *Failure of Continental System*

Britain's will to resist. Loss of trade following the Berlin Decrees caused considerable distress, but this was progressively offset by increased trade across the oceans to America and India—from which (as from the West Indies) the French were totally expelled. Moreover, even Napoleon himself had to make exceptions to his rules: he permitted his army to be supplied with 50,000 West Riding overcoats and 200,000 pairs of Northampton boots. Britain's counter-measures, on the other hand, proved increasingly effective, for prices rose rapidly in countries starved of manufactured goods, and this helped to turn popular feeling more and more against Napoleon.

Effect of Orders in Council

2. *The Peninsular War and the Downfall of Napoleon*

Among the challenges to Napoleon's Continental System could be counted the Spanish rising. At first he did not take it very seriously, but then disturbing news arrived. A French army had been forced to surrender to the Spaniards at Baylen, down in the south. Meanwhile, in Portugal a small British force under Sir Arthur Wellesley had been landed and had defeated the French at Vimiero. Unfortunately, after the victory Wellesley was relieved by two uninspired senior officers who concluded a treaty unduly favourable to the French, whereby the latter were to evacuate Portugal but to be carried back to France in British ships.

Rebel success in Spain
The British in Portugal, 1808

After this, Napoleon soon sent large reinforcements to Spain. Towards the end of 1808 he then arrived in person to crush all resistance. The Peninsular War, as it is termed, lasted six years and demanded great endurance and toughness from those who fought. The bare rocky mountains and arid plains, the extremes of heat in summer and cold in winter, made Spain a harsh land for the soldier. It was a land, as a Frenchman once said, where 'a small army is beaten and a large army starves'. And the inhabitants were no kinder than the country. As regular soldiers they were no match for the French, but in their hatred of the invader they resorted to general and completely ruthless guerrilla

Napoleon in Spain, 1808
Nature of Peninsular War

warfare. One captured French general was boiled alive, another sawn in half; and for nearly four years Napoleon's daily losses averaged a hundred men. The priests, angered by Napoleon's seizure of the Papal States and harsh treatment of the Pope, took an active part in spurring on resistance; one Franciscan friar boasted that he himself had slain six hundred of the enemy. For their part the French treated the Spanish with equal cruelty. Only between British and French were the courtesies of war observed.

In October 1808 the new commander of the British forces in Portugal, Sir John Moore, led his army into Spain to help the Spanish insurgents. He found co-operation with them almost impossible—one British officer wrote that they were 'intractable as swine, obstinate as mules, and unmanageable as bullocks'. Meanwhile Napoleon, having defeated several Spanish armies, advanced south and restored Joseph to Madrid, whence he had been expelled. His move drew Moore to march across northern Spain in an attempt to cut Napoleon's communications with France. Napoleon turned on him; and Moore, with a much smaller force, had to retreat hurriedly to the coast at Corunna, where British vessels were ordered to meet him. It was a terrible march along snow-covered tracks over the great mountains of northern Spain in the depth of winter. Many of the troops did not survive. At Corunna Moore beat off a French attack, but he himself was killed. They 'buried him darkly at dead of night' and next day the British army embarked. It had been a costly retreat, yet the British in Portugal and the Spaniards in the south still kept alight the flame of resistance. Moreover, after this campaign Napoleon himself departed from Spain and was never able to return.

Even more than leading this heroic escape from the jaws of the enemy, Moore's greatest contribution to the eventual British victory in Spain was the new spirit and training he had given to the Army. Both in England and Spain he insisted on having officers who knew their job—he had no patience with those whose only qualifications were their family connections or their love of ceremonial. At

Moore in Spain

The retreat to Corunna

Work of Moore

The Light
Brigade
(of infantry)

Shorncliffe he trained the Light Brigade. These troops were equipped with a rifle, effective at 300 yards, instead of the musket which was still the normal issue to troops of the line and which had a range of only 100 yards. They were taught to move quickly, to operate in loose formation for scouting, to make use of natural cover, and to carry their own supplies.[1]

Wellesley
(Wellington)
in the
Peninsula

Moore's successor, Sir Arthur Wellesley—later Duke of Wellington—found these riflemen invaluable. He returned to Portugal in 1809 in command of all the British forces in the Peninsula. He was a man of middle height, with a large beaked nose and little charm. Severely practical, he had a great command of detail, and although not one who suffered fools gladly, he never lost his temper—a great asset in Spain, where the Spanish generals were usually infuriating. On one occasion he went down on his knees to persuade the Spanish commander-in-chief to retreat from a hopeless position: the Spaniard boasted of his humiliation, but Wellesley got his way, and that was all he cared about. On the battlefield Wellesley was so cool that some doubted if he possessed any nerves at all. And personal comfort in a campaign, as is not always the case with those of exalted rank, meant little or nothing to him. A Spaniard on his staff learnt to dread his answer to the question at what hour the Staff would move and what there would be for dinner. It was so often 6 a.m. and cold meat. No one but a Spartan like Wellesley could have commanded with such success in Spain.

British
success and
failure in
Peninsula,
1809

In 1809 the task of driving the British from the Peninsula was handed over by Napoleon to his marshals, only for Wellesley first to drive the French from Portugal and then win a big success in Spain at Talavera. For this he was created Viscount Wellington. Soon, however, he was compelled to retire into Portugal. Elsewhere in the same year the allied cause went badly. Napoleon once more beat the Austrians, who had again entered the conflict, and forced them to enter into an alliance with him and apply the

Napoleon
defeats
Austria
again

[1] For a fine novel of the Peninsular War in which one of these riflemen is the hero, read C. S. Forester's *Death to the French*.

Continental System. And a British expedition to Holland Failure of British expedition to Holland got no further than the island of Walcheren, where it suffered appalling losses from disease and incompetent supply.

Meanwhile Wellington was on the defensive in the Peninsula. After beating off an attack by Marshal Masséna, he had retreated behind strongly fortified lines at Torres Torres Vedras Vedras, near Lisbon. He had carefully stripped the country in front of supplies, with the result that the French, who had difficulty in bringing up provisions from any distance owing to the activities of the Spanish guerrillas, came near to starvation. Unable to penetrate the lines and running short of supplies, Masséna was forced to leave Portugal early in 1810. The next year Wellington freed all Portugal British successes: and in 1812 sallied into Spain and beat the French at Salamanca. Once more he was forced back into Portugal, Salamanca, 1812 but this time southern Spain remained in the hands of the Spanish rebels.

To add to Britain's problems she now became involved War between Britain and U.S.A., 1812–14 in war with the United States. The Americans objected to Britain's exclusion of their trading vessels from French-controlled ports; and though they were eventually exempted from the operation of the Orders in Council, the concession came too late to stop war. The fighting included an unsuccessful American attempt to invade Canada, a number of clashes at sea in which the Americans more than held their own, and the burning of the public buildings in Washington by a British expedition. All this built up further ill-will against Britain in the United States, but fortunately did not affect the issue of the main struggle in Europe.

By the end of 1812 that struggle had taken a decisive turn against Napoleon. He had launched an attack which Napoleon's Moscow campaign, 1812 led to his own destruction. In 1812 he marched an army of 600,000 men into Russia, for the previous year Alexander I had abandoned the Continental System and allowed British goods once more to enter his country. Unlike Hitler, Napoleon reached Moscow—after a bloody victory outside at Borodino—but Moscow was bare of supplies (and large

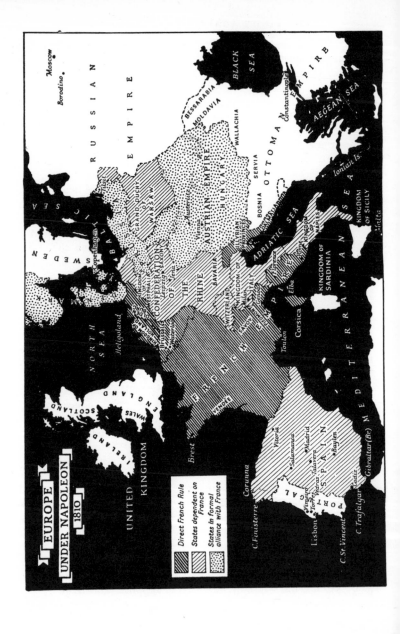

EUROPE UNDER NAPOLEON 1810

Direct French Rule
States dependent on France
States in formal alliance with France

parts of it on fire) and the Russians failed to surrender. Without supplies he could not winter in Moscow, so he had to retire. He did not leave until the end of October. It was too late. The Russian armies, avoiding a major battle, constantly harassed the retreating enemy, and the Russian winter gradually seized them more and more remorselessly in its grip. By December there were sixty degrees of frost and the retreat was a rout. In the end only some 20,000 men of the whole vast expedition escaped from Russia. It was disaster on a scale almost unparalleled in history.

To amass so large a force as he led into Russia, Napoleon had withdrawn troops from many places, including Spain. Of this, Wellington was quick to take advantage. In 1813 he struck out from Portugal on what proved to be his final advance across the Peninsula. Rapidly he expelled Joseph Bonaparte from Madrid, followed up his retreating forces towards the Pyrenees, and smashed them at Vitoria. Within a few months not a French soldier was left in Spain. *Wellington frees Spain*

Vitoria, 1813

That same year, despite superhuman efforts, Napoleon was eventually beaten at a great battle near Leipzig and driven back across Germany by the Russians, Austrians, Prussians and Swedes, who with the British had formed yet another coalition. By 1814 these troops were invading France from the east while Wellington attacked from the south. The end was now near, and eventually Napoleon agreed to abdicate. This left the way open for the restoration of the Bourbons, the brother of the executed king being given the throne. As a consolation prize the former Emperor of the French was awarded the little island of Elba in the Mediterranean. Here, and here alone, could he rule. *The Fourth Coalition, 1813*

Abdication of Napoleon: banishment to Elba, 1814

The delegates of the various European states then met at Vienna to discuss a final settlement. It was not long before their deliberations were rudely interrupted. On March 1st, 1815, Napoleon and a few companions, having left Elba, landed in southern France. 'The Hundred Days' that now followed provided the final and perhaps the most remarkable scenes of his career. Troops sent to arrest him fell in behind him, and in three weeks France was once more in his power and the Bourbons had fled. But the British Foreign *Congress of Vienna meets, 1814*

Napoleon lands in France: The Hundred Days, 1815

Minister, Lord Castlereagh, quickly took a lead in re-
constructing the alliance against him, and Napoleon found
that he had to fight the European Powers all over again.

He marches into Belgium Deciding to take the offensive, he marched into Belgium,
where he defeated the Prussians at Ligny, while Marshal Ney

Ligny and Wellington clashed nearby at Quatre Bras. Imagining
that he had driven the Prussians hopelessly out of touch with

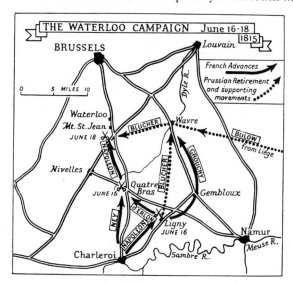

THE WATERLOO CAMPAIGN   June 16-18
1815

BRUSSELS   Louvain

French Advances
Prussian Retirement
and supporting
movements

Dyle R.

Waterloo
Mt. St. Jean   BLUCHER   Wavre
JUNE 18   BÜLOW
                                                from Liège
NAPOLEON

Nivelles   BLUCHER   CROUCHY

Quatre
JUNE 16   Bras   Gembloux
NEY   D'ERLON

Ligny
JUNE 16   Namur
NAPOLEON
                                    Meuse R.
Charleroi   Sambre R.

their allies, Napoleon then pressed on to attack Wellington,
who had retired from Quatre Bras to cover Brussels and preserve the possibility of contact with the Prussians.

Waterloo, 1815 On Sunday, June 18th, Napoleon launched his attack on
Wellington's army, of whom only a third were British. They
were drawn up behind a ridge at Waterloo, near Brussels.
The battle raged all day, but the French could not penetrate
the allied position. Towards evening Napoleon threw his
Old Guard into one last desperate attack. He could not break
the British line. Seeing the enemy reeling back, Wellington
then sent his troops surging forward. They were aided by the
Prussians under Blücher, who true to promise had now forced

his way to the scene despite his earlier reverse. The result was utter defeat for the French. Nevertheless, the margin of victory was very narrow. 'A damned nice thing—the nearest run thing you ever saw in your life', as Wellington put it. As for Napoleon, all he could do was to surrender and once more abdicate—to be sent this time to the lonely island of St. Helena in the South Atlantic, from which there would be no escape. And at St. Helena, after furbishing up the story of his career to appear in the best light to posterity, he died six years later.

At the Congress of Vienna, resumed after Waterloo, the Allies claimed the rewards of victory and much of the old European order was restored. Amongst those who had helped to defeat Napoleon and preserve Europe from domination by one man, none had borne a stouter or more *The British* successful part than Britain. Thanks to her island position, *contribution to the war* her sea-power, and her commercial and manufacturing strength, allied to her unfailing courage and tenacity, she had been able to hold on after others faltered, rebuild the shattered coalitions, and become the main architect of the Allied success. She had subsidized the Allied armies, mastered the enemy fleets, swept up the enemy colonies, brought about rising prices and dissatisfaction in French-occupied territory by her blockade, and finally, by the deeds of her troops in the Peninsula and at Waterloo, had made a powerful military contribution by land on the Continent. For all these reasons, when the victors fell to dividing the spoils, she did not feel herself unjustified in retaining the Cape of Good Hope, Mauritius, Ceylon, *Britain's* Heligoland, Malta, the Ionian Islands, Trinidad, St. Lucia *gains* and Tobago. So the Napoleonic War finished with Britain enjoying more prestige and power abroad than ever before —the almost unchallenged ruler of the seas and the possessor of a still greater Empire.

At home, however, as we shall see, the picture was far less satisfying to British self-esteem.

CHAPTER FIFTEEN

THE ARTS IN THE GEORGIAN PERIOD (I)

1. *Eighteenth Century Literature*

The high level of artistic achievement

THE rapidly growing wealth of Britain during the reign of the first four Georges not only brought increased comfort; it also helped to inspire a great achievement in the arts. Later, under Queen Victoria, wealth became widely spread among people who had no family background of culture and little artistic taste, and were therefore liable either to ignore art altogether or to spend money on buildings and pictures of little merit. In the eighteenth century, wealth was still piling up in the hands of the landed **The influence of the aristocracy** aristocracy, who with their great houses and their 'Grand Tours' abroad had by now a traditional interest in art. These noblemen established admirable standards of taste in painting and architecture which others were generally content to follow. And in literature, where authors came to depend as the century progressed not on the patronage of an individual nobleman but on the favour of a small, cultured upper and upper-middle class, the achievement was no less brilliant.

The influence of the classics

To much of the literature of the eighteenth century, as to much of its architecture, it is possible to apply the word 'classical'. During this century many writers produced work in a style which owed a great deal to the Latin authors of the classical world. No writer was more influenced in this **Pope** way than Alexander Pope (d. 1744), the greatest poet in the early part of the century. He published a verse translation of both *The Iliad* and *The Odyssey*, and the couplets (rhymed pairs of lines) in which he wrote were in many ways like those of Ovid. Above all, Pope's verse had the strong sense of form and the conciseness of the classical style. Here are a few lines culled from various poems, all

expressing a profound truth with the minimum of words—
and so familiar that we usually do not realize their source:

> A little learning is a dangerous thing.
>
> Hope springs eternal in the human breast.
>
> For fools rush in where angels fear to tread.
>
> For forms of government let fools contest;
> Whate'er is best administered is best.

Pope was a great artist in words. Perhaps through his
having absorbed the classics so thoroughly, however, his
ideas often seem unoriginal. Moreover, he inspired many
imitators who carried on his style without his genius. As a
consequence a good deal of early eighteenth-century poetry
now seems to us artificial and lifeless and much too dependent on a set 'poetic' language. The sun, for instance, is all
too often 'Phoebus', a ship 'a bark', and countrymen
'swains'. Yet Pope cannot be blamed for the defects of his
imitators, and his own supreme skill must always be
admired.

Among the next generation of poets was Thomas Gray Gray
(d. 1771). He was prone to melancholy and for much of
his manhood lived a retired life at Cambridge. His best
known work, *An Elegy Written in a Country Churchyard*,
appeared in 1751. It is simpler and less full of classical
allusions than most of his poems; in feeling it is stronger and
deeper than most of the earlier work of the century. The
love of the countryside, which in Pope and his followers
though frequently expressed tends to sound unreal, in Gray
seems truly sincere. Very unusual in a man of his generation,
he even sought out mountains, visiting the Alps, the Lake
District, and the Scottish Highlands. As a result he was
considered by the orthodox opinion of the day, including
that of Dr. Johnson, to be rather wild.

Dr. Samuel Johnson (d. 1784), lexicographer, poet, critic, Johnson and
essayist, and editor of Shakespeare, was the greatest literary his circle
figure of the century. Today, however, he owes his fame
to his character and conversation rather than to his books,
which are largely unread. He was born at Lichfield, the son

Dr. Johnson and Boswell in Edinburgh
From a drawing by Samuel Collings.

of a bookseller. After a short period at Oxford and then as
an unsuccessful schoolmaster he went up to London, where
he earned a precarious living by writing. Gradually he was
able to abandon hack journalism and concentrate on more
congenial tasks. It was *A Dictionary of the English Language*,
published in 1755 after eight years of labour, that really
established his reputation—with the result that he later
obtained a government pension that freed him from want.

Boswell's
Johnson
　　　It is the successful Dr. Johnson that we meet in the
famous biography by James Boswell. Boswell was a Scot of
noble family, a much younger man than Johnson, and a
deplorable chaser of women. He had excellent descriptive
ability, the industry to maintain a diary over large periods
of his life, and the determination to cut a figure in literary
society. He set himself out to cultivate Johnson's acquain-
tance and to record his opinions. From the pages of Bos-

well's biography there emerges a remarkable personality. Johnson was large, almost burly, and his naturally good features were marred by the scrofula from which he had suffered as a child.[1] He appeared uncouth from the peculiar way in which he rolled his head and body from side to side as he walked, and from various other eccentric habits, such as beating time with his feet, that sometimes led those who did not know him to think him an idiot. His clothes were always dark and worn in some disorder. Yet in conversation he had no equal, even among friends who included many well-known writers and artists. His talk was irresistible— full of vigour, prejudice and wit, yet with a great deal of underlying common sense.

It was at 'The Club', founded in 1764 on the suggestion of the great painter Joshua Reynolds, that Johnson shone most brilliantly. This group of distinguished men, including Edmund Burke and Oliver Goldsmith, for some years met once a week in the evening at the Turk's Head in Soho. Here over wine and food the conversation went on till late into the night. Johnson's remarks there and elsewhere have come down to us through Boswell. Not surprisingly, many of them were judgements about people. Of Lord Chesterfield, a nobleman of literary ambitions who had failed him as a patron, he said: 'This man I thought had been a lord among wits; but I find, he is only a wit among lords.' Of a woman preaching he remarked: 'Sir, a woman's preaching is like a dog's walking on his hinder legs. It is not done well; but you are surprised to find it done at all.' Of a well-known republican lady he told this story. 'One day when I was at her house, I put on a very grave countenance, and said to her, "Madam, I am now become a convert to your way of thinking. I am convinced that all mankind are upon an equal footing; and to give you an unquestionable proof, Madam, that I am in earnest, here is a very sensible, civil, well-behaved fellow-citizen, your footman; I desire that he may be allowed to sit down and

[1] In the early eighteenth century many still believed that this disease could be cured by the royal touch, and in Johnson's early years his mother took him to London to be touched by Queen Anne.

dine with us." I thus, Sir, showed her the absurdity of the levelling doctrine. She has never liked me since. Sir, your levellers wish to level down as far as themselves; but they cannot bear levelling up to themselves. They would all have some people under them; why not then have some people above them?'

As this last extract shows, Johnson was a great enemy to every form of humbug—'cant' he called it—and a great conservative. As long as he was alive he maintained in literature the classical tradition that we have seen appearing so strongly in the work of Pope.

The drama: Goldsmith and Sheridan

Two of Johnson's friends, the Irishmen Oliver Goldsmith (d. 1774) and Richard Brinsley Sheridan (d. 1816), were dramatists who wrote plays that have been regularly performed ever since. In this they were unlike their immediate predecessors; for between 1715 and 1770 there was no play written (apart from *The Beggar's Opera*) which is now acted more than very occasionally. Goldsmith, who was also poet, essayist, novelist and literary jack-of-all-trades, wrote *She Stoops to Conquer*; and Sheridan, who later became a theatrical manager, a Whig politician, and a brilliant debater in Parliament, wrote *The Rivals* and *The School for Scandal*. These plays are comedies of manners in which there is a great deal of fun at the habits of fashionable —and unfashionable—society. Unlike most of the similar comedies of Charles II's and William III's reign, they were not obscene; and unlike the fashionable comedies of 1715– 1770, they were not over-sentimental.

Other prose writing

On the whole, English literature throughout the greater part of the eighteenth century excelled in prose rather than in verse. Edward Gibbon, the historian of *The Decline and Fall of the Roman Empire*, and Edmund Burke the politician, Adam Smith the economist, and David Hume the philosopher were all masters of smooth and balanced yet vigorous prose. But it was in a more popular form of literature that the most important development took place.

The novel

Novels—extended stories in prose—appeared and grew rapidly in favour. They were new in that such prose stories as had appeared in the sixteenth and seventeenth centuries had either been short or, like *The Pilgrim's Progress*, intended to point a moral rather than simply to tell a tale. This new form of writing was eagerly devoured by a much wider public than was attracted to poetry or the drama.

At a Comedy

From a satirical engraving, about 1797, by Thomas Dighton.

In the early decades of the eighteenth century two famous novels were written which we still read—*Robinson Crusoe* (1719) by Daniel Defoe and *Gulliver's Travels* (1726) by Jonathan Swift. The idea of the first came from the adventures of a real person, the second was a satire on contemporary politics and the ways of mankind. We have now forgotten the satire, and the story is enjoyed for itself in numerous editions specially 'cut' for children—a result far from Swift's intentions. Swift, in fact, was not a novelist at all but an effective and bitter political writer.

The novels written later in the century bore a much greater resemblance to modern fiction. Often leisurely in

Defoe's Robinson Crusoe

Swift's Gulliver's Travels

pace and sometimes ramshackle in construction, they
delighted to retail a love-affair at enormous length or to
follow their hero's adventures all over the English countryside. They were pure stories written almost entirely to
entertain, and they supplied a new diversion to the literate

The first great novelists: Richardson

members of the public. Samuel Richardson (d. 1761),
Henry Fielding (d. 1754) and Tobias Smollett (d. 1771)
are the best known of these novelists. Richardson was the
son of a London joiner. He became a master printer, and
took up novel-writing later in life. By modern standards his
novels are fairly dull, extremely detailed, and too moralizing
and sentimental. He excelled at portraying women and
delving deep into feminine ways of thought; and his best
novels—*Pamela, or Virtue Rewarded* and *Clarissa Harlowe*—
are named after their heroines.

Fielding

Fielding, though at first impoverished, came of aristocratic stock. He was handsome, gay, and full-blooded, and
he took a broad view of human life and pleasure. Tom
Jones, the vigorous character who is the hero of his novel
of that name, is 'no better than he ought to be'; and
Joseph Andrews starts as a skit on Richardson's *Pamela*. At
the same time there is in Fielding's work a note of protest
against the coarseness and crudeness of eighteenth-century
life. Fielding had great experience of this side of affairs,
particularly after he had become a magistrate at Bow
Street.

Smollett

The third great novelist of this period, Smollett, was a
doctor who had served as surgeon's mate in a battleship.
He combined extraordinary vigour and coarseness, particularly in his humour, with a passionate concern for more
hygienic conditions in everyday life. In *Roderick Random* he
showed up the hardships both in Bridewell prison and in
the Navy. And here is a typical extract from his *Humphry
Clinker*, a novel written (like Richardson's) in the form of
letters. The writer, a confirmed countryman, describes
first the water he finds in London: 'If I would drink water,
I must quaff the rankish contents of an open aqueduct,
exposed to all manner of defilement, or swallow that which
comes from the river Thames, impregnated with all the

filth of London and Westminster. Human excrement is the least offensive part of the concrete [mixture], which is composed of all the drugs, minerals and poisons used in mechanics and manufacture, enriched with the putrefying carcases of beasts and men, and mixed with the scourings of all the wash-tubs, kennels and common sewers. . . . This is the agreeable potion extolled by the Londoners as the finest water in the universe.' And the writer has no better opinion of London milk: 'the produce of faded cabbage-leaves and sour chaff, lowered with hot water, frothed with bruised snails, carried through the streets in open pails, exposed to foul rinsings discharged from doors and windows, spittle and tobacco quids from foot passengers, spatterings from coach wheels, dust and trash chucked into it by roguish boys for the jokes' sake, the spewings of infants who have slabbered in the tin measure . . . and finally the vermin that drop from the rags of the . . . milkmaid.'

2. The Romantic Revival

From the middle until nearly the end of the eighteenth century the novelists were much more vital in their art than the poets; and they were able to reach a fair-sized public through the new subscription or 'circulating' library. Suddenly, however, just before the end of the century, new *New life* life burst into English poetry, with the result that the fifty *in poetry* years after Dr. Johnson's death mark one of the greatest periods in English verse-writing. Wordsworth, Coleridge, Shelley, Keats, Byron and Scott all belong to these years. The movement they set in train is often called 'The *The* Romantic Revival'.[1] The Romantics turned their backs on *Romantic Revival* the immediate classical tradition, on the clever but rather artificial poetry of Pope and his followers. They also turned their backs on the urban life of the Britain of the Industrial

---

[1] 'Romantic' is derived from 'romance', a tale in the old French language full of incidents of a strange or unusual kind, and remote from everyday life. It is often used as the opposite of 'classical'. There had been a great period of 'romantic' literature before in England during the Elizabethan Age.

Revolution. It was the Lake District with its wild and solitary scenery or the Mediterranean. with its wine, warmth and leisure that they sought. Yet their work was intensely creative. Inspired by imagination and sympathy rather than logic, their poems had a new depth, passion and power.

The publication of *The Lyrical Ballads* by William Words-worth and Samuel Taylor Coleridge in 1798 is usually considered to mark the beginning of the Romantic Revival. There were, however, several poets who in many respects were forerunners of the Romantics. Two of these have an important place in our literature. William Blake (d. 1827), an eccentric genius who was also a fine artist, wrote not only long religious poems of great obscurity, but also short religious poems of charm and simplicity. *The Lamb*, *The Tiger*, and 'Jerusalem'[1] are well-known examples. And the poems of Robert Burns (d. 1796), the son of a small farmer in Ayrshire, also owed nothing to the classical tradition. They were mostly written in Scottish dialect and drew their strength from the old love for song in the Scottish country-side. They, too, are both simple and beautiful.

Romantic forerunners:

Blake and Burns

Wordsworth   The main stream of the Romantic Revival, however, started with Wordsworth (d. 1850, aged eighty) and Samuel Taylor Coleridge (d. 1834). Born and brought up in Cumberland, Wordsworth became a great enthusiast for the Revolution in France—in which country he lived for a short time. Disillusioned by the Reign of Terror he turned from politics to poetry, and it was in the beautiful scenery and the simple people of his native country, to which he returned, that he found his inspiration. He had little taste for the ordinary life of business and concern for material things, as is apparent from one of his most famous sonnets:

> The world is too much with us; late and soon,
> Getting and spending, we lay waste our powers.

---

[1] This poem, beginning 'And did those feet in ancient time/Walk upon England's mountains green', is not in Blake's long poem called *Jerusalem* but in his *Milton*.

Real delight, Wordsworth thought, could best be found in Nature: happiness—or rather, satisfaction—in the fulfilment of duty.

Coleridge, philosopher and brilliant literary critic as well as poet, was the son of a Devon clergyman. He gradually ruined his health by taking opium, but not before he had written some of the most remarkable poems in our language. He had a wonderful imagination, and he was fascinated by the mysterious and the eerie. It was distant lands and seas or the medieval world that drew him—all remote from the classical tradition. This fondness for the strange and the unknown is well seen in such poems as *The Ancient Mariner* and *Kubla Khan*. Coleridge

In the next decade came two more great poets, Percy Bysshe Shelley (d. 1822, aged thirty) and John Keats (d. 1821, aged twenty-six). They were friends who had much in common, and both died young in Italy. They came, however, from very different backgrounds. Keats was the son of a stable-keeper and served an apprenticeship as an apothecary; Shelley, educated at Eton, was the grandson of a baronet. But both alike met rebuffs in England. Keats's work was scorned by some of the most powerful literary critics, and Shelley was sent down from Oxford (after writing a pamphlet on *The Necessity of Atheism*) and was later cold-shouldered by society on account of his unconventional opinions and behaviour. Both wrote poems of a beauty and an imaginative power that have rarely been surpassed. Shelley
Keats

In addition to being a great poet, Shelley was an ardent reformer. He had a natural dislike of most authority and he nursed a bitter hatred against the British Government when the Cabinet after 1815 carried still further its policy of repressing radical, reformist, and working-class movements. He did not pull his punches. In *The Masque of Anarchy*, Lord Castlereagh, one of the ministers, came in for a very sharp couplet:

> I met Murder on the way—
> He had a mask like Castlereagh.

And Shelley disposed of George III in one line:

> An old, mad, blind, despised, and dying king.

But Shelley's opinions were far too wild for him to be a good guide in politics, and his best work was done·in deeper realms. No one can forget, once felt, the power and the passion of poems like the *Ode to the West Wind*.

Byron Almost an exact contemporary of Shelley was Lord Byron (d. 1824, aged thirty-six). Though a nobleman, he was as great an enthusiast as Shelley for reform and liberty. *Childe Harold*, his long and colourful poem of his travels through Europe, made him for a short time the leader of the romantic movement and the darling of society; but his highly questionable morals made a rapid departure from England advisable, and he took up residence in Italy. He died of fever in Greece while aiding the Greeks in their struggle against the Turks. As a poet he was esteemed at the time far above Shelley and Keats, but few would now consider him their equal.

Scott The foremost novel-writer of the Romantic Revival was Walter Scott (d. 1832), a Scotsman who lived his life in Edinburgh and the neighbourhood. His Waverley Novels, called after the first in the series and published anonymously after he had already won fame as a poet, achieved an immense success in both Scotland and England. Attracted by the ancient ballads of Scotland and the Border, he found a new world in the past, and, like Coleridge, he was especially drawn to the Middle Ages. His stories are mostly tales of romance and adventure of earlier times. He brought history to life and created the historical novel. An author with a prodigious reputation, he incurred big debts in a publishing venture, and hastened his death by slaving away at his writing over long years in order to repay them.

After Scott, the best-known novelist of the period was Jane Austen (d. 1817). Her novels, such as *Pride and Prejudice*, centre on the middle- and upper-class society of her day, and owe nothing to the Romantic Revival. Their quiet humour, accuracy of observation and delicacy of touch have endeared them and their author to many generations of readers.

John Keats

Aged 24—from a miniature by
Joseph Severn.

Lord Byron in Albanian Dress

Aged about 25—from a painting by
Thomas Phillips.

William Wordsworth

Aged about 28—from a sketch by
R. Hancock.

Sir Walter Scott

Aged about 53—from a painting
by Landseer.

In this brief sketch there has been no space to recall more than the very greatest among the writers of the period 1715–1830. There were also, of course, scores of other notable authors: great letter-writers like Horace Walpole (the son of Sir Robert) or essayists like Charles Lamb and William Hazlitt, or hymn-writers like Isaac Watts, William Cowper and Charles Wesley. All told, then, the years 1715–1830 were years of great richness for our literature. And within them were two phases distinguished by work of supreme originality: the years 1740–70, which saw the sudden rise of the novel, and the years 1790–1830, when 'romantic' poetry blossomed in new and glorious profusion.

Letters:
Horace
Walpole

Essays:
Lamb, etc.

Hymns

3. *Music*

In an earlier volume we saw how English music, of supreme quality during the reigns of Elizabeth I and James I, declined from about 1625, blazed up again in full glory in the late seventeenth century through a single genius, Henry Purcell, and then paled before foreign competition in the form of opera from Italy. The manager of the Italian opera company which took London by storm in the reign of Queen Anne was not an Italian but a young German, George Frederick Handel (1685–1759); and he liked England so well, and was so well appreciated by George I and George II, that he settled here, became naturalized, and here produced his greatest work. Originally best known for his operas in the Italian style, in 1720 he began a fresh departure by writing his first sacred oratorio, *Esther*. The sacred oratorio, or musical relation of a Biblical story by means of recitative, arias, choruses and instrumental interludes, was a new form of art; and it culminated in one of the world's supreme masterpieces, Handel's *Messiah*, first performed in Dublin in 1741.

Handel

Oratorio:

Messiah

The eventual success of this wonderful work, which the British some time later took to their hearts and began ceaselessly performing, had its unfortunate side. For a large part of the nineteenth century serious British composers could not get it out of their heads that they should be

Handel in Old Age

From a modern imaginative drawing by 'Batt'.

composing oratorio; and on the whole their efforts to do so were lamentable. This later result, however, was not yet apparent. During the rest of the eighteenth century British composers strove not so much to write great oratorio, as to write much less ambitious works—mainly anthems, short orchestral pieces and suites, songs, glees and ballad-operas (after the great success in 1728 of Gay's *Beggar's Opera*, which employed well-known British tunes). In this minor kind of work they were reasonably successful. Pleasant orchestral music was written by Dr. Thomas Arne (d. 1778), who also composed such fine songs as *Rule Britannia* and his well-known settings of Shakespeare (*Where the bee sucks, Blow, blow, thou winter wind*, etc.). Similar work was done by William Boyce (d. 1779), who also wrote fine anthems and whose songs included *Heart of Oak*, the verses for which were by David Garrick, the great actor. Other notable

Ballad-opera: The Beggar's Opera

Arne

Boyce

composers were Samuel Wesley (the younger), a son of
Charles Wesley, with some good anthems to his credit, and
Charles Dibdin, who wrote successful ballad-operas and is
perhaps best remembered by *Tom Bowling*.

Dr. Arne

From a coloured etching after F. Bartolozzi. He is seen
playing his best known composition ('Rule Britannia')
on an organ.

On the whole, however, it must be confessed that all this
was small beer compared with the towering genius of
Handel. Not till the end of the century did Britain produce
a composer whose work was in any marked degree original;
and then the musician concerned, the Irishman John Field
(d. 1837), whose 'nocturnes' for the pianoforte helped later

Field

to inspire the great Chopin, spent most of his working life on the Continent. In these nocturnes, it may be remarked, 'romantic' feeling is again evident, while the work of the earlier composers mentioned—Arne, Boyce and Handel— is, in its adherence to a stricter or more regular form, much more 'classical' in spirit. 'Romanticism'

So far as music is concerned, it would be fair to say that eighteenth-century Britain shows a better record for performance than composition. Music-making was still a favourite occupation in town and countryside; some noblemen such as the Duke of Chandos, the patron of Handel, maintained a private orchestra; and public concerts in the larger towns were becoming a regular feature. The orchestra at Vauxhall Gardens was for a time under the direction of no less a musician than Arne. The Three Choirs Festival, held successively in the cathedrals of Gloucester, Worcester and Hereford, began in 1724 and has continued ever since. Foreign musicians of the eminence of Mozart and Haydn visited London to perform—the former as a child prodigy on the keyboard, the latter to conduct symphonies which a London concert-promoter had specially commissioned from him. Performance

Such facts show that Britain in the eighteenth century was far from being unmusical. Nevertheless, it remains true that from the death of Purcell in 1697 to the emergence of Edward Elgar round about 1900, Britain produced not a single composer of the highest calibre. The falling-off is seen clearly enough in the 'glees' or 'catches' that became so popular in the late eighteenth and early nineteenth centuries. They were often pleasant, fresh and gay; but they are simply not in the same class as their earlier counterparts, the Elizabethan and Jacobean madrigals.

CHAPTER SIXTEEN

THE ARTS IN THE GEORGIAN
PERIOD (II)

1. *Painting and Sculpture*

THE eighteenth century was a notable period for British painting. In earlier times such artists of the very first rank as had worked in England had all been foreigners —Holbein, for instance, in the time of Henry VIII, or Rubens and Van Dyck in the time of Charles I. But in the second quarter of the eighteenth century there appeared for the first time native British painters who could challenge comparison with the finest masters from abroad.

The end of foreign domination

The oldest of these was William Hogarth (d. 1764), a Londoner and the son of a schoolmaster. His most original work, apart from some of his portraits, took the form of oil-paintings done in a series to illustrate such themes as *The Rake's Progress*, *Marriage à la Mode*, and *The Election*. Some of these series he later engraved, and sold widely in that form. He also made original engravings with a moral, showing, for instance, the *Four Stages of Cruelty*, or pointing the contrast between *Beer Street* and *Gin Lane*, *Industry* and *Idleness*. In all these pictures he portrayed with vigorous caricature and great dramatic force some striking (and usually regrettable) aspect of the life of his day. Such work owed little or nothing to any foreign source. It was a native product; and Hogarth was the first truly great English artist.

Hogarth

Reynolds

After Hogarth the next great name is that of Sir Joshua Reynolds (d. 1792). Reynolds took a leading part in the formation of the Royal Academy in 1768 and was its first president. A Devon man, he owed much (unlike Hogarth) to Italy, where he spent three years studying the great masters. Indeed, in his *Discourses* on painting delivered at the Academy, he proclaimed that by studying the work

The Election

From a series of paintings by Hogarth. This one shows the polling on the open hustings, with two voters taking the oath on the Bible under the rival flags. The crippled, the paralysed, the dying and the blind have all been brought along to vote.

General Sir George Eliott (later Lord Heathfield)

As Governor of Gibraltar, Eliott defended the Rock against the Spaniards during the American War of Independence. In this superb portrait, Reynolds characteristically shows the General holding the keys of the fortress, and against a background of cannon, sea and smoke.

of the past an artist could absorb the best features of many different painters and so achieve a kind of composite excellence. Yet his portraits—his finest work, as a rule much better than his subject pictures—always have a style and an air of their own, and are far from being imitations of the old masters. They combine fine composition and colouring with a striking glimpse of the sitter's personality, usually brought out in relation to something in the setting—an admiral seen against the ocean, a mother seen playing with her child, and so on. Not surprisingly, they brought him wealth and the friendship of the famous, from Johnson, Garrick and their circle to great noblemen. Reynolds, who greatly esteemed social success, would doubtless have been delighted to know that at his funeral in St. Paul's his body was borne by nine peers, including three dukes and two marquesses.

The greatest rival of Reynolds was Thomas Gainsborough (d. 1788). A native of Suffolk, he first established himself as a painter in Ipswich, then transferred to Bath, where he won instant success as a portraitist in the fashionable world. From Bath he moved on to London, and became the favourite painter of the Court and a member of the Academy—with which he soon quarrelled over the hanging of his pictures. He had little of Reynolds's self-control, genius for friendship, or knowledge of the past; but he had a highly individual technique (described by one critic as a 'scratchy, thunder-and-lightning form of art'), a subtle sense of colour, an extraordinary lightness of touch, and a great gift for giving his sitters an air of aristocratic refinement while at the same time catching their personal features and characters. He was also a fine painter of landscapes—but these he found it much more difficult to sell. *Gainsborough*

Portrait-painting, in fact, remained the great road to fame for a British artist throughout the century: there were many noblemen and flourishing men of commerce who desired pictures of themselves and their families, and the camera was not yet invented. In addition to Hogarth, Reynolds and Gainsborough, others who achieved fame as portrait painters—mainly in the latter half of the century—included John Hoppner, George Romney (who fell in love with Nelson's mistress, Lady Hamilton, and repeatedly painted her), Sir Thomas Lawrence (at the end of the *Other portrait painters*

Heneage Lloyd and Sister

A characteristic portrait by Gainsborough, in which the landscape setting
almost as important as the human subjects.

century), and two Scotsmen, Allan Ramsey and Sir Henry
Raeburn.

Landscape

Though not nearly so fashionable or profitable, there was
also a rising school of landscape painting. The 'father of

Wilson

English landscape painting' was Richard Wilson (d. 1782),
but he remained neglected and poor. Some of the finest
work in this sphere was done by artists who were mainly

The water-colourists

water-colourists—among whom may be mentioned Alexander and J. R. Cozens (father and son), and Thomas Girtin
(whose bold effects in some of his last pictures capture
strikingly various 'moods' in the countryside and are closely
akin to the work of the Romantics in poetry). The water-
colour tradition was continued in the following century by

Morland and others

John Sell Cotman (d. 1842). Meanwhile other artists, including Gainsborough, George Morland and John Crome, explored the possibilities of landscape in oils. The crown and summit of English landscape painting, however, came not in the eighteenth century but in the early nineteenth, in the work of Turner and Constable.

The Fighting *Temeraire* Being Tugged To Her Last Berth

Turner's picture of the old man-of-war, which had fought at Trafalgar, being towed up the Thames for breaking up, shows his delight in the atmospheric effects of sun, shadow, sky, light, cloud, water, smoke.

The older by one year of these two men was J. M. W. Turner (1775–1851). The son of a barber and of a mother who became insane, Turner first exhibited at the Academy when he was only fifteen. By 1802, at the age of twenty-seven, he was elected a full R.A.—after which he made the first of his many continental tours. Landscape scenes of all kinds, in both oils and water-colours, came readily from his brush, as well as subject pictures in an outdoor setting. Many of the latter went to the classics for their subject—

for example, *Dido Building Carthage*, or *Ulysses Deriding Polyphemus*—but though the subject-matter might be classical, the treatment, with its absence of strongly marked outline and its reliance on a dramatic use of colour, became increasingly romantic. Pictures with a sea background— such as *The Fighting Temeraire*—usually called forth his highest genius. After 1840 he became a recluse, living secretly in London under an assumed name, and allowing the specially built gallery in which he hoarded vast quantities of his work (which he later left to the nation) to fall into disrepair. In these last years he pushed his most characteristic qualities to their limit, making his art more and more abstract and impressionistic, till many of his pictures became simply light and atmosphere, with no other subject. These developments were beyond the period under review in this chapter, but were profoundly important for the history of painting later in the nineteenth century.

The other great master of this period was John Constable
Constable (1776–1837). The son of a prosperous Suffolk miller, he established himself only slowly, and it was not until he was in his forties that he really began to make money from his work. Between 1816 and his death he painted many of the most beautiful landscapes ever produced by a British, or indeed any, artist. *View on the Stour, The Hay Wain, The Lock, The Leaping Horse, The Cornfield, The Valley Farm*—these are some of his masterpieces. His most original quality came from his feeling for the flicker of light, the movement of clouds, and other atmospheric effects, and his supreme ability to render these in paint. For this reason Constable was an artist who, like Turner, greatly influenced later painters—and in particular the French Impressionists of the late nineteenth century.

Caricature During the late eighteenth century important work was also done in caricature. We have seen that Hogarth had made use of this; and it also appeared in the drawings and
Rowlandson engravings of Thomas Rowlandson (d. 1827), a superb artist who delighted to poke fun at high and low society alike. He had a strong vein of coarse humour, combined— in the drawings at least—with a marvellous lightness of

Flatford Mill

One of Constable's many superb landscapes, in which he gives characteristic care to the effects of cloud and light.

touch. His cruder work, in engravings for a large popular sale, has a nightmare quality; in it appalling disasters befall people who are all monstrously fat, thin, or deformed. Some of this cruder work was used for political ends; and another caricaturist of the same period, James Gillray (d. 1815), made the engraved print a really powerful weapon in politics.

Yet another field of eighteenth-century artistic activity was the sporting picture, usually in the form of a print. This in general did not achieve any very high standard. But in the oils of George Stubbs (d. 1806), a superb painter of horses and the author of an illustrated work on the anatomy of the horse, outdoor subjects of this kind reached the level of great art.

Sporting pictures

Stubbs and the horse

John and Sophia Musters on Horseback

A splendid example of a Stubbs' outdoor scene with horses, painted in 1777.
Some years later John Musters had the figures of himself and his wife painted out,
and two grooms at the horses' heads added by another painter. The picture was
restored to its original state in 1936.

Away from these main streams of artistic work there also
existed a strange and unregarded artist in a class of his own.

Blake

William Blake, besides being a poet and prophet, was a
book illustrator and engraver whose ideas and techniques
were quite personal to himself. Hating Reynolds, fashionable portraiture, and everything that smacked of the
'worldly' in painting, Blake regarded art as an activity of
the spirit; and his pictures (notably his illustrations to
Dante, Milton and the Book of Job) do in fact show an
intensely spiritual quality. Little heeded in his own day,
Blake is now regarded as one of England's greatest, and
certainly one of her most original, artists.

Sculpture

If we turn from painting and engraving to sculpture, the
eighteenth century has no comparable wealth to show from

British artists. There was splendid portrait-sculpture from two foreign sculptors, the Fleming J. M. Rysbrach and the Frenchman L. F. Roubiliac, but much of the other work of the time, notably in the ornamental tombs, is too florid and artificial for our taste nowadays. The foremost British sculptors included John Flaxman (d. 1826), who for a time worked for Wedgwood, the potter, and Joseph Nollekens (d. 1823)—and the latter was of Flemish extraction.

2. *Architecture and Furniture*

Most ages have some form of building which is specially characteristic. In the eighteenth century, the golden age of the landed aristocracy, it was the country houses of the lords and squires on which architects spent most of their energy. Town houses, too, of great artistic merit were built, both for the landed gentry who also kept a house in London and for the ever-growing commercial classes. *A great age of house-building*

Like literature, architecture was inspired throughout much of the century by the traditions of the classical style. Sir John Vanbrugh (d. 1726), playwright and soldier, turned to architecture in the later part of his life and designed the most notable buildings in England since Wren. Castle Howard (finished 1714) and Blenheim Palace, his two largest constructions, are gigantic places with immensely impressive exteriors. Theirs is not the pure or sedate type of classicism, but the much more vigorous, imaginative and florid form which developed in seventeenth-century Europe during the last stages of the Renaissance. There is a lack of homeliness about these buildings which Pope hit off in his lines inspired by Blenheim: *Baroque classicism* *Vanbrugh*

> 'Thanks, Sir,' cried I, ''Tis very fine:
> But where d'ye sleep, or where d'ye dine?
> I find, by all that you've been telling,
> That 'tis a house, but not a dwelling.'

Yet the grandeur of Blenheim and its park still catches the breath of the visitor, and Vanbrugh is one of the most original, if not one of the most completely successful, of our architects.

The Strand in 1792

Showing in the foreground St. Mary le Strand, built by James Gibbs in the second decade of the century, and on the right the new Somerset House, built by Sir William Chambers in the 1770s and 1780s.

Another of the foremost architects in the early part of the century who worked in this free-flowing, 'baroque' type of classicism was Nicolas Hawksmoor (d. 1736).[1] At Hawksmoor first one of Vanbrugh's assistants, he built many of the fifty new churches voted by Parliament in Queen Anne's reign, and he also worked extensively in Oxford. With him may be mentioned James Gibbs (d. 1754), who built two more Gibbs of the fifty churches—St. Martin-in-the-Fields and St. Mary-le-Strand—and the Senate House and part of King's College at Cambridge.

In the 1730s and 1740s there was a strong movement in 'Purer' favour of a much 'stricter' classical style. The patron of this classicism: was Lord Burlington, a nobleman who had studied in and Kent Italy the work of the great Renaissance architect Palladio. In Burlington's opinion Wren and Vanbrugh had departed too far from the regularity favoured by Palladio and his English disciple Inigo Jones, and he set himself to lead taste back towards a 'purer' classicism. One of the architects most closely connected with him was William Kent (d. 1748), who had also spent a long time in Italy. His best-known buildings that still survive are Holkham Hall in Norfolk and the Horse Guards in Whitehall. Unfortunately his talents as a painter and a furniture designer, on which he also prided himself (as he did on his excellent landscape gardening), were inferior to his architectural ability, with the result that an 'all-Kent' room can easily appear too heavy and oppressive.

Greater as an architect than Kent and much greater as a Robert decorator and designer was Robert Adam (1728–1792), who Adam worked with his brother James. Like Kent, Adam had closely studied Roman models—especially in his case the remains that were discovered at Pompeii when he was twenty years old. Among his greatest houses are Kedlestone in Derbyshire and Syon House and Osterley in Middlesex. All have great classical pillars that from certain aspects make them look rather like Roman temples. Indeed, in the case of Syon House the pillars had been dredged from the

[1] Baroque = irregularly shaped (probably from a Spanish word for a rough pearl).

Tiber and brought to England. The suitability of such features for the entrance hall of even the greatest private house is admittedly questionable, and Dr. Johnson remarked of Kedlestone: 'The house would do excellently well for a town hall: the large room with the pillars would do for the judges to sit in at the assizes; the circular room for a jury chamber; and the room above for prisoners.' Nevertheless, inside an Adam house—once the great reception hall, if any, is passed—all is of a most refined and tasteful elegance; gone is Kent's ponderousness, and the total impression is one not only of richness but also of lightness, grace and comfort. Above all, everything is consistent, however varied in pattern, and perfectly conceived to the last detail. The plaster-work or the decorative scenes on the oval ceilings, the fanlights over the doors, the carved marble chimney-pieces, the specially constructed furniture, the lamps, even the carpets—all are designed, using shapes and patterns derived from classical remains, to harmonize with the architecture and increase its effect.

Town houses

The glory of Georgian architecture does not lie only in the great houses. Some of the best architecture of the period is to be found in the smaller houses that can still be seen in many places both in town and country. Built usually in red brick, they have large sash windows, a porch with light classical decoration, and often some graceful wrought iron work in their balconies or their torch-lit gardens. Their proportions are unerring. Such houses have classical balance combined with an unpretentious English charm.

Town schemes: terraces and squares

The town houses are most impressive when they are grouped in terraces and form part of a larger plan. Good examples can be seen in Bath, where the Circus and the Royal Crescent, built by the two John Woods, father and son, have been much admired. Cheltenham and Brighton, too, can show many fine terraces and squares, mostly of a somewhat later date In this later work the façades were usually covered with stucco and painted, to give a light and uniform effect. Planning on a still bigger scale, using this type of house, was attempted by John Nash (d. 1835) in London with the support of the Prince Regent. The plan

Nash

Country Life Ltd

The Gallery, Syon House

The original Jacobean long gallery of Syon House, Brentford, was given this
elegantly classical appearance by Robert Adam around 1763–64. Note the em-
broidery-like delicacy of the ornamentation, and how walls, ceiling and carpet
are kept in harmony by closely related geometric designs.

The Circus, Bath

Built by John Wood (the elder) around 1740. One of the earliest examples,
outside London, of classical domestic architecture used on an extended
scale for town development.

was to make the present Regent's Park into the centre of a
magnificent housing estate. The park was to be dotted with
villas and around it great terraces were to be built. The
whole was to be connected with Carlton House, the Prince
Regent's house, by a new street—Regent Street. Much of
this was accomplished. Regent Street with its quadrant at
the bottom leading into Piccadilly Circus is Nash's design
in shape, though the actual buildings now in it date from
the 1920s, when the old houses and shops were demolished.
Further north many of Nash's terraces around Regent's
Park still stand. Nash's work, combined with the development during the eighteenth century of other great estates
like the Bedford, the Portman, and the Portland, gave to
western London a splendid dignity and grandeur—which
even today is still a little evident.

As the century drew to its close, and, later, in the Regency
period, other and stranger styles crept in. During the period
when classical influence was at its strongest, the Middle
Ages with its Gothic buildings was regarded with some
scorn, but as in literature there came the Romantic

Revival, so in architecture taste began to interest itself again in the medieval. The Gothic style of building originally used for churches and cathedrals began to be applied to country houses—and with much less success. The earliest important example of this style can be seen in the alterations Horace Walpole made to Strawberry Hill, his house in Middlesex. These began by being whimsical and ended by their owner taking them seriously. On the whole, however, they were superficial, concerning embellishment rather than fundamental design. A good deal later came Fonthill Abbey, in Wiltshire, which cost its strange owner, William Beckford, over a quarter of a million pounds (a very large sum in 1802). Its central point was a great Gothic tower 278 feet

Strawberry Hill

and Fonthill Abbey

Country Life Ltd

The Library, Strawberry Hill

Horace Walpole, son of Sir Robert, was one of the earliest patrons of revived Gothic architecture, based on the pointed arch. Here we see the 'Gothic' chimney piece and bookcases added to his Library at Strawberry Hill, Twickenham, in the 1750s.

high. Unfortunately the contractor scamped the foundations and after twenty-three years it crashed down and wrecked most of the house.

Wyatt

The designer of Fonthill Abbey was James Wyatt (d. 1813), who developed from a 'Classical' architect into the chief pioneer of the Gothic revival. In addition to new buildings, he was also responsible for 'restoration' work at three or four cathedrals, and for remodelling in the Gothic style the interiors of several great country houses. He made a ruthless job of it, and was commonly known among his critics as 'The Destroyer'. His nephew, who added a fancy

Wyatville

ending to his name and became Sir Jeffry Wyatville, carried out some big schemes in Gothic for George IV at Windsor Castle, but with less displeasing results.

The full tide of the Gothic revival did not arrive until the mid-nineteenth century. Before it, from about 1820 onward, the vogue was more for a Classical style based on a heavy imitation of Greek models, such as may be seen in the exterior of the St. George's Hall at Liverpool or of the British Museum. But other, more exotic styles also came in, the result of Britain's trading and imperial interests. The Pavilion built for the Prince Regent at Brighton was a strange mixture of Indian and Chinese styles with a dash

Competing styles: the end of Classical supremacy

of Russian. By 1830, in fact, it was clear that the Classical style had lost the supremacy it had held for so long. Though still alive, it was breaking down. And with its passing there ended, so most people think, the greatest period of domestic architecture that Britain has ever known.

In conclusion, it is worth remembering that the beauty of a fine eighteenth-century house was usually greatly increased by that of the articles to be found in it. The kitchen copperware was very handsome—with plenty of servants to keep it well burnished. Silver and plate for the

The great days of English porcelain

dining table were extremely elegant in design. Fine English porcelain for dinner services, tea-sets, snuff-boxes and the like, as well as in the form of vases and small figures purely for ornament, also began to appear. Inspired at first by Chinese, German or French porcelain, it yet had special qualities of its own, and within a few years reached a

Derby Porcelain Figures (Minuet Dancers)

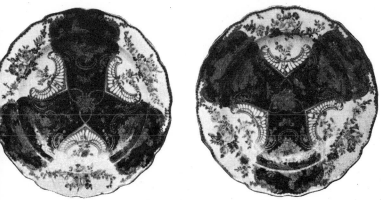

Chelsea Porcelain Plates

perfection hardly since approached in this country. In the middle years of the century were established all the four factories which have made the finest English porcelain—Chelsea, Bow, Derby and Worcester—as well as many of those of excellent but lesser achievement.

Wedgwood Vase, 1788

This vase (white jasper, sage-green and blue dip) shows a typical Wedgwood classical scene and motives designed by the sculptor John Flaxman.

Pottery: Wedgwood   The same period, too, saw the rise of the great potter Josiah Wedgwood, who at Stoke, Burslem and finally in his famous Etruria factory near Hanley, produced earthenware which was cream-coloured throughout and of much greater strength and fineness than any previously known. A man of great business as well as inventive genius, he employed artist-designers (whose light classical decorations are still reproduced) and marketed his wares so cheaply and extensively that they soon spread all over Europe. From the 1760s onwards, attractively designed and coloured

Wedgwood tea-pots, tea and dinner ware, jugs and coffee-pots began to appear on thousands of British tables, elegant Wedgwood cameos and plaques to decorate the walls and cabinets of thousands of British drawing-rooms. Fine porcelain was still a privilege of the rich, but Wedgwood's pottery brought beauty into a wide range of middle-class homes. It even became so fashionable that in some great houses Wedgwood dinner services replaced porcelain.[1]

Wedgwood Pottery Sandwich Set
in Queen's Ware, hand painted, c. 1780.

Furniture, too, reached a new standard of excellence Furniture during the eighteenth century. The splendid walnut furniture of Queen Anne's reign, so much finer and lighter than the oak furniture of the previous century, was succeeded before long by mahogany furniture which became increasingly elegant. The best work came after 1754, when Thomas Chippendale published *The Gentleman's and Cabinet* Chippendale *Maker's Director*. The designs in this, inspired by a considerable variety of sources and including some in the 'Gothic' and 'Chinese' tastes, were in many cases far too

[1] Broadly speaking, the term 'pottery' covers all articles made by heating natural clays. The term 'porcelain' is reserved for articles (distinguished by a special fineness, hardness, whiteness of substance and translucence) which are made from particular clays mixed with other minerals and fired at a very high temperature.

fancy to be carried out in practice; but the simpler among them were successfully followed both by Chippendale's own firm and by craftsmen elsewhere, and did much to spread fashionable ideas in cabinet-making throughout the country.

Chair: *c.* 1775
In a Chippendale style.

Chair: *c.* 1778
In a Hepplewhite style.

Chippendale, who was regarded in his own day as only one among many fine cabinet-makers, and who made only a tiny fraction of the thousands of pieces to which his name has since been attached, died in 1779. After his death the greatest figures in furniture-design during the century were probably those of George Hepplewhite, the brothers Adam (who designed, for craftsmen to make, much highly elegant painted and other furniture), and Thomas Sheraton. The last-named, who died in 1806, was important not as a maker—very few pieces can be definitely ascribed to him —but as a designer. The three books which he issued during his lifetime contain an immense variety of designs the distinguishing features of which are complexity, light

Sheraton

An Adam Cabinet

A cabinet inlaid with rosewood and satinwood veneers,
designed by Robert Adam about 1771 to incorporate eleven
Italian pictures in marble mosaic.

classical ornament, and the determination to achieve
slenderness at all costs.

Between them, these and other great cabinet-makers and
designers of the period 1715–1830 familiarized Britain with
a host of attractive and useful pieces of furniture, from
dozens of different kinds of tables, desks, chairs and settles
to bow-fronted chests of drawers, tallboys, toilet-mirrors,
dressing-tables, wash-stands, sideboards, wine-coolers and
dumb-waiters. The hundred years which followed were to
see the production of a still wider variety of articles; but
after 1830 inventiveness in furniture design abounded, as
in architecture, only for taste to run out.

CHAPTER SEVENTEEN

GREAT BRITAIN AFTER WATERLOO

1. *The Years of Repression*

DURING the century that followed the defeat of Napoleon, Britain became not only the greatest imperial power in the world but also the main centre of international commerce. The tonnage of her merchant navy surpassed that of all other nations put together. Everywhere on the Continent and across the seas, British engineers built railways and other useful works, often with money provided by British investors. On all sides the British constitution was increasingly envied, admired and imitated. Yet, for long years after Waterloo, unrest and discontent stalked the land, and it was not until after the middle of the century that there was any general feeling of peace and prosperity.

Causes of post-war discontent:

—difficulties of readjustment to peace

—effects of Industrial Revolution

—price slumps and unemployment

What were the causes of the discontent that lasted so long after 1815? They were of two main kinds, economic and political. The period after a great armed conflict is often difficult, for industry has to turn over from wartime to peacetime requirements. At the same time large numbers of men are released from the forces and have to find civilian employment. Between 1815 and 1816, for instance, Britain's naval manpower was reduced by two-thirds. Difficulties of this sort were much increased in 1815 by the fact that Britain was still in the throes of the Industrial Revolution. There was already hardship in the old-fashioned trades; and though the new world markets had caused an enormous growth in some industries, notably iron and cotton, they had also brought great uncertainty. Trade fluctuated violently, and the slumps that came in 1816 and 1818–19 caused much unemployment and distress—particularly in the northern factory districts. There was distress, too, in the rural districts of the South, where the small domestic industries were dying and the fall in the price of corn after 1814 led to less corn being grown and so to a slackening in the demand for agricultural labour.[1]

The first five or six years of the peace were in many ways the worst, for in time industry and agriculture settled down to the new conditions of lower wages and prices. In fact, after the big fall in prices during 1820–21 the ordinary worker was better off than he had been in the period just before the wars. Skilled workers in many trades also fared reasonably well, for their wages fell very little, while prices steadily declined. On the other hand, skilled workers in the domestic industries, such as hand-loom weavers, who were trying to compete with the new machines in the factories, earned less and less. The distress was to some extent lessened by poor-relief, which in the South was still for the most part operating under the Speenhamland system. In 1818, the most expensive year, £8 million was paid out by the local authorities to help the poor—nearly eight times as much as all other expenditure by the local authorities put together. —high cost of poor relief

This high cost of poor-relief was a special grievance of the farmers—though, had the relief not been given, they would certainly have had to pay more in wages. Among many other grievances, two for which Parliament was directly responsible—the abolition of Income Tax and the passing of a new Corn Law—were greatly resented by the poorer sections of the community. The war had left Britain with a big load of debt (£850 million), and taxation had to be kept high to pay the interest: so it was particularly unfair that at the end of the war Parliament insisted on abolishing Income Tax (on the ground that it had been introduced only as a wartime measure) and that in its place taxes were imposed which fell on the poor as well as the better-off. Moreover, in order to protect the landlords and farmers who were frightened by the low price of corn at the end of the war, a new Corn Law in 1815 excluded foreign —abolition of Income Tax

—Corn Law of 1815

[1] Chalk-downland, for instance, which had been ploughed up during the war when high prices for wheat were obtained, now reverted to pasture.

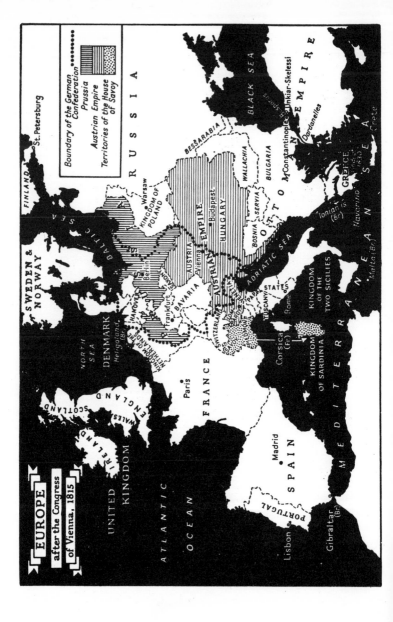

EUROPE after the Congress of Vienna, 1815

Boundary of the German Confederation
Prussia
Austrian Empire
Territories of the House of Savoy

UNITED KINGDOM
SCOTLAND
IRELAND
ENGLAND
WALES
Paris
FRANCE
SPAIN
Madrid
PORTUGAL
Lisbon
Gibraltar (Br.)

ATLANTIC OCEAN
NORTH SEA
BALTIC SEA

SWEDEN & NORWAY
FINLAND
RUSSIA
St. Petersburg

DENMARK
Heligoland (Br.)
NETHERLANDS
HANOVER (Br.)
Berlin
Frankfurt
SAXONY
BAVARIA
SWITZERLAND
SAVOY
PIEDMONT
SARDINIA
Corsica (Fr.)
KINGDOM OF SARDINIA

KINGDOM OF POLAND
Warsaw
BESSARABIA
AUSTRIAN EMPIRE
Vienna
Hungary
Budapest
WALLACHIA
BULGARIA
SERVIA
BOSNIA

PAPAL STATES
TUSCANY
Rome
KINGDOM OF THE TWO SICILIES

MEDITERRANEAN SEA
ADRIATIC SEA

OTTOMAN EMPIRE
Constantinople
Unkiar-Skelessi
Dardanelles
BLACK SEA
GREECE
Navarino (1827)
Ionian Is. (Br.)
Malta (Br.)
Crete

corn altogether until home-produced wheat rose above the fairly high price of eighty shillings a quarter. This tended to keep the price of home-grown corn, and therefore of bread, higher than it need have been, and so was resented by those who were not landowners or farmers.

All these economic grievances brought into disrepute the political system which allowed or encouraged them. As we have seen, there had been attempts to reform the parliamentary system, thirty years earlier.[1] The criticisms that applied then applied now with redoubled force. It was impossible for fair-minded men to rest content with a House of Commons in which neither Manchester nor Birmingham nor Leeds, all leading towns in the Britain of 1815, was separately represented. Representation of districts, in fact, remained on an eighteenth- (or even seventeenth-) century basis, and certainly no longer corresponded with the distribution of the population or of wealth. It was the landed classes who still held unchallenged sway in the House of Commons and who had pushed through the Corn Law of 1815, unpopular with manufacturer and workman alike. The manufacturing classes, for all their energy and wealth, counted for little in Parliament: their workmen for scarcely anything at all. *Demand for reform of Parliament*

These facts naturally produced a demand for reform, and it was to changes in the political system, as the key to all else, that the majority looked. During the difficult times of the French Revolution, Fox and the few Whigs who followed him had kept alive the demand for parliamentary reform. Of Fox's friends, Earl Grey had been a keen supporter of the movement, but by 1815 his ardour had cooled. He loathed the fuss and bother of politics and loved his house and library in Northumberland. 'How I long', he once wrote, 'to return to Tacitus and our own comfortable home.' *Grey and the Whigs*

There were also, however, reformers much more extreme than most of the Whigs—the men known as Radicals, because they wanted radical or fundamental changes. They were middle-class rather than aristocratic, and in many cases were inspired by the philosopher Jeremy Bentham. *The Radicals*

[1] Pages 164, 173–175.

Bentham believed that much less respect should be paid to privilege and tradition, and that politics and law should be rearranged on a logical system which would always seek to produce 'the greatest happiness of the greatest number'. The proposals of the Radicals were sweeping. They demanded not only a redistribution of seats, but also the vote for all male householders (sometimes for all male adults), and annual parliaments.

During 1815 and 1816 the character of the movement for parliamentary reform changed. Through lack of moderate leaders, extremists came forward and the movement tended to pass from the middle class to the working class. Above all, two great agitators, Henry (or 'Orator') Hunt and William Cobbett, made a successful appeal to the masses—who until the Wilkes affair had normally taken little interest in politics.

Cobbett

Born at Farnham in Surrey, William Cobbett was the son of a small farmer. He had a flair for journalism and was never afraid to speak his mind. This had brought him into trouble. By 1815 he had been fined in the U.S.A. (whither he had emigrated) and imprisoned in Britain—on both occasions for newspaper articles, and in the latter case for criticizing the practice of flogging in the Army. By 1816 the newspaper he ran—the *Weekly Register*—had achieved a large circulation through its violent attacks on the government. Cobbett was a great lover of the old rural England, and his *Rural Rides* gives us as good a picture of the England of the 1820s as Defoe's of Britain a century earlier. He was also a great hater of new-fangled ideas—among which he numbered factories, the growth of towns, the National Debt, paper money and potatoes! He hated, too, the *nouveaux riches* who had made their fortunes in the war. At heart he wanted a return to the old rural England, peaceful and prosperous as he imagined it—an impossible dream for nineteenth-century Britain. Nevertheless, having suffered from the government, he thought the whole political system monstrously unjust, and eagerly urged such radical demands as that all adult males should be allowed the vote.

While Cobbett often looked back longingly to the old

ways, 'Orator' Hunt was a more thorough-going Radical. 'Orator'
His life thus far had been nothing if not colourful. He had Hunt
eloped with a friend's wife, challenged his colonel in the
yeomanry to a duel, and been imprisoned for assaulting a
gamekeeper. After 1800 he became a leading Radical and

Conspirators, or Delegates in Council

From an engraving by Cruikshank in 1817 satirising the Government's use of spies
and *agents provocateurs*. On the left a renegade Irishman, Thomas Reynolds,
reveals imaginary plots and proposes hare-brained schemes to the Home Secretary,
Lord Sidmouth. On the right, Castlereagh and Canning confer with two notorious
spies, Castle and Oliver, and discuss suitable rewards for them. John Bull, over-
hearing (behind Castlereagh) is extremely indignant.

was the principal speaker at the first great mass meeting
for parliamentary reform, held at Spa Fields in London in The Spa
1816. A vast crowd attended, and Hunt appeared preceded Fields
by two men, one carrying on a pike the red cap of the meetings,
French Revolution, the other a tricolour, the flag of the 1816
future British republic. A second meeting a fortnight later
ended in riot, and an attempted march on the Tower of
London. Meanwhile there had been disturbances in other
areas, caused by economic distress as much as political

agitation, and both in Nottinghamshire and Lancashire the Luddites had been active.

Attitude of the government:
Lord Liverpool

Eldon, Castlereagh, and the 'pigtails'

The government was alarmed. It was still Tory. Since 1812 the Prime Minister had been the Earl of Liverpool, a man completely lacking in originality, though skilful at keeping the peace between his ministers. The two most powerful influences in the Cabinet were Lord Eldon, the Lord Chancellor, and Viscount Castlereagh, the Secretary of State for Foreign Affairs—an office created in 1782 when the division of Foreign and Home was substituted for North and South. Eldon was the leader of the extreme Tories nicknamed 'pigtails' (from the fact that the pigtail was a very prim and old-fashioned method of doing the hair, long-preserved for soldiers, but recently abolished even for them). Castlereagh, an Irish peer, was Leader of the House of Commons as well as Foreign Secretary, and was supposed rather unfairly to favour despotic rule as practised on the Continent.

Once reform appeared to have any connection with revolution—as the violence in the North and the behaviour of Hunt and the Spa Fields mob seemed to indicate—a government of this kind would soon favour repression.

Habeas Corpus suspended, 1817

Early in 1817 it accordingly suspended Habeas Corpus—the Act which ensures arrested persons a trial. Men could now be held in jail on suspicion only, or for purely preventive reasons. Nevertheless the troubles continued, especially in the North, whence groups of 'Blanketeers' (each carried a blanket to sleep in) attempted to march on London and present a petition demanding reform.

The 'Blanketeers', 1817

'Peterloo', 1819

Two years later, in 1819, partly because of a falling off in trade, there was further trouble. Meetings were held in the towns and on the moors to demand reform. Among other demonstrations, a mass meeting was called in St. Peter's Fields, Manchester. Hunt was to be the main speaker. A crowd of 60,000 assembled, bearing revolutionary slogans such as 'Reform—or Death', and Hunt began. There was no disorder, but the magistrates watching the proceedings unfortunately decided to send troops to arrest him. These were impeded by the crowd; whereupon

Massacre at St Peter's or "BRITONS STRIKE HOME"!!!

Britons Strike Home!

A satire on 'Peterloo' by Cruikshank. The well-fed yeomanry go eagerly to work on the defenceless crowd. The officer in charge urges them on with the words 'Remember, the more you kill, the less poor rates you'll have to pay'.

the order was given for a detachment of the local mounted yeomanry—a volunteer body of cavalry—to ride to the rescue of the soldiers. In the sword-slashing and stampede that followed, eleven people were killed and over four hundred injured. The government, of course, backed the magistrates, but there was a chorus of protest from all over Britain, and the incident was nicknamed in mockery 'Peterloo'.

This did not stop the government from introducing six Acts to stamp out this type of agitation. Two of these restricted the freedom of the Press, and one the right of public meeting—meetings to draw up petitions were to be confined to the residents of the parish in which the meeting was held. The next year there was only one serious incident. Arthur Thistlewood, an extreme Radical who had helped to organize the second Spa Fields meeting and had challenged the Home Secretary to a duel, devised a hare-brained plot to assassinate most of the Cabinet at a dinner-party. The conspiracy was discovered and Thistlewood and his accomplices, who were operating from a house in Cato Street, off the Edgware Road, were arrested. Five, including Thistlewood, were later executed.

The government's general policy of repression has usually been condemned by later generations. It was certainly a negative policy when constructive measures were badly needed. Also, it failed to distinguish properly between peaceful reformers and violent revolutionaries. It has also been condemned for excessive harshness—though its actions were very mild compared with those taken by governments in many countries nowadays. Objection has also been taken to the use it made of *agents provocateurs* (spies who pretend to be in league with the watched person and spur him on to violent action). The employment of such men was certainly stupid as well as discreditable, yet the government was in a real difficulty. It had to ensure order and protect property, but it had no police and no reliable sources of information. It was the government's genuine ignorance, coupled with the weakness of the security forces, that made intelligent ministers liable to panic. Also,

The Six
Acts,
1819

Cato Street
Conspiracy,
1820

Within the image:
- A FREE BORN ENGLISHMAN!
- THE ADMIRATION of the WORLD!!!
- AND THE ENVY of SURROUNDING NATIONS!!!!!

A Free-born Englishman

A satirical print of Cruikshank's after the Six Acts of 1819. The shackled Englishman, with a padlock on his mouth marked 'No Grumbling', stands on Magna Carta and a torn Bill of Rights. In the background a family is left destitute after the tax-gatherers have arrested the breadwinner; and debtors beseech alms from prison.

of course, the revolutionary talk of the popular leaders goes far to explain the government's fright. Once more, memories of the horrors of the French Revolution stood in the way of peaceful progress.

Agitation
subsides,
1820

In 1820 and the years immediately after, the agitation subsided—more perhaps owing to improved economic conditions than to any action by the government. Moreover, in 1820 there occurred a first-class royal scandal, to which the public turned all its attention. George III, who had been permanently insane since 1811, at last died, and was succeeded by his son the Prince Regent, who became George IV. The new monarch, a selfish fop who had the one merit of being a discriminating patron of the arts, had long been notorious for his extravagance and self-indulgence. In a time of hardship he spent recklessly on his various pleasures, the most respectable of which was building. In addition to sponsoring Nash's great plan in London he built the Pavilion at Brighton and virtually rebuilt Buckingham Palace and Windsor Castle. Money was no object. The chandeliers for the Music Room at the Pavilion alone cost over £4,000, and the feasts he gave sometimes consisted of more than a hundred dishes. His unpopularity explains the warm popular welcome given to Caroline of Brunswick, his discarded wife, when in 1820, on the accession of her husband, she returned to England to claim her place as queen.

George IV
king:
affair of
Queen
Caroline,
1820

Caroline had been selected for George IV by his father. The parent's choice did not appeal to the son. When they first met, he was so shaken that he said to a friend, 'I am not well; get me a glass of brandy.' He had gone through with the marriage, but it had broken up almost immediately. Recently Caroline had been leading a disreputable life abroad. She now demanded to be crowned as George IV's consort. He demanded a divorce, and in the course of the proceedings in Parliament much dirty linen was washed, to the discredit of both king and queen. The Radicals and some of the Whigs championed the queen, and great were the rejoicings when the divorce proceedings were dropped. However, enthusiasm for her waned as the novelty of the scandal wore off. In 1821, to the cheers of the mob, she set off with a male companion for Westminster Abbey, where George IV was being crowned, to demand her share in the ceremony; but when both were not admitted—they had only one ticket between them—she gave up her attempt to enter, and was promptly booed.

But whichever way popular favour turned, two facts about the episode could hardly be contradicted. It greatly lowered the prestige of the monarchy, and it distracted attention from matters of much greater importance.

2. *Reform under the Tories*

For the next few years domestic politics entered into calmer waters. As violent agitation died down, reform made progress, and after 1822 it was taken up in a mild way by the Tory party. Round about then there were important changes in Liverpool's Cabinet. In 1822 Canning succeeded Castlereagh (who had committed suicide) as Foreign Secretary and Leader of the House of Commons; and in the same year Sir Robert Peel replaced Viscount Sidmouth (Addington) as Home Secretary. The next year William Huskisson entered the Cabinet as President of the Board of Trade. These three newcomers were all more open to reforming or liberal ideas, and they pushed the 'die-hard' Eldon into the background.

The Tory Cabinet becomes more progressive

George Canning was reckoned the best speaker in the House of Commons. A follower of Pitt, he had become Foreign Secretary in 1807 at the age of thirty-seven, but since falling out (and duelling) with Castlereagh in 1809 he had not had much success in the political world. He was very ambitious and had once or twice missed office by demanding too much. He was also disliked in various quarters for his uncertain temper, his reputation for double-dealing, his social origin—his mother became an actress— and his biting wit. On one occasion, when there was a proposal to elect as Speaker of the House of Commons a certain politician who had a high, piping voice,

Canning

Canning suggested that he could be addressed as 'Mr. Squeaker'.

Canning's foreign policy

Canning proved to be one of the most important Foreign Secretaries in the whole of the nineteenth century. He first made clear both at home and abroad that Britain was not prepared to give automatic support to the other victors of Waterloo in any attempt to put down further revolutionary movements in Europe. To understand the significance of this, we must turn back to the treaties of Vienna. In addition to rewarding the victors and enlarging Prussia, Holland and Piedmont, with the idea of enabling them to withstand France, the Vienna Settlement had contained another feature of great importance. The great powers of Russia, Austria, Prussia and Great Britain had not only agreed to maintain an alliance against any further French aggression, but had also undertaken to meet together at intervals in Congresses, to consider any question which might threaten the peace of Europe. This was an entirely new idea, for no congress of the great powers had ever met except at the end of a war. The use to which her allies wished to put this arrangement, however, soon aroused Britain's opposition.

The Vienna Settlement and the Congress system

Congress of Aix-la-Chapelle, 1818

The first congress after Vienna, held at Aix-la-Chapelle in 1818, produced excellent results. It ended the military occupation of France—who had by that time paid off her war indemnity—and allowed her to participate in the Congress System. But from 1820 onwards it became clear that the despotic monarchies of Russia, Austria and Prussia, and even France under her restored Bourbon king, were in favour of using the alliance as a general weapon against revolutions. Wherever these might occur, and whatever wrongs had produced them, the great monarchs of Europe were anxious to intervene and nip them in the bud. In France during the 1790s they had seen a movement for constitutional reform develop into a violent revolution which set half Europe ablaze, and they were determined to extinguish similar outbreaks at the start.

Policy of the despotic powers

Austria suppresses Italian revolution

It was not long before liberal parties were trying to limit the ruler's power in Naples, in Piedmont, in Portugal and in Spain (where another Bourbon king had been restored). The Austrian Emperor, who had territories in Italy, thereupon intervened to put down the revolutions in that country. Castlereagh, British Foreign Secretary at the time, approved of this, but at congresses in 1820 and 1821 refused to associate Britain in Austria's action. This was not because he sympathized with revolutions but because the British Parliament would not have supported British intervention. Then came Castlereagh's breakdown and suicide, and his replacement by Canning. The latter at once went a stage further in opposition to the policy of the despotic rulers. When a Congress was called at Verona in 1822 to consider helping the monarchy in Spain, where a revolutionary movement had restricted the royal power, Britain not merely declined to give the Spanish king any support, but also opposed the whole idea of intervention. *Attitude of Castlereagh* *Congress of Verona, 1822* *Canning opposes intervention in Spain*

Canning's policy had little effect in Spain, where French armies soon helped the king to recover full power. But the British Foreign Secretary was much more successful over Spain's colonies. Some of these had broken away from Spanish control during the Napoleonic wars; and they had no intention, if they could help it, of surrendering their newly won freedom. Canning accordingly warned France, on pain of war, not to extend her intervention on the Spanish king's behalf to any territories across the Atlantic. This policy agreed with that of President Monroe, of the United States, who issued a 'hands off the American continent' warning to all Powers. Shortly afterwards Canning recognized three of the late Spanish colonies— Buenos Aires, Colombia and Mexico—as independent republics. All this was very gratifying to British merchants, for as independent states these countries traded freely with Britain, whereas under Spanish rule trade with Britain had been severely restricted. Of course the recognition was a blow to the principle of monarchy, but in England only George IV felt this strongly. He was so upset that he avoided reading the King's Speech in Parliament which referred to the decision—on the excuse that he had gout and had mislaid his false teeth. *Canning and the Spanish colonies* *The Monroe Doctrine, 1823* *Trading advantages for Britain*

Canning
supports
the
Portuguese

Canning was also able to check Spanish intervention in Portugal—in this case by despatching a British force to Lisbon. He also gave aid to the Greeks in their struggle for

—and the
Greeks

independence against the Turks, who had long ruled them. In 1827 British and other warships were sent out to enforce an armistice and self-government for the Greeks within the Turkish Empire. There followed a clash in Greek waters

Navarino,
1827

at Navarino and the destruction of the Turkish fleet—an action which virtually decided the struggle in favour of the Greeks. Such developments showed that with Canning as Foreign Secretary or Prime Minister (as he was for a short time before his death in 1827) the policy of the Tory government was very far from one of blind repression.

Peel

Sir Robert Peel, who later became one of England's greatest Prime Ministers, was a Tory, but with industrial rather than landed interests. His father—also Sir Robert—had been a successful cotton manufacturer and had been responsible for the first Factory Act. Peel's nickname was 'The Spinning Jenny'—for a 'factory' background was scorned by the more snobbish Tories. Peel was the first Home Secretary to make much of the position. In 1815 the laws of England were still antiquated and barbarous. There were about 220 offences for which the death penalty could be imposed, including stealing five shillings from a shop; the number had been continuously increased during the eighteenth century in a vain effort to check the growth in crime. Bentham and others had pointed out the absurdities of this, for juries frequently declined to convict where the penalties were so severe. Nevertheless, all change was resisted by Eldon and most of the judges and lawyers. Fortunately, Peel was not a lawyer, and together with one or two Members of Parliament he strove to make the legal

Reduction
in number
of offences
punishable
by death

system worthy of a civilized country. During his period of office he abolished the death penalty for over a hundred offences. The movement continued, and from 1838 to the end of the century no one was hanged except for murder (or—until 1861—attempted murder).

Prison
reform

Peel also took a number of steps to reform the larger prisons. He ensured that female prisoners, for instance, should no longer be supervised by male warders, and that jailers should be paid instead of living on fees from their prisoners. These reforms were largely the result of investigations into prison conditions by two private persons, John Howard in the eighteenth century and Elizabeth Fry, a Quaker, in the early nineteenth.

Perhaps the greatest of all Peel's achievements as Home Secretary was the foundation of the Metropolitan Police Force. We call the police 'Bobbies' to this day after Peel's first name. The police which he set up in 1829 were limited to London, with Scotland Yard as their headquarters. But other areas soon imitated London's example —especially when criminals flocked there to avoid the new police in the capital. More than anything else, an effective police system ended the disorder and crime that had been so prevalent in London and other large towns, and brought about the settled and secure conditions in which most of us now live.

Metropolitan Police Act, 1829

After 1822 the government also relaxed the Navigation Acts and lowered the import duties on goods entering the country. These changes, which continued the pre-war work of Pitt, were largely due to Huskisson. Like Pitt, Huskisson had been convinced by the economists who, since Adam Smith, had taught that government interference in economics was usually misguided, and that trade should be unrestricted and free—the doctrine of *laissez faire*. Accordingly, Huskisson introduced some drastic reductions in duties: the general tariff of 50 per cent on the import of manufactured goods, for instance, fell to 20 per cent. This policy was welcomed by commercial circles (who had agitated for it) but was disliked by 'the pigtails', who saw in Free Trade a danger to the Corn Laws.

Huskisson: lowering of duties

The decrease in duties encouraged trade and so helped to improve general conditions. Round about the same time another Tory measure, too, proved of benefit. In 1824, following a campaign organized by the Radical tailor and writer Francis Place, the Combination Laws of 1799 and 1800 were repealed. Under these, trade unions and all other similar associations of working men had been forbidden. The new-found freedom promptly produced a wave of strikes, with the result that the government somewhat

Repeal of Combination Laws, 1824-5

restricted it the following year. Associations for peaceful bargaining about wages and hours of labour remained legal, however, and were later to prove of untold benefit to working men.

Canning, Prime Minister, 1827

In 1827 Lord Liverpool was laid low by a stroke. Canning became Prime Minister and there seemed some prospect of further reform. The 'pigtails', with Wellington and Peel, both of whom disliked Canning, left office, and four Whigs were included in the new government. Canning, however, died within a few months. An attempt to keep the ministry going under a less able figure of similar views, Viscount Goderich, was a failure, and in 1828 George IV turned to the Duke of Wellington.

Wellington, Prime Minister, 1828–30

Until his recent resignation, Wellington had been in the Tory Cabinet since 1819 as Master General of the Ordnance. Though in some ways an old-fashioned Tory, he disliked party politics and took office in 1828 mainly because the king asked him and he thought it his duty. He promptly brought back Peel into the Cabinet, but the four Whigs refused to serve, and in general the new government was far from enthusiastic for reform.

Nevertheless, Wellington's ministry soon introduced one very important change. It passed 'Catholic Emancipation' —the freeing of the Roman Catholics from the various laws restricting their political rights. It did this in the teeth of the 'pigtail' Tories, who of course wished to keep the Church of England in a privileged position.

Two events led to the decision. First, on the motion of the young Whig Lord John Russell, the seventeenth-century Test and Corporation Acts, by which admission to state or borough office was dependent on taking the Church of England Communion, were permanently repealed in 1828. This gave the Protestant Nonconformists full political privileges—which many of them had already enjoyed unofficially for some time—and left the Roman Catholics as the only large body deprived of the right to hold political office on account of their religious opinions.

Repeal of Test and Corporation Acts, 1828

Daniel O'Connell and the County Clare election

Secondly, Daniel O'Connell, a Roman Catholic landlord, had in 1825 founded the Catholic Association in Ireland to agitate for emancipation. By 1828 O'Connell was so successful that he defeated the government candidate and was returned at the County Clare election—illegally, for he was a Roman Catholic. Though he was not allowed to sit, it seemed certain that at the next general election O'Connell or his supporters would everywhere be chosen, so making a farce of the government of Ireland. Peel and Wellington, who were both practical men, thereupon decided to beat a retreat before it was too late. The Roman Catholic Relief Act, passed in 1829, threw open to Roman Catholics practically every political and administrative post throughout Great Britain and Ireland. So at last was secured the measure which Pitt had intended to introduce in 1801, after the achievment of the parliamentary union with Ireland, and from which George III had held him back. *Catholic emancipation, 1829*

Wellington's ministry, however, soon foundered on another controversial topic—parliamentary reform. In 1830, after a period of comparative quiet due to better economic conditions, this question again came to the fore. Parliament had to discuss the future of two boroughs convicted of corruption; and a revolution in Paris, in which the autocratic Charles X was overthrown almost without bloodshed in favour of a limited monarchy under his cousin Louis Philippe, revived interest in constitutional change in England. But to all demands for fairer representation or the extension of the right to vote, Wellington returned a blank refusal. In one speech he even went so far as to declare that the British parliamentary system could not be improved. This was too much. His enemies combined to defeat him, and he resigned. *Renewed demand for parliamentary reform* *1830 revolution in Paris*

Wellington had not proved nearly so great a statesman as he had been a general. He knew his mind clearly and spoke it too forcibly, caring little for public opinion—which he had often in the past found mistaken. Nor was he good at handling his supporters in Parliament and the Cabinet. He was used to an army, not a party. 'The party!' he once exclaimed: 'What is the meaning of a party if they don't follow their leaders? Damn 'em! Let 'em go!' But in the end it was the Duke who had to go. By 1830 the Whigs were in power and the gateway to parliamentary reform was at last open. *The Whigs in power*

CHAPTER EIGHTEEN

REFORM UNDER THE WHIGS

1. *The Great Reform Bill*

William IV
(1830–37)

SHORTLY before Wellington's resignation George IV died and was succeeded by his brother William IV. William was simple, affable, and rather empty-headed. He was quite without royal dignity. When signing a declaration at his first Privy Council he exclaimed, 'This is a damned bad pen you have given me!' Soon after his accession he went out alone for a ramble in the London streets. A large crowd followed him, a woman kissed him, and friends had to escort him back to the Palace.

Grey's
Whig
ministry,
1830

Having accepted Wellington's resignation, William turned to the Whigs and asked Earl Grey to form a government. It was a difficult task, for the Whigs were disunited and had not held office in a body since early in George III's reign. However, Grey succeeded—and the result of his efforts was one of the most aristocratic Cabinets of the century. Of the thirteen members, no fewer than eleven were peers.

Among those selected for office were some Canningite Tories who had broken with Wellington. The most important of these was Palmerston, who became Foreign Secretary. Grey also included his son-in-law, Lord Durham, who was an extreme reformer—'Radical Jack' the Durham miners called him. He was an impetuous and awkward colleague. The Whig leader in the House of Commons was Lord Althorp, a man trusted and liked by everyone. To him, as to Grey, the taking of political office was a personal sacrifice: they both much preferred staying at home. Grey used to describe London and Parliament as 'the places I hate most'. Althorp's view may perhaps be seen from his

Palmerston
Durham
Althorp

reply to a friend who commiserated with him on his acceptance of office again in 1832. 'Yes,' answered Althorp, 'and after ordering my new gun, too, and thinking I was going to have a really good shooting season.'

When the Whigs came into power in 1830, the country was again seething with unrest. The days of Peterloo seemed to be returning. Early in the year Thomas Attwood, a banker, had founded the Birmingham Political Union to demand the reform of Parliament. Radicals all over the country founded other unions (or societies) with the same programme. Dearer bread, following bad harvests in 1828 and 1829, added to the discontent, and this and the increasing power of the trade unions led to strikes and violence in the cotton districts of the North. In the autumn there followed disturbances in the rural areas of the South, where threshing machines were smashed and ricks burned. These outbreaks, while to a great extent caused by poverty, were also aimed at the system of government. The Whig Home Secretary, Lord Melbourne, put down all such rioting with a stern hand, but at the same time his colleagues hastened a Reform Bill which they hoped would quieten popular feeling.

The demand for parliamentary reform

Attwood

The Radicals

Mob violence

There were gasps of astonishment and bursts of ironical laughter when early in 1831 Lord John Russell, soon to be a member of the Cabinet, introduced the proposed measure to a crowded House of Commons. It was far more sweeping than most had expected, although Durham had been the chairman of the committee that drafted the Bill. By its proposals, for instance, sixty boroughs with tiny populations were to lose both their seats and forty-seven one seat; and most of these seats were to be given instead to the counties (many of which were to have their representation doubled) and to the bigger towns which had never enjoyed separate representation before.

Russell introduces Reform Bill, 1831

Small boroughs to lose their seats

With the seats of so many members threatened, the second reading of the Bill passed by only one vote, and soon the government was outvoted in the 'Committee' stage, when Bills are considered clause by clause. Grey thereupon asked William IV for a dissolution of Parliament and new

Bill defeated in Committee; Grey asks for general election

elections. His wish was granted, with eminently satisfactory results. Wherever the elections were contested the triumph of the Reformers was complete. Families who had regarded seats as their own preserve for generations were turned out if they tried to oppose the surging tide of reform.

When the new Parliament met, a slightly modified Bill accordingly passed through the House of Commons without much difficulty. Its opponents, however, had not given up: there was still the House of Lords. After a debate lasting five days, in the early hours of October 8th, 1831, Grey rose to make the final speech. His eloquence was in vain: the Lords rejected the Bill. At once a storm of indignation swept the country—not least against the bishops, who had all opposed the Bill. At Bristol there were angry demonstrations not only against the bishop but also against the Recorder, another opponent of the Bill, and for thirty-six hours the city was given over to rioting and mob rule. Many lesser disturbances occurred elsewhere.

Persevering in his intention, Grey then introduced the Bill again, with changes which spared some of the threatened boroughs. Still the Lords would not pass the measure intact. So Grey asked William IV to create fifty new peers to swamp the Tory majority and see the Bill through. The king stuck at twenty, Grey resigned, and William appealed to Wellington to take over the government and carry a lesser measure. This the Duke would have done, though reluctantly—but Peel and other Tory leaders refused to support so barefaced a change in their party policy. Unable to form a suitable ministry, the Duke also found himself faced by a clever move on the part of a leading Radical, Francis Place, who with Thomas Attwood organized a 'run on the banks', or, in other words, encouraged Reformers to withdraw deposits and cash their bonds. 'To stop the Duke, go for gold', was Place's slogan. In this sort of atmosphere William IV had little choice but to recall Grey and promise to create all the peers necessary. Only then, when this promise was known, did the Tory majority in the House of Lords give way and permit the final passage of the Bill.

Whigs returned with increased majority

Second version of Bill passes Commons and is defeated in Lords

Riots in Bristol and elsewhere

Third version of Bill

Grey asks king to create fifty peers

William IV turns to Wellington

The Duke unable to form ministry

'The run on the banks'

William gives in

The Bill passes the Lords, 1832

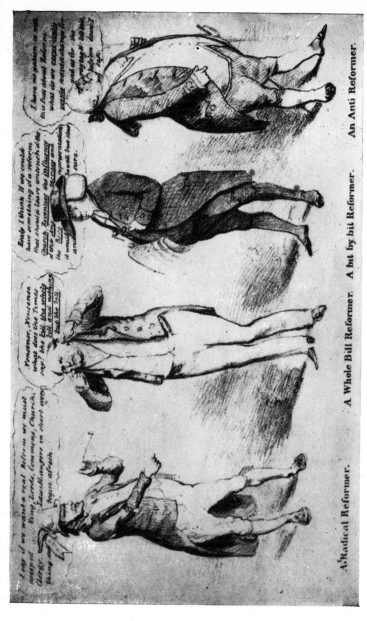

Four Specimens of the Political Public, 1831

Four different attitudes to the Reform Bill, as seen in a print of the day.

Terms of
the Great
(First)
Reform Act,
1832
Representa-
tion:
Seats from
small towns
to bigger
towns and
to counties

The new Act at last brought some sense into the distribution of seats. The smallest boroughs lost their separate
representation, and their seats were given instead to the
new England of the Industrial Revolution—for the most
part to the fast-growing towns of the Midlands and the
industrial North, like Birmingham, Manchester, Leeds and
Sheffield. Sixty-five extra seats were also given to the English
and Welsh counties, which had a large and independent
electorate. So far as the franchise, or vote, was concerned,
it was the middle class and not the working class which
benefited. For the county seats, the right to vote had thus

Franchise:
40s. free-
holders, £10
copyholders,
£50 lease-
holders in
counties;
£10 house-
holders in
towns

far been confined to freeholders of land of forty shillings or
more annual (i.e. rentable) value. Leaseholders and copyholders (an old form of tenure) were now also admitted to
the vote, but only if they held land to the value of £50 per
annum in the former case, £10 per annum in the latter.
For the borough seats, where the qualification had varied
from the mere ownership of a hearth (the 'potwallopers')
to membership of the Borough Corporation, a new uniform
franchise was laid down—the privilege of voting was to
belong to those who owned or leased a house of the annual
value of £10 a year or more. These amounts appear very
small now, but were then high enough to debar most
people from the vote. All told, the immediate effect of the
new franchise was to increase the number of voters in
England and Wales from 435,000 to 652,000, out of a male
adult population of about three million.[1]

Opinions on
the Act

There were plenty of misgivings about the Bill. The
Tories, and even some of Grey's government, including
Palmerston, thought it much too sweeping a measure. On
the other hand, the Radicals thought it not nearly sweeping
enough, for it did not grant their demands of manhood
suffrage (a vote for all men) and annual elections. It was
denounced by Orator Hunt and many of those who had
agitated for reform throughout the country. Their disappointment was soon to vent itself in Chartism, a movement which we shall examine later.

[1] Separate Reform Acts were passed for Scotland and Ireland by
which the former gained eight new members and the latter five.

2. *Other Whig Reforms in the 1830s*

Except for one short break, the Whigs remained in office till 1841. There was soon, however, a new leader of the government. In 1834 Grey resigned and Melbourne took his place as Prime Minister—a change he described as 'a damned bore'. He did not find it so boring, however, after 1837 when William IV died and the late monarch's niece, Victoria, became queen.[1] At her accession she was a girl of only eighteen, and Melbourne, a man-of-the-world nearing sixty whose own home life had been full of tragic disappointment, found himself powerfully attracted towards his unsophisticated and high-spirited young sovereign. He spent hours with her, and performed a considerable service to the nation by the tactful and sensible way in which he introduced her to her new duties. *Melbourne, Prime Minister, 1834*

Accession of Queen Victoria, 1837

The first House of Commons elected after the Reform Act met in 1833. Its members were very much the same kind of people as before, though there were more middle-class Radicals. Of the extreme Radicals Cobbett was returned and Hunt defeated. The measures the government brought forward had important and beneficial results for the future, though they did little to relieve distress at the time. The Municipal Corporations Act of 1835, for instance, reformed the government of the boroughs just as the Reform Act had reshaped Parliament. It abolished 'close' corporations, where vacancies were filled merely by co-option, and laid down a uniform system under which every borough council was to be elected, all male rate-payers of three years' standing being entitled to vote. This slowly produced a more efficient, as well as a fairer, type of town government. Similar Acts were passed for Scotland and Ireland. *The new Commons*

Reforms

Municipal Corporations Reform Act, 1835

More controversial in its effects was the Poor Law Amendment Act of 1834. Its main object was to check the widespread granting of poor-relief and so restore the labourer's self-respect, force manufacturers and farmers to *Poor Law Amendment Act, 1834*

[1] She did not succeed to Hanover, where the law barred women from the throne, and where her uncle the Duke of Cumberland now became king.

Poor Laws—Old and New
From a satirical print of 1836.

pay a living wage, and reduce the heavy burden of poor-rates on the ordinary householder. With these ideas in view it restricted the granting of 'outdoor' relief (including the supplements to wages paid in accordance with the Speenhamland system) and decreed that in future the only form of relief normally available to the able-bodied should be maintenance in a workhouse. A central Poor Law Board was set up to administer this scheme, which was rather like a necessary surgical operation carried out with quite unnecessary brutality. Its long-term effects were on the whole good; the numbers on relief dropped, as did the poor-rates, and slowly the level of wages rose. But the immediate effects were in many places very bad—and would have been worse still had not several northern districts, where outdoor relief was regularly given during slumps, allowed

'The workhouse test' for poor-relief

many years to pass before applying the Act. Conditions in the workhouses were also made needlessly harsh. The loss of liberty suffered by an unemployed man when he had to enter one of these establishments in order to avoid starvation was quite enough, without rules which entirely separated the sexes and broke up families. In their bare walls, Spartan furniture and low diet, workhouses were made as much like prisons as possible and little care was taken to give the aged, the young and the sick the separate privileges to which they were entitled.

Certain reforms passed by the Whigs during the 1830s were directly inspired by great philanthropists. In 1833, following many years of agitation by Sir Thomas Fowell Buxton, a brewer who had taken on the leadership of the anti-slavery movement from William Wilberforce, an Act abolished slavery throughout the British Empire. The news was brought to Wilberforce, then in his eighty-fourth year, *Abolition of slavery, 1833*

Factory Children in 1814

From 'Costume of Yorkshire'. The stunted figures seem only too well suited to the bleak landscape and the blasted tree.

Lanark, 1825

Showing Robert Owen's New Lanark Mills in the foreground.

just before he died. So the work which his deep Christian faith had prompted him to undertake, and which had first resulted in the Act of 1807 prohibiting the slave-trade to British subjects, was completed. In 1834 the slaves became officially free though most of them were still made to serve some years of apprenticeship with their former owners.

Factory Act, 1833 Another measure similarly inspired was a further Act to control young people's labour in the factories. As we have seen in Chapter X, the first Sir Robert Peel had succeeded in getting an Act passed to limit the hours of pauper apprentices in cotton factories to twelve a day, but it was **The Act of 1819** not much observed. Since then a further Act, passed in 1819 by the combined efforts of this same Sir Robert Peel and another great manufacturer, Robert Owen, had extended the benefit of the twelve-hour day to all children under sixteen years of age working in cotton-mills, whether apprentices or 'free'. By the same Act, children under nine years of age were not to be employed in these mills at all.

But like those of the Act of 1802, these regulations were very little observed, for there was no one except the local unpaid magistrate to enforce them—and he rarely visited factories.

As time went on, indeed, Owen came to be increasingly regarded as a mere 'crank'. The son of a saddler and postmaster of Newtown, in Montgomeryshire, he had entered the cotton industry as a youth, become a mill-owner at the age of seventeen, and by twenty-eight was the manager and leading partner in Dale's great mills at New Lanark in Scotland. There he had stopped the employment of children under twelve—for whom he arranged excellent schooling—and had provided good housing and recreation for all his workers, whose hours of labour he reduced from thirteen to ten and a half a day. All this produced not only a satisfied community but also greater profits than ever before for the partners. Nevertheless, though Owen's methods were at first acclaimed in important circles, they were little applied outside New Lanark. Moreover, Owen had other ideas which gave offence to

A great factory reformer—Robert Owen

ESSAYS

ON

THE FORMATION OF THE HUMAN CHARACTER.

A Tract by Robert Owen

This is the illustrated heading, contrasting the upbringing in two different types of home.

many serious and well-meaning people at the time: he believed, for instance, that the education of children under ten should include a high proportion of the lighter subjects (such as music, dancing and drill), that divorce should be made easier, and that a large part of the accepted Christian religion was nonsense. Encountering a good deal of opposition to his views, in 1824 Owen had therefore emigrated to the United States. There he spent a large part of his fortune in founding an 'ideal community' at a place in Indiana which he named New Harmony. Unfortunately, the idle there tried to live on the efforts of the industrious, and the harmony was short-lived. Returning to Britain a poorer but little less optimistic man, Owen then strove to foster in this country schemes of 'co-operative' production, in which joint ownership of factories and plant by the workers would replace the existing system with its harsh and glaring distinctions between employer and employed.

Meanwhile, more and more people in Britain were becoming aware of the dreadfully long hours worked and the brutal discipline enforced in the new textile factories. In 1833 a great Christian, Lord Ashley (better known under his later title—the seventh Earl of Shaftesbury), became the leader of a movement to protect at least the women and children. In response to his pressure Grey's government produced a measure, introduced by the Home Secretary, Lord Althorp, which carried the protection of children a stage further than the Act of 1819. Though it was by no means all that Ashley had hoped for, it continued the ban on the employment of children under nine, limited the working hours of children between nine and thirteen to forty-eight a week (with a maximum of nine a day) and laid down a maximum of sixty-nine hours a week (or twelve in any one day) for 'young persons' between thirteen and eighteen. For the first time the Act also applied to other textile factories besides cotton-mills—though silk-mills were excepted. Most important of all, for the first time paid factory inspectors were appointed to see that the regulations were carried out.

The new Factory Act and the other measures described

Ashley (Shaftesbury) presses for new Factory Act

Althorp's Factory Act, 1833: Protection extended to 'young persons'

Paid inspectors

HAS

DEATH

(IN A RAGE)

Been invited by the Commissioners of Common
Sewers to take up his abode in Lambeth? or, from
what other villanous cause proceeds the frightful
Mortality by which we are surrounded?

In this Pest-House of the Metropolis, and
disgrace to the Nation, the main thoroughfares
are still without Common Sewers, although the
Inhabitants have paid exorbitant Rates from time
immemorial!!!

" O Heaven! that such companions thou'dst unfold,
" And put in every honest hand, a whip,
" To lash the rascals naked through the world."

Unless something be speedily done to allay
the growing discontent of the people, retributive
justice in her salutary vengeance will commence
her operations with the *Lamp-Iron* and the
Halter.

SALUS POPULI.

Lambeth, August, 1832.

J. W. PEEL, Printer, 9, New Cut, Lambeth.

A Handbill in the Fight for Better Sanitation, 1832

in this chapter touched only the fringe of the problems of
the new industrial Britain. They did little to lessen popular
discontent, which began to show itself in attempts to form
bigger and stronger trade unions. Among these was the
Grand National Consolidated Trades Union founded in
1833 on the inspiration of—but not actually by—Robert
Owen. Soon numbering half a million members, this aimed
at co-operative production as well as the more usual objects
of trade-unionism. Little proper thought, however, had

The Grand National Consolidated Trades Union, 1833-4

been given to such an ambitious policy, and the life of the Grand National was short. Its inevitable failure was hastened by the hostility both of employers and of the government—whose attitude can be seen from the famous case of the 'Tolpuddle martyrs'. In 1834 six labourers of Tolpuddle in Dorset were prosecuted for swearing men into an agricultural lodge which was intending to join the Union. The oaths were held to be illegal and the men were all sentenced to transportation—from which they were recalled two years later only as a result of a lengthy public agitation.

The
'Tolpuddle
Martyrs'

Though the Whigs were responsible for a number of useful reforms during the 1830s, the party as a whole had little more sympathy for working-class movements than had the Tories. On the other hand, the condition of the country gave genuine concern and alarm to Whig and Tory alike, especially after cholera came to England in 1831. In that year Greville, an official of the Privy Council, wrote: 'The reports from Sunderland [where cholera had first broken out] exhibit a state of human misery such as I hardly ever heard of and it is no wonder when a great part of the community is plunged into such a condition that there should be so many who are ripe for any desperate scheme of revolution.' Later on, when cholera had come to London, he wrote: 'Government is ready to interpose, but what can Government do?' That was the point. Even when the government was willing—and that was not often, while theories of *laissez faire* held sway—there was very little it could do to produce immediate results in social and economic problems. The total number of civil servants was extremely small, and for this type of work there were practically none. The factory inspectors and the poor-law commissioners—these were a small and useful beginning. But a considerable army of officials, backed in the last resort by a considerable number of police, would be needed before increased government regulation could be really effective. For the government merely to lay down additional regulations which it was unable or unwilling to enforce would be a hindrance rather than a help to the social and economic life of the nation.

Need for
bigger
government
organization
—civil ser-
vants, etc.—
if govern-
ment regula-
tion to be
effective

CHAPTER NINETEEN

RAILWAYS AND STEAMSHIPS

1. *The Coming of the Railways*

ON September 15th, 1830, the Duke of Wellington and Sir Robert Peel were among those who took part in the opening ceremony of the Liverpool and Manchester Railway. Except for a fatal accident to William Huskisson, who was flustered by the approach of an engine and knocked down just after he had shaken hands with the Duke, everything went well. 'The flying machines', reported one paper, 'sped through the awful chasm [a cutting] at the speed of 24 m.p.h.' The Railway Age—the next great phase of the Industrial Revolution—had begun.

The coming of the railways will always be linked with the work of a father and son, George and Robert Stephenson. George, born in 1781 at Wylam near Newcastle upon Tyne, was the son of a 'fireman' who tended the stationary steam-engines used in the colleries of that area. George was first employed looking after cows at twopence a day, but his ambition was always to work the engines. In his fourteenth year he became assistant fireman to his father at a shilling a day. Four years later he started going to village night schools to learn reading, writing and arithmetic, and by the age of twenty he was in charge of an engine—a job known as brakesman. At twenty-four he became brakesman at the West Moor pit at Killingworth, north of Newcastle. Here it was that, some years later, he built his first locomotive.

George Stephenson

Yet, as Robert Stephenson once said: 'The locomotive is not the invention of one man but of a nation of mechanical engineers.' The remark might almost as well have been made of railways, for which the track is quite as essential as the locomotive. In the colleries of Tyneside, for instance, extensive use of 'tramways' or 'railways' had already been

Rails

made for a century or more; and one such railway ran outside the cottage where Stephenson was born. To begin with,
the rails were made of wood. Later, iron was used, and
often the rails were given a raised flange at the edge to keep
the wheels of the wagons on the track. About 1790 a new
idea came in, and the flange was transferred from the rail
to the wheel. So was born the edge-rail of the modern
railways. These rails, being at first still made of cast iron,
tended to break under heavy weights. In 1820, however,
the Bedlington ironworks succeeded in producing the new
edge-rail in wrought iron.

Locomotives   For the locomotive, too, Stephenson could draw on
considerable experience. There was the very first of all,
already mentioned—Richard Trevithick's 'Uncle Dick's
Puffer', built for colliery work in 1804.[1] Then, in 1812,
John Blenkinsop had constructed locomotives for collieries
near Leeds. These worked successfully for many years, but
they were very slow, for they were of the 'rack' type, with
cogs engaging on a toothed line. A locomotive of this kind
was built and brought to Wylam. It failed to move. Its
maker became impatient. Exclaiming, 'Either she goes or
I shall', he clamped down the safety valve on the boiler.
As soon as the machinery was set in motion, 'she' flew to
pieces. A second model was rather more successful.

Stephenson's first locomotive was placed on the rails at
Killingworth in 1814. It did at least move and drag coal-
wagons, but it used so much coal that it was reckoned to be
no cheaper than equivalent power in horses. In 1815
Stephenson hit on the idea of the steam blast. The steam
that had driven the piston was led out into the chimney
and its force gave a greater draught to the fire, thereby
enabling more steam to be raised. His new locomotive built
on this principle proved more economical and powerful.
By this time Stephenson was beginning to get a reputation,
and in 1819 he was commissioned to build a railway from
Hetton Colliery to the banks of the Wear.

Stockton   The first public railway to use locomotives was the
and
Darlington   Stockton and Darlington, opened in 1825. Before this there
Railway,
1825   [1] Page 139.

A Collier in 1814

From 'Costume of Yorkshire'. In the background, the pit shaft and an early
colliery locomotive and trucks.

had been a number of scattered public railways, such as
the Surrey Iron Railway between Wandsworth and Croy-
don opened in 1803, but they all used horses. In 1817,
largely through the work of Edward Pease, a Quaker
banker of Darlington, a company was formed for the
Stockton and Darlington. Money was raised, an Act of
Parliament permitting the line was obtained in 1821, and
shortly afterwards George Stephenson was appointed as
engineer.

The company had not intended to use steam-engines.
The virtue of the railway, they thought, was that 'a horse
upon an iron road would draw ten tons for one ton on a
common road'. However, in addition to stationary engines
with ropes for two uphill sections of the line, Stephenson in
the end persuaded the directors to order a locomotive from
him. He also induced Pease and a friend to lend him
enough money to set up a locomotive factory at Newcastle. On Stephenson's advice much of the track was laid

The *Northumbrian*

One of Stephenson's locomotives for the Liverpool-Manchester line, 1830.

in wrought iron, with a gauge of 4 feet 8½ inches. This had been the gauge of the earlier 'tramways' for it was the normal axle-span of the carts that used them.[1] The line was single track with sidings. It was successfully opened in 1825 when the *Locomotion*, Stephenson's engine, drew a train over a large part of the route. To begin with, the company itself did not run the services but simply charged tolls on traffic in the same way as a turnpike trust. For some years horses did most of the work on the line.

Liverpool and Manchester Railway, 1830

The Liverpool and Manchester Railway was a much more ambitious affair. It connected two large industrial towns, it had double track, and it included some very difficult engineering work. Sponsored mainly by Liverpool merchants, it had been bitterly opposed by other local

[1] The axle-span of carts was traditional and possibly stretched back to the days of Roman chariots. A constant width was preserved to enable carts to travel in the great ruts which they made on tracks and roads.

interests such as landowners and canal-owners. It was even said, for instance, at the Parliamentary enquiry that the trains would stop cows grazing and hens laying, that any bird flying over a train would be killed, and that Stephenson must be mad if he thought that a locomotive would travel at twelve miles an hour. However, he got the better of one of his critics. 'Suppose now,' he was asked, 'one of these engines to be going along a railroad at the rate of nine or ten miles an hour, that a cow were to stray upon the line; would not that, think you, be a very awkward circumstance?' 'Yes,' replied Stephenson in his strong Northumbrian accent, 'very awkward—for the cow.'

Because of the amount of opposition, the preliminary survey of a new railway such as the Liverpool and Manchester could thus be very difficult, for landlords and farmers were not above chasing off the surveyors. When Robert Stephenson was surveying the London and Birmingham route, one of the strongest objectors who refused all entrance to his land was a clergyman. The surveyors on this occasion waited until the obstinate cleric began his sermon in church. Then, at a given signal, they swarmed on to his estate, surveyed it, and managed to decamp before he left the pulpit.

So far as the Liverpool and Manchester was concerned, the greatest difficulties Stephenson had to surmount were in the actual construction of the railway. There was a long entrance tunnel into Liverpool, a deep stone cutting in some places fifty feet deep, and the crossing of Chat Moss, a great bog of peat. This was the worst part of all, and several of the directors of the company despaired of success. Stephenson's idea was to build across the moss a floating embankment, heather, branches, turf and hurdles forming the foundations for the track. At the Manchester end it was for long impossible to get the embankment to stay on top of the bog—it kept disappearing underneath. In the end Stephenson was successful, though it was said later that onlookers could see the rails sag as trains passed over Chat Moss.

There was still the question of what type of power to

A Viaduct on the Liverpool–Manchester Railway, 1831

This viaduct carrying George Stephenson's line across the Sankey valley is typical
of the splendid work of the early railway engineers.

use. Many wanted stationary steam-engines, but Stephenson's enthusiasm persuaded the company to offer a prize for the best locomotive to complete certain tasks. The trials were held at Rainhill on the company's line in 1829. Stephenson's *Rocket* won easily. Among other improvements on earlier models, it had a tubular boiler, so allowing the production of more steam. After the triumph of the *Rocket* the company adopted the locomotive and it was Stephenson's engines that drew the trains on the opening day.

The success of the Liverpool and Manchester started off railway-building in earnest. In 1833 a railway (the later Great Western) was projected between London and Bristol; it reached the latter town in 1841. The London and Birmingham railway completed its last section of line and started through-traffic in 1838. By 1841 people could travel by rail from London to Newcastle by way of Birmingham and Derby, and could reach Glasgow by the west coast—though there was a sea passage from Fleetwood to Ardrossan. By this time there were 2,000 miles of route. Ten years later, continuous railway stretched north as far as Aberdeen, and there were nearly 7,000 miles of route in operation.[1]

This expansion was at its most intense in 1836–7 and in 1845–6. The latter years witnessed an especially severe bout of 'railway-mania', when the public eagerly paid inflated prices for shares, often in companies that had only modest prospects of success. One of the greatest figures of these years was George Hudson, the 'Railway King'. A draper and Lord Mayor of York, he began by encouraging railway development in the North-East, then set out to gain control of as many lines as he could. In particular he strove to establish a stranglehold over traffic from London through the Midlands to York and beyond. He overplayed his hand and went bankrupt, but one result of his activities was that a number of the small lines amalgamated to form larger companies, either as part of his schemes or in opposition to them. In 1844, for instance, an amalgamation produced the Midland Railway; and in 1847 the London and Birmingham, the Grand Junction (Manchester–Birmingham), and the Liverpool and Manchester united to form the London and North Western Railway. Larger groupings of this kind were able to give much better service to the public than hundreds of small companies, particularly in the matter of long-distance traffic.

George Hudson

Amalgamations in the 1840s

During all this time the name of Stephenson continued to be the greatest in railway engineering. George, after building the Grand Junction, the London and Birmingham (with Robert) and many other lines in the Midlands and the North, spent his last year or two of life as a country gentleman in Derbyshire. He was consulted on the railway problems of various countries, and everywhere was held in

[1] The route mileage in Great Britain reached its maximum round about 1920, when there were about 24,000 miles in operation. Nowadays, owing to the competition of road transport, the figure is much less— about 18,000.

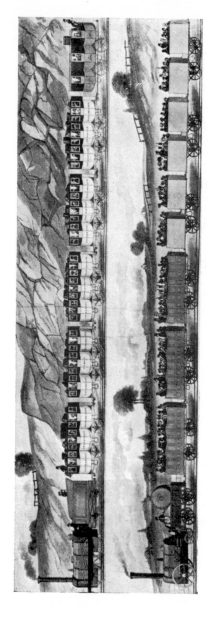

First and Third Class Carriages on the Liverpool–Manchester Railway, 1831

great esteem as one whose genius had brought fame and riches to himself and great benefit to mankind. He died in 1848. Robert lived a few years longer, dying in 1859. Early in his career he had taken charge of the Stephensons' locomotive factory in Newcastle and the *Rocket* owed much to him. His, too, was much of the credit for the successful construction of the London and Birmingham. Later he was consulted about railways all over the world. He also showed his engineering genius in designing important railway bridges, such as the Royal Border at Berwick, the High Level at Newcastle, and the two famous tubular bridges on the Holyhead Line, the Conway and the Britannia over the Menai Straits. In addition he designed the Victoria tubular bridge over the St. Lawrence at Montreal —a structure practically two miles long. Member of Parliament for Whitby and President of the Institution of Civil Engineers, he, too, like his father, was one of the great figures of early Victorian England. *Robert Stephenson*

The other great engineer of the early railways was Isambard Kingdom Brunel. The son of a brilliant French engineer and inventor who had left his own country on account of the French Revolution, he was the constructor of the Great Western Railway. Brunel worked on a grand scale. The gauge he chose for the Great Western was seven feet, the gradients were all made very gentle, and the entrances to the tunnels were given impressive architectural façades. The longest of these tunnels, and for some time the longest in the world, was at Box, near Bath. Brunel's Great Western was also the first railway to use the recently invented electric telegraph for controlling its traffic, with the result that the Great Western could for some time run trains much faster than any other company. By 1848 the morning mail-train was timed to do the fifty-three miles from Paddington to Didcot in fifty-six minutes.[1] Brunel's methods, however, involved the Great Western in much expense, and before the end of the century the Company decided to change their track to the standard gauge of 4 feet 8½ inches. Famous as a railway engineer, *I.K. Brunel* *The Great Western: the 'broad gauge'*

[1] The fastest train nowadays (1960) takes seven minutes longer.

The Royal Albert Bridge, Saltash
Brunel's last great railway masterpiece.

Brunel was almost equally well known as a designer of docks, piers, guns, steamships and bridges. Among the last, his most brilliant achievements included the Royal Albert bridge at Saltash, the Maidenhead railway bridge, and the Clifton suspension bridge.

The effect of the railways on the national life was very great. Once built, they offered a new opportunity for regular employment: by 1850 the various companies had a staff of over 50,000. New 'railway' towns were created, including Crewe, Swindon, Woking and Middlesbrough (to which the Stockton and Darlington was extended). Above all, the railways brought quick and cheap travel for passengers and goods alike. By coach the journey from London to Glasgow could easily take a week: by train, in 1841, it took twenty-four hours, in 1850 thirteen hours. Fares, too, were much cheaper than by coach. At one time in 1856, during a 'railway war', the return fare from London to York fell to five shillings, but in any case the railways after 1844 were bound by Act of Parliament to carry passengers on at least one train a day over each section of route at not more than one penny a mile. Thus the railways, by enabling people to move much more freely from district to district, made Britain much more of a single unit. They broke down local barriers, familiarized people with machinery, and immensely stimulated the growth of trade, both at home and abroad. The price of coal and food fell in many home districts owing to the cheaper transport, while abroad British goods could reach new markets along the railways of the world. All British exports felt the benefit of this, including those on which railway construction itself depended—coal, iron, locomotives.

Results of railway development

2. Steamships

In the locomotive may be seen one of the greatest applications of the power of steam—the steam-engines for pumping in coal-mines having been the first great application, and the steam-engines for driving textile machinery the second. Other applications soon followed, among them being the steam-engines which by 1830 drove threshing-machines in Northumberland and south Scotland. None of these perhaps quite equalled in importance the next great development, the ocean-going steamship.

Steamships   Considering the speed with which the railways spread during the twenty years after 1830, the development of steamships was comparatively slow. The first use in Britain was in 1802, when a steam-tug ran on the Forth and Clyde Canal. This experiment was stopped because of damage to the canal banks. Paddle-steamers were then built and used successfully on the rivers and lakes of the United States, and by 1812 Henry Bell's paddle-steamer *The Comet* was running in the mouth of the Clyde. Thus far ocean voyages had not been attempted, though in 1816 a steamboat service was started across the English Channel and coastal traffic soon followed. Longer voyages were then made using steam as an

The *Sirius*, 1837

In 1837 the paddle-steamer *Sirius* made the first crossing of the Atlantic (Cork New York) under continuous steam power. The passage took 18½ days, at a average speed of 6·7 knots.

aying the First Submarine Cable across the English Channel, 1850
ae *Goliah* is seen paying out the wire, while H.M. packet *Widgeon* stands by.

auxiliary to sail, but it was not until 1833 that a vessel—
the Canadian *Royal William*—crossed the Atlantic entirely First all-steam Atlantic crossing, 1833
under the power of steam.[1] By this time iron was coming
into use for the hulls of vessels—the first iron river-steamer
had been launched eight years earlier—and it was not long
before Brunel and others were building iron ocean-going
steamships. Brunel's first great project was a steamship Brunel
named the *Great Western*, intended to carry railway passengers on from Bristol to New York. A medium-sized
paddle-steamer, it came into successful service in 1838,
making the first crossing in thirteen days. Thereafter Brunel
moved to ever more ambitious projects, the next being a
much larger vessel, the *Great Britain*. Not only was this
built of iron, but it also had a screw propeller. The great
efficiency of this device had been proved by an Admiralty
test earlier in the same year, when a paddle-steamer and a

[1] The engines were stopped every fourth day to clear the boilers of salt.

screw-steamer of comparable power were secured stern to
stern. Both then went full speed ahead—and the screw-
steamer pulled the paddle-steamer along at the rate of
2½ knots.

By 1850, however, steamship traffic was still in its
infancy. Regular routes were being followed, and Samuel
Cunard of Liverpool and Canada had a contract to carry
mail to America, but the total steamship tonnage was
still very small. Britain was more advanced than any
other country, but even in the British merchant navy (of
3,000,000 tons) only 100,000 tons were as yet propelled by
steam. But the next ten years, with the invention by
Thomas Elder of the expansion engine (which used the
steam a second time), saw the development of steamships
of much greater reliability and power. Wooden sailing-
ships of improved design, including the clipper, still
played a part for long to come—as late as 1870 they made
up four-fifths of the world's tonnage—but the future clearly
lay with iron, steel, and steam. And with the development
of better and better steamships, came a still further growth
in overseas trade, emigration and all the other things that
linked Britain with the rest of the world.

* * * * *

It is against this background of rapid improvement in
the means of communication, both by land and sea, that
we must now study the great political movements of the
1840s.

CHAPTER TWENTY

CHARTISM, THE CORN LAWS, AND SIR ROBERT PEEL

1. *Chartism and the Anti-Corn Law League*

DESPITE the popular term 'the hungry 'forties', people in Great Britain—though certainly not in Ireland—were on the whole better off during the 1840s than in the previous ten or twenty years. This, however, did not make the 'forties a time of contentment. On the contrary, they were a time of great agitation and disturbance. Two big movements—Chartism and the Anti-Corn Law League—attacked the government relentlessly, and for the first time the nation was subjected to large-scale political propaganda. This was possible because the new railways and the penny post (introduced in 1840) provided much better means of communication than ever before. *Two great popular movements*

Chartism was the first sustained political movement of the industrial working class. Strongest in the North and Midlands, it was in spirit a protest against the inequalities and injustices resulting from the new industrial system. Outwardly, it took the form of a demand for extreme parliamentary reform, so that the voice of the working class should be heard in Parliament. *Chartism* *Inspired by economic grievances* *Its political programme*

Industrial workers had plenty of other grievances apart from the rigour of factory life or the lack of a vote. The Poor Law Amendment Act of 1834—the 'Poor Man's Robbery Bill' as Cobbett called it—was bitterly resented. The cotton trade was uncertain, and now in a time of unemployment there was officially no relief except in the workhouses—'Bastilles', as they were called. General living conditions, too, were still very bad in many of the towns. Friedrich Engels, co-founder with Karl Marx of *Grievances of the working class*

Communism, here describes the view from a bridge in the centre of Manchester in 1844:

> At the bottom flows or rather stagnates the Irk, a narrow coal-black, foul-smelling stream full of debris and refuse which it deposits on the shallower right bank. In dry weather, a long string of the most disgusting, blackish-green slime-pools are left standing on this bank. Below the bridge you look upon the piles of debris, the refuse, filth, and offal from the courts on the steep left bank; here each house is packed close behind its neighbour and a piece of each is visible, all black, smoky, crumbling, ancient, with broken panes and window frames.

Many another town could display similar scenes.

The 'People's Charter'—the programme of the Chartists —was published in 1838. The main force behind it was at first the London Working Men's Association, a society founded two years earlier by William Lovett, a cabinet-maker, who held extreme radical views but was no believer in violence. The Charter, drawn up in the form of a Bill to be put through Parliament, contained six demands: annual parliaments, manhood suffrage, vote by ballot, no property qualifications for M.P.s, payment of members, and equal electoral districts—a programme which has since been achieved in every point except the first (and to a slight extent the last), but which at the time seemed revolutionary indeed. It soon became the rallying point of all the extreme Radicals. It was adopted by nearly all the parliamentary reform societies, by the Birmingham Political Union, and by most of the anti-Poor-Law agitators who had been threatening death and destruction in Yorkshire and Lanca-shire to the 'hellhounds' (the Poor Law Commissioners) to such an extent that in most areas no workhouse could be opened.

The Chartist campaign was aided by the support of an important Leeds newspaper, *The Northern Star*. Its founder and editor, Feargus O'Connor, was a doubtful asset. Born in 1794 of an Irish landed family, he had entered Parliament as one of O'Connell's supporters. He lost his seat and took up extreme radical politics in England. He was a big, heavily built man, full of Irish blarney, a good journalist

The
'People's
Charter',
1838

Lovett

The Six
Points

Feargus
O'Connor

Manchester by Night

From an engraving of about 1850–60.

and speaker, with a ready and effective flow of abuse. He was once hissed by some wealthy-looking people in his audience. His reaction was immediate. He turned to them and said, 'Yes—you—I was just coming to you when I was describing the materials of which our spurious aristocracy is compŏsed. You gentlemen belong to the big-bellied, little-brained, numbskull aristocracy. How dare you hiss me, you contemptible set of platter-faced amphibious politicians?' He was, however, much too vain and unreliable to be a good leader.

The Chartist Convention, 1839

The first great climax in the activity of the Chartists came after they decided to hold a Convention, or parliament, with representatives from the various districts. These assembled in London in 1839. Many of them placed M.C. after their names in rivalry to M.P.s, for the Convention claimed to be more truly representative of the people. Its members were to organize a mass petition to the House of Commons demanding the Six Points, and if this were not accepted, to consider calling a month's general strike. They found they had not yet enough support for their petition and so began a widespread campaign for signatures throughout the country. They also transferred the Convention to Birmingham—where riots in the Bull Ring were soon followed by the arrest of Lovett, who had signed a protest against the repressive measures taken by the town authorities. When at length the petition was presented to Parliament, it was of course overwhelmingly rejected, and the Convention then called for the general strike—only to cancel the order before it could take effect.

Riots in Birmingham: arrest of Lovett

Petition rejected

Collapse of Convention

By this time the Convention was hopelessly split between those who favoured violence and those who did not, and soon it adjourned. With many of the leaders in prison, Chartism was now a disorganized force. It was not, however, as yet a broken one. There was much drilling and arming in factory and mining districts, but fortunately General Napier, the officer in command of the troops in the North, by sensible tactics managed to prevent a rising. Only in the West did a really serious outbreak occur. Towards the end of the year some three thousand miners tried to seize

Newport, in Monmouthshire, and release an imprisoned Attack on Newport, 1839 Chartist leader. The move was defeated by the garrison of twenty-eight soldiers, who had been forewarned. The miners, it seems, had hoped for help from the North, but O'Connor's bark was much worse than his bite, and he gave the plot no support. This did not stop his being arrested, in common with most of the other Chartist leaders.

Chartism, however, though now disgraced in the eyes of the middle classes, was not yet dead. In its later stages O'Connor, who had quarrelled with Lovett, came into increasing prominence. He allowed his vanity full play. This is how *The Northern Star*, after listing the various banners, described his entry into Huddersfield:

Then came:

Operatives sixteen abreast

The Carriage

drawn by four greys; postillions, scarlet jackets, black velvet caps, and silver tassels; containing the People's Champion

FEARGUS O'CONNOR ESQUIRE

In 1842 O'Connor organized another mass petition for The second mass petition, 1842 the Charter. It was signed by over three million persons. The House of Commons gave it a chilly reception, even one of its supporters in the House declaring that O'Connor was 'a foolish, malignant, and cowardly demagogue'. Its opponents claimed that, if manhood suffrage were granted, it was people like O'Connor who would be returned to Parliament, and the petition was easily rejected.

In 1845 O'Connor launched out on a fresh line—a land O'Connor's land scheme scheme. He bought an estate in Hertfordshire and divided it up into smallholdings for Chartist supporters. Like Cobbett, he imagined that the only real remedy for industrial distress was a return to the land—in fact, he even supported the Corn Laws.

By 1848 O'Connor was an M.P. again. Spurred by the revolutions on the Continent which began that year with the overthrow of Louis Philippe and the proclamation of a French Republic, he set about organizing another national petition for the Charter. He obtained fewer than two million signatures—and these were later found on examination to include such obvious fakes as Victoria Rex, the Duke of Wellington, Mr. Punch, Pugnose, and No Cheese. A big rally on Kennington Common gathered to launch the petition on its way, but the government had banned the intended procession to Westminster and O'Connor and one or two others had to take the document to the House alone in three cabs. Later efforts in 1848 by other leaders to raise riots in London were frustrated, and soon afterwards O'Connor's land scheme failed financially. Four years later, by which time Chartism was already dead and done for,

he was judged to be insane. The movement had failed through poor leadership, disunity, and the sweeping demands of its programme, which went much too far for responsible opinion at the time. It was difficult to make out a case for a reform that might have given O'Connor and the other Chartist leaders charge of the government of Britain. After 1850 increased prosperity and a continuation of the slow rise in the standard of living, already perceptible in the 'forties, prevented any revival of the movement.

Having gained nothing (except experience) from Chartism, the working classes now turned towards smaller and more practicable schemes, which brought them greater benefits. 'Friendly' societies like the Oddfellows and the Foresters grew in number and provided useful help to

members in time of sickness, or for burial. Trade unions of the modern type, for the most part confined to one naturally associated group of trades and aimed primarily at improving conditions in those trades, also increased in number, the most important being the Amalgamated Society of Engineers founded in 1851. In addition, the

Co-operative movement in its modern form, as an association whose members benefit in proportion to the extent of their purchases, found its starting point in 1844 when a successful Co-operative store was founded in Toad Lane, Rochdale, by twenty-eight men with a total capital of £28. In thirty years' time its profits were nearly £50,000 per annum. The idea caught on, and many other places started

Co-operative shops on the 'divi' principle. These proved to be much more enduring than previous co-operative ventures, confined to actual producers, or those which had tried to set up depots for the exchange of goods.

The second great popular movement of the mid-nineteenth century, the Anti-Corn-Law League, appealed not only to the working class but to the middle class as well. To the Chartists the villain of the piece was the manufacturer, to the Anti-Corn-Law Leaguers the landlord. The struggle for the repeal of the Corn Laws was a straight fight between the leaders of the new industrial Britain and the leaders of the old rural Britain. A movement with middle-class support —the Anti-Corn-Law League, 1839

Renewed agitation against the Corn Laws (which had been much modified since the law of 1815 but still retained heavy duties on imported grains) began in 1838. The following year the Anti-Corn-Law League was formed. Two of its three leading spirits were Richard Cobden and John Bright, both Lancashire cotton manufacturers. Cobden, a Sussex man who had been a commercial traveller before he took over a business in Manchester, became a Member of Parliament in 1841 and was the chief spokesman of the League. A skilful agitation, directed from Manchester, was carried on throughout the country. Cobden and other lecturers toured first the towns in England and Scotland, then the country districts. In some places they were hounded out through the influence of the local landlord, but during 1842–3—thanks to the recently introduced penny post—pamphlets were distributed to over nine million people. The campaign soon took on something of the quality of a religious crusade, for Bright and Cobden believed that Free Trade had a great moral as well as a material value. They thought it wrong to increase the cost of necessities like bread by Customs duties; and they imagined that Free Trade, by breaking down national barriers and bringing a higher standard of living, would help to prevent wars. Suddenly in 1846, as we shall see, Sir Robert Peel's Conservative government, which had fought the League's arguments for five years, gave way to its demands. Unlike Chartism, the League had been well Cobden and Bright The League's victory, 1846

led and united on a simple and perfectly practicable
programme—the repeal of the Corn Laws. Also unlike
Chartism, it had enjoyed the support of many who, if not
of the aristocratic governing class of the time, were nevertheless men of wealth, responsibility and influence.

Reasons
for success

2. *Peel, the Conservative Party, and the Repeal of the Corn Laws*

Sir Robert
Peel

Though Peel was educated at Harrow and Christ Church,
Oxford, he came, as we have seen, from an industrial background and had little in common with those Tories whose
thoughts did not go beyond their lands and such pastimes
as hunting and shooting. With the rest of the Tories he went
out of office in 1830. In the elections at the time of the
Reform Bill the Tories were badly beaten; and Peel soon
saw that there was little hope for a party whose only programme was either to keep the clock where it was or, if
possible, to put it back. On the other hand, he disliked
sweeping changes. He had already made a name for
himself as a moderate reformer, a man who considered
measures on their merits. At the election of 1834, when he
was the acknowledged leader of the Tories, he accordingly
issued a manifesto to his constituents at Tamworth in which
he committed his party to this type of reform. He also made
it clear that the Tories accepted the Reform Act. To mark
the change, he and others started to call themselves
Conservatives, and from this time onwards the Tory party
became the Conservative party. At this period—1834-5—
he was briefly in office as Prime Minister, but, lacking a
majority in the Commons, his government was unable to
survive.

The Tam-
worth
Manifesto,
1834

Tories into
Conserva-
tives

Peel's
second
ministry,
1841-6

The Conservatives won a good majority in the elections
of 1841, and Peel became Prime Minister for the second
time. This time he had power as well as office, and his
ministry, which lasted till 1846, was one of the most important in the nineteenth century. Peel was a big red-haired
man whose energy was almost inexhaustible. In office he
often worked sixteen hours a day, and he had a mind which

Wellington and Peel in 1844
From a portrait by Winterhalter.

could readily master the complicated business of government. Twice, though he had a Chancellor of the Exchequer, he introduced the Budget himself. The first time, in 1842, he took the House by storm in a speech lasting nearly four hours, and even the Opposition found little to criticize. It was perhaps his great intellectual superiority that was responsible for his chief fault. In public—though not among his friends and family—he seemed reserved and awkward. George IV, annoyed by his manner, once said to him, 'Damn you, sir, don't stand there pawing the air, put your hands in your pockets.' Peel, nettled, promptly replied, 'Damn you, sir, I have no pockets.' Queen Victoria at first described him as a 'cold odd man', though later she came to admire him. Wellington summed up the situation with his usual terseness, saying, 'I have no small-talk and Peel has no manners.'

Economic policy

Peel's main effort was in financial affairs. He sorted out the problems left by the Whigs, who had for some years failed to secure enough revenue to balance the Budget. His master policy was to reintroduce Income Tax (sevenpence in the pound on incomes over £150 a year) and at the same time to simplify and reduce the various Customs and Excise duties. By the time he resigned, he had cut by half the number of articles that paid duty, yet the greater volume of trade brought in an increased revenue from those duties which remained. In 1844, to secure a stable currency, he also passed an Act to limit the notes issued by the Bank of England and other banks—which were becoming increasingly important with the rapid development of commerce and industry. So successful were his financial measures that he was able to make a considerable reduction in the burden of the National Debt. All told, his efficient administration greatly encouraged trade. His reduction of duties, however, including those on corn, soon made some Conservatives fearful for the general principle of 'protecting' home agriculture by Corn Laws—a principle which the party was pledged to preserve.

Reintroduction of Income Tax, 1842

Approach to Free Trade—mass reduction of duties

Bank Charter Act, 1844

The question of the Corn Laws

The crisis of Peel's government came in 1846. In that year, despite his previously expressed views and the fact that his party was the stronghold of the agricultural interest, Peel decided to repeal the Corn Laws. He had taken office as a supporter of these laws. What made him change his mind?

There were two reasons. After 1841 the success of the Anti-Corn-Law League and the strength of Cobden's arguments gradually converted Peel. The Corn Laws, by taxing imports of foreign corn, were intended to keep the price of home-grown grain high in order that British agriculture might thrive. Though a flourishing agriculture was highly important to the nation, the Laws could also be regarded as a tax on the necessities of the whole community, and in particular of the great new industrial classes, for the benefit of one section of the community—the landed classes. As Britain became more and more industrial, with an ever greater proportion of her people gathered in towns away from any direct connection with agriculture, it became more and more difficult to resist the demand for repeal. Moreover, as Cobden pointed out, with cheaper food the level of industrial wages could be kept low enough for British manufacturers to produce cheaply and so sell their goods in great quantities abroad. To Peel, a student of economics and the son of a manufacturer, this was a particularly convincing argument. His belief in Free Trade, already very strong as far as manufactured goods and raw materials were concerned, thus began to extend to foodstuffs as well. *Reasons for Peel's change of mind*

There was, however, a more immediate cause for repeal in 1846 that finally tipped the scale in Peel's mind. He had long been worried by events in Ireland. Catholic emancipation had not solved the Irish problem, and O'Connell had immediately launched a campaign for the repeal of the Union. Peel managed to hold this in check by various measures, including the banning of the Irish leader's meetings. But in 1845 a new and unexpected crisis broke in Ireland—a terrible famine. Following a disastrously wet summer, three-quarters of the potato crop—the staple food of the Irish peasant—was destroyed by blight in that year. The situation was made much worse by the recent growth in the Irish population. In the thirty years since 1815 the *The Irish potato famine, 1845* population had increased from six million to eight and a half million with no corresponding increase in food production. For over a hundred years there had been no serious famine. Now that one had arrived, there was no plan to deal with it. The Irish landlords, among the worst of their class in Europe, continued to export their corn, though in certain cases hunger was staved off by private charity. Faced by the prospect of mass starvation among the peasantry, Peel decided that the government must take action. He imported maize from America and organized relief works. He also decided that the corn duties must be lowered immediately to encourage the import of corn from the Continent—for there had been a poor harvest in England as well.

The last measure was political dynamite, and Peel found himself opposed by several members of his own Cabinet. Still less did the rank-and-file of the Conservatives see the need for their own party to take the lead in jettisoning their cherished Corn Laws. Peel accordingly offered to resign in favour of a Whig government which would repeal the Laws —only to find that Russell, now the Whig leader, could not form a satisfactory ministry. So Peel continued in office, with the support of nearly all his old ministers, and himself undertook the task of repeal. His proposal, supported now by nearly all the best brains in his party, was that the corn duties should be reduced forthwith, and in three years totally abolished. At once it became clear that he would not be able to carry with him the whole of his party. The rift between the reforming Conservatives and the old-style Tories quickly reappeared, and on all sides the landed families hotly protested against a policy that pandered to the industrial areas.

This opposition within his own party might not have mattered so much to Peel had the Tory rank-and-file not found a brilliant spokesman in Benjamin Disraeli, to whom Peel had refused office in 1841. Disraeli, Jewish by descent but not by religion, had little in common with the Protectionists (the Conservatives who opposed repeal) but they applauded with great gusto his slashing attacks on Peel.

Peel proposes repeal of Corn Laws

Opposition within Conservative party

Disraeli

Their nominal leader in the Commons was Lord George Bentinck, a well-known figure on the Turf, who had rarely spoken before. Prompted by the feeling that Peel had 'sold' the party by adopting the policy of its opponents, he surprised and bored everyone on the night of the crucial vote for repeal by rising at midnight and speaking for three hours. His speech, however, showed a remarkable command of the subject, and thereafter he continued to devote his whole energies to attacking Peel—so much so that he worried himself into an early grave. Nevertheless, the real leader of the opposition to Peel in the Commons was Disraeli, whose motive must remain a matter of opinion. Was it genuine dislike of a measure which in his opinion had betrayed the interests of the landed classes— or was it spite and the promptings of ambition? *Bentinck*

Though the Protectionists made up the majority of the Conservative party in the Commons they were unable to stop the passage of repeal, for over these proposals Peel had the support of the Whigs. The Protectionists, however, were now determined to oust Peel in order to teach him the lesson of loyalty to party doctrines. On the night that the repeal of the Corn Laws went through the Lords, they therefore united with the Whigs in the Commons to defeat a Coercion Bill (suspending trial by jury, etc.) for Ireland —a policy they would normally have supported. Peel then resigned and the Whigs under Russell took over. *Repeal of Corn Laws, and defeat of Peel over Coercion Bill, 1846*

What were the effects of Corn Law repeal? It reduced the price of bread, though not by a large margin. The years of very high prices disappeared. It removed the last great obstacle to Free Trade, which in the particular conditions of the third quarter of the nineteenth century brought Britain great commercial prosperity. It did not immediately ruin British farming in accordance with the Protectionists' prophecies; not until the opening up of the virgin lands of Australia and North America in the fourth quarter of the nineteenth century was there enough spare foreign corn to swamp the British market. *Results of repeal*

As far as Ireland was concerned, repeal did not cure that country's ills. It is doubtful if anything proposed at the *Effect on Ireland* time could have done. Large sums of money were spent by the government on Irish relief, but this was by no means effective. At one time in 1847 three million people were supported from public funds, but even so there were many deaths from starvation and exposure. In the next fifteen years over two million Irish folk emigrated, mainly to the U.S.A., and by 1871 Ireland's population had fallen to five and a half million. Emigration was probably the only solution to Ireland's maladies. But the conditions in which the emigration was carried out, like those which the emigrants left behind them, were appalling, and left a long legacy of ill-will to Britain among the Irish Americans.

Justification of Peel's policy
On the whole, it is difficult to dispute the wisdom of Peel's measure. Free trade suits a country with a large and vigorous manufacture but without all the necessary raw materials, and for the rest of the century Britain gained greatly from it. In fact not even the Protectionists tried to reintroduce Protection—which Disraeli was soon referring to as 'not only dead but damned'. Admittedly the method that Peel used was open to criticism. To get the measure through he was prepared to wreck his party, with the result that the Whigs came into office and remained there (sometimes in coalition with Peelites) for all but two of the next twenty-eight years. On the other hand, a Prime Minister must in the last resort decide an issue on national and not on party lines. Moreover, the landed classes were too narrow a basis for any large party in Britain in the nineteenth century. Peel could see this but the Protectionists could not. 'Against stupidity even the gods fight in vain.'

Before his resignation Peel turned on the Protectionists. He paid a deliberate tribute to Cobden, their most-hated enemy, and he gave vent to his feelings about them in these words: 'To be . . . the tool of a party—that is to say to adopt the opinions of men who have not access to your knowledge, and could not profit by it if they had, who spend their time in eating and drinking, hunting and shooting, gambling, horse-racing and so forth—would be an odious servitude to which I never will submit.' Four years later, in 1850, Peel died as the result of a fall from his horse—'the greatest statesman of his time', as he was described in *The Times*. Of his followers, Aberdeen and Gladstone later became Prime Ministers.

Death of
Peel, 1850

Children Working in a Coal Mine

From a print of the early 1840s. Note the 'trapper' on the right.

During the 'forties a number of other reforming measures were carried in Parliament, thanks more to the work of private individuals than to any impulse from government, Whig or Tory. In 1842 a Commission, set up largely as a result of Ashley's agitation, published its report on female and child labour in the mines. It profoundly shocked the country. The Commissioners revealed that the employment underground of children as young as seven was common and that in some pits children were employed at six or even five. The smallest often worked as 'trappers', operating the trap doors that controlled the ventilation of the mine. On them, therefore, depended the safety of the miners. Many of these trappers had to sit for sixteen hours a day in darkness, damp and solitude. In some districts little girls were harnessed to trucks by a girdle and chain and made to drag the coal to the bottom of the shaft, whence women

Other
reforms
of the
'forties

The Mines
Act, 1842—
no female
or child
labour in
mines
carried it in great baskets up ladders to the surface. As a result of these and other disclosures Ashley obtained the passing of an Act prohibiting the employment of all female labour and of boys under ten in the mines. Inspectors were appointed to see that the new law was carried out.

Further
Factory
Acts
With this vitally important measure in force, Ashley then concentrated again on factory reform. In 1843 the government, spurred by his agitation, produced a factory bill. One of its clauses aimed to introduce compulsory education for factory children. This part was soon wrecked by that rivalry between Churchmen and Nonconformists which was the downfall of so many educational schemes in the nine-

1844
(12-hour day
for women
and young
persons)
teenth century. However, an Act was passed in 1844 which brought at least two improvements: the daily hours of the youngest children were reduced from nine to six and a half, and for the first time grown women were given the protection of a 'twelve-hour day'. This did not satisfy Ashley, who as leader of the 'Ten Hours Movement' went on campaigning for a maximum ten-hour day for women and young people. (It would have been quite against the economic doctrines of the time to seek such protection for men, who were supposed to be capable of looking after themselves; but in point of fact running a cotton-mill by male labour alone would have been too costly, and the men therefore hoped to benefit from whatever restrictions in hours were laid down for the women.)

1847
(10-hour day
for women
and young
people)
Three years more of campaigning eventually resulted in the 'Ten Hours' Act of 1847, which limited the labour of women and of young people aged thirteen to eighteen in the textile factories to ten hours a day. It was piloted through the Commons not by Ashley, who had temporarily ceased to be an M.P., but by his fellow-campaigner John Fielden, the great cotton manufacturer of Todmorden who had agitated against the new Poor Law. Unfortunately the benefit which the men had hoped for did not immediately come about; many employers, while limiting the work of any one woman or young person to ten hours, began to 'stagger' this labour throughout a fifteen- or sixteen-hour day, for the whole of which time the men were still required

to work. This practice was stopped by a further Act in 1850, which laid down that all female and child labour must be worked within the period 6 a.m.–6 p.m. So the men, too, at last got indirect protection. To secure this, however, Ashley had to agree to a concession to the employers which was also embodied in the Act—that the '10-hour day' laid down in 1847 should be increased to a 10½-hour day.

1850 (10½-hour day, all between 6 a.m. and 6 p.m.)

In 1848 Parliament approached another field in which reforms were urgently needed, when it passed the first Public Health Act. This was largely the work of the Benthamite Radical, Edwin Chadwick, who had been one of the original Poor Law Commissioners. Chadwick was a great believer in efficiency and was horrified by the bad conditions and the administrative chaos in the towns. The Act set up a central Board of Health, of which both Ashley

Public Health Act, 1848

Chadwick

A Refuge for the Destitute, 1841

At this 'Refuge for the Destitute and Houseless Poor', in the heart of London, here were 9,000 applicants for a night's shelter within twelve months. Soap and water, half a pound of bread, and clean straw were provided for each shelterer.

and Chadwick were members, and together they began the long-delayed attack on bad sanitation and housing. Unfortunately they were far from tactful, and went at a faster pace than opinion would then accept. At any rate, in his efforts to set up local boards of health (one of the main objects of the Act) and to get healthier water supplies, sewage systems, cemeteries and the like, Chadwick, who was the main executive officer of the Board, ran up against strenuous opposition. This came not only from owners of threatened property but also from the municipalities, the justices of the peace, and the various 'improvement commissions' which existed in the towns, and which in many cases were doing good work along their own lines. After only six years of the Board's activity a public outcry against its 'interference' secured the resignation of Chadwick and a reduction in its very limited powers.

Four years later the same forces of public opinion swept it away entirely. A further ten years were then needed, and another great cholera outbreak in 1865-6, before the central government again attempted any major inroad into local 'freedom' in these matters. The whole story of the struggle to secure measures for the protection of the public health is thus a striking example of the main difficulty which confronted reformers in all spheres during the mid-nineteenth century—the prevailing belief that State direction in economic and social matters could only be achieved at the cost not only of liberty but also of efficiency.

Opposition to central Board of Health

The Board disbanded, 1858

CHAPTER TWENTY-ONE

PALMERSTON AND BRITISH FOREIGN POLICY 1830–1851

1. *Belgium and the Eastern Question*

FOR sixteen of the twenty-one years between 1830 and 1851 the position of Foreign Secretary was held by the same man—Viscount Palmerston. This long spell in office enabled Palmerston to play the main part in shaping British foreign policy during this period.

1830–51 Foreign Secretary.

Born in 1784, Palmerston was heir to a title in the peerage of Ireland. At fifteen he left Harrow for Edinburgh University, before passing on to Cambridge. Edinburgh was an unusual choice for the son of a nobleman. The subjects taught there included new studies, such as Economics, which were frowned on by those who thought that education should be limited to Christianity and the Classics. These years at Edinburgh helped to implant in Palmerston a number of liberal opinions.

Palmerston, 1784–1865 Education

After succeeding to his father's title at the age of eighteen, Palmerston decided to take up politics. As an Irish peer he was not a member of the House of Lords, so in 1807 he entered the Commons by way of a 'pocket borough'. His ability and influential connections soon brought him office, and from 1809 to 1828 he served the various Tory governments as Secretary-at-War—a junior post concerned with the finance of the Army. During this time he was more prominent as a man of fashion than as a politician. One of the more liberal Tories and a supporter of Canning, he disliked the 'pigtails' and eventually resigned with Huskisson from the Duke of Wellington's government after a dispute over a minor piece of parliamentary reform. During the next year he travelled and became a keen student of

Tory Secretary-at-War, 1809–28

foreign affairs. When the Whigs came into power later in

Whig
Foreign
Secretary,
1830

1830, the Prime Minister, Grey, being anxious to secure the
help of the more liberal Tories, accordingly offered Palmerston the Foreign Secretaryship. From this time onward the
ex-Tory was a major figure in the camp of the Whigs.

Reasons for
Palmer-
ston's
successes

As Foreign Secretary, Palmerston was to enjoy many
successes. These were possible because from the defeat of
France in 1815 to the unification of Germany in 1871 there
was no one predominant military power on the Continent,
and because Britain had unique industrial resources and
an unchallengeable navy. But they were also due to
Palmerston's own courage, determination and ability. A
man of great vigour and directness, he never minced his

Palmer-
ston's
character

words—'Lord Pumicestone' was one of his nicknames.
Over one despatch from a diplomat abroad he wrote
'Goose! Goose! Goose!'—his opinion of the author. To
foreign statesmen he was equally blunt, and he caused much
resentment among those of whom he disapproved. Louis
Philippe, King of France, finally described him as the
'enemy of my house', and Metternich, the Austrian
Chancellor, as the 'son of the devil'. In England, too, he
was many times attacked for his lack of tact and his light-
hearted methods. Yet he was very far from being a fool,
worked extremely hard when in office, and usually got what
he wanted.

'Pam', as he was known, had another great asset—his
immense popularity among ordinary Englishmen. England
was still a lord-loving country, and Palmerston was just
the type of jovial, high-spirited, sporting peer whom few
except intellectuals could dislike. Handsome and well-
built, he cut a dashing figure in society with his top hat
tilted slightly backwards and a flower in his buttonhole—
'Cupid' was another of his nicknames. He was a great
eater and a great horseman, his racing colours being seen
on most English courses. He was considerate to the less
fortunate. To his tenants, especially in Ireland, he was a
generous landlord, and he was very active in the suppression
of the slave-trade. He took considerable trouble to enlist
the support of the British Press. The popularity he gained in

'Susannah and the Elders'

From a sketch by J. Doyle. Queen Victoria riding in 1837—between Lord Melbourne (Prime Minister) and Lord Palmerston. The title refers to a well-known incident in the Bible.

these ways enabled him more than once to carry out policies distasteful to many of his colleagues in the government.

At the beginning of 1830 the map of Europe was that laid down by the Vienna settlement of 1814–15. The long-established dynasties—the Bourbons, the Habsburgs, the Romanoffs—still held sway. Like Humpty-dumpty, the ruling families of Europe had taken a great fall, but, unlike Humpty-dumpty, they had managed to put themselves together again. Now they were extremely anxious not to suffer another tumble. Having seen what followed from royal weakness in the early days of the French Revolution, they withheld any share of government from their peoples and strove to stifle opposition at birth—or preferably before birth. Compared with their despotisms, even the unreformed

Europe in 1830

government of Britain shone out as a model of progress and freedom.

Not all the despotic rulers, however, sat securely on their thrones. In France the Bourbons, reimposed by the allied armies in 1815, got little support from the nation. They pursued much the same old policies, having in exile 'learnt nothing and forgotten nothing'. Not surprisingly, then, in July 1830 came another revolution in Paris, and Charles X, the Bourbon king, was chased out. Here was a challenge to the Vienna settlement. Were the French on the warpath once more? Would 1830, like 1789, lead to a revolutionary struggle throughout Europe? The despots were alarmed, especially when popular risings followed in Belgium, Poland, Italy and Germany. Their fears, however, on this occasion proved groundless. France proclaimed not a republic but a constitutional (or limited) monarchy on the pattern of Britain. Louis Philippe, of the Orleanist or younger branch of the French royal family, became king. His régime quickly earned British support, which Palmerston continued when he came into office—and did not withdraw until many years later.

The country that we now call Belgium presented a trickier problem. A part of the Netherlands ruled in the seventeenth century by Spain and in the eighteenth by Austria, it had been united with Holland under the rule of the Dutch monarch by the Vienna settlement. This was in order to form a stronger state on the boundaries of France. The Belgians, however, differed in religion and language from the majority of their new masters, and they resented being ruled, as they considered, in the interests of the Dutch. When they rose in revolt in 1830 they became an international problem. On the one hand, the despots wanted to help the Dutch king against the rebels; on the other, Louis Philippe was pressed by some of his subjects to fish in troubled waters and bring Belgium under the control of France. In this situation Palmerston thought the best solution would be complete independence for Belgium under a constitutional monarchy. He secured Louis Philippe's support for this proposal, and made sure that the king of

The Revolution in Paris, July 1830

Other revolutions follow

King Louis Philippe

—supported by Palmerston

The Belgian question, 1830–39

Palmerston's solution

the new state was a German princeling (Leopold of Saxe-Coburg-Gotha) and not one of Louis Philippe's sons. Together, British and French then protected Belgium from a Dutch attack. After some years the independence of Belgium was finally recognized in 1839 by all parties, including the Dutch, and the neutrality of the new country was guaranteed by the Great Powers.[1]

Belgian independence

Belgium was the most successful example of Palmerston's policy of supporting, where he considered it possible, the setting up of constitutional monarchies abroad. A follower of Canning in this respect, he was thus generally popular with nationalists and liberals on the Continent, but not with despotic rulers. Other instances of his support for the constitutional side were soon to be seen in both Spain and Portugal, where joint British and French action helped to defeat the 'absolutist' parties in civil wars. Elsewhere in Europe, however, Palmerston usually confined his support of the liberals to mere words of encouragement. The liberals and constitutionalists who had risen in 1830 in Italy and Poland he left, unaided, to the tender mercies of Austria and Russia—for these two powers were not within such easy reach of the British fleet, nor did events in their territories so directly affect British interests.

Palmerston supports constitutional parties in Spain and Portugal

Apart from the quarrel between despot and liberal in Europe, Palmerston's main concern during the 'thirties was with the Turkish Empire. In name this empire still extended from the Persian Gulf to Morocco and from Egypt to the southern borders of Austria. But in fact its ruler the Sultan, whose capital was Constantinople, had little control over the outlying provinces, and even in the centre the great nobles often disregarded his orders. In 1808 Mahmud II had become Sultan. He was an energetic and in some ways an enlightened ruler. He reduced many of the rebellious beys and pashas to obedience, and introduced a number of Western reforms in the face of considerable

The Eastern Question: The Turkish Empire

Mahmud II

---

[1] Three-quarters of a century later, in 1914, Germany was to violate this neutrality by attacking France through Belgium, and the German Chancellor was to refer to the guarantee treaty as 'a piece of paper'! ('scrap' in the contemporary British translation).

opposition—sanitary reform, for instance, was resisted on the ground that disease was the will of God and ought not to be prevented.

Revolt of
Mehemet
Ali of
Egypt

Mahmud's vigorous policy unfortunately brought him face to face with the strongest of his vassals, Mehemet Ali, the Pasha or Turkish viceroy of Egypt. Mehemet Ali had built up an efficient army and navy, trained mainly by French officers, and had extended his dominions far south into the Sudan. He had also given powerful but finally unavailing help to the Sultan against the Greeks in their war of independence; and at Navarino he had lost his fleet on the Sultan's behalf. When, after all this, he was denied the promised reward for his services, on the ground that they had not been successful, he rebelled and sent his armies north. Very soon they had overrun Syria and the Sultan was at the mercy of his victorious vassal. In despair, the Turkish ruler looked for help to Russia, Turkey's traditional foe; for, as one of his advisers said, 'A drowning man in his despair clings to a serpent.' Russian ships and troops then arrived at Constantinople and the Sultan was saved. He had, however, to assign the government of Syria and Palestine to Mehemet Ali and—as the price of her help—to give Russia important rights of control over the Dardanelles. By a secret clause of the Treaty of Unkiar-Skelessi Turkey agreed to close these straits to foreign warships whenever Russia demanded.

Turks
secure
Russian
help

Treaty of
Unkiar-
Skelessi,
1833

Palmerston
and Russia

The clause was soon revealed, and of course alarmed Palmerston. To him, as to the younger Pitt before him, the danger of expansion by Russia seemed serious. She had already conquered vast stretches of Asia and had established herself on the northern shores of the Black Sea. Control of the Dardanelles would now enable her to extend her southward thrust still farther. This would threaten British control of the Mediterranean and—if carried far enough—Britain's possessions in India. These fears, together with dislike of Russia's despotic government, explain the increasing hostility which Palmerston and Britain now showed towards Russia.

Renewed
war between
Turkey and
Mehemet
Ali, 1839

In 1839 a new crisis broke when once more the Sultan

and Mehemet Ali came to blows. Again Mehemet triumphed, but the Sultan died before news of the disaster reached him. His successor was an ineffective youth. This was Russia's as well as Mehemet's opportunity—so to foil Russia Palmerston decided to bolster up the Turkish Empire. He also wished to curb Mehemet Ali, who was pro-French, and through whom the French were hoping to extend their own influence in the Near East. Palmerston's policy meant disregarding a threat from France to back up Mehemet Ali, and to Melbourne he gaily wrote: 'If France begins a war, Mehemet Ali will just be chucked into the Nile.' Backed by Austria, he then coolly ordered the Egyptian ruler to abandon his conquests. Mehemet of course refused, the British navy with Austrian support promptly went into action, and France—as Palmerston had anticipated—climbed down and did not intervene. Within a few weeks Mehemet Ali was forced to acknowledge defeat (1840) and in future his rule was confined to Egypt. A new international agreement with Turkey then closed the Bosphorus and Dardanelles to the warships of all foreign powers during peacetime, thus ending the privileged position which Russia had acquired eight years earlier. Once more Palmerston had triumphed all along the line!

Palmerston supports Turks, France Mehemet Ali

Defeat of Mehemet Ali, 1840

The Straits Convention, 1841

Shortly after this the Conservatives under Peel took over from the Whigs and Palmerston left office. He was succeeded as Foreign Secretary by the Earl of Aberdeen, a cultured and pacifically-minded nobleman. During Aberdeen's years in office two disputes about the Canadian–U.S.A. border came to a head, one over the boundary in the extreme east, between New Brunswick and Maine, and the other over the division of the Oregon territory in the far west. The latter had been for some time jointly administered by both countries. Agitators in the U.S.A. were now claiming all of it, with the cry of 'Fifty-four forty or fight.'[1] Both disputes were settled peacefully, the first by the Ashburton Treaty of 1842, the second by the Oregon Treaty of 1846. This latter treaty defined the boundary in the far west as the

Aberdeen, Foreign Secretary, 1841-6

The Maine and Oregon disputes

---

[1] i.e. they claimed that the U.S.A. should control the territory up to the line of latitude 54° 40′ N.

49th parallel, along which it already ran from the Great Lakes to the Rockies, except that Vancouver Island was to be British. Though this was a great deal less than the American claim, Palmerston denounced the settlement, considering that Peel and Aberdeen had made too many concessions. However, it was fortunate in the long run that they rather than the belligerent 'Pam' were in office at this time, for the agreements paved the way to better relations with the U.S.A.—whose support has been so vital to Britain during the present century.

2. *The Revolutions of 1848 and the Dismissal of Palmerston*

Palmerston Foreign Secretary again, 1846–51

In 1846 the fall of Peel following the repeal of the Corn Laws brought the Whigs back to office. Lord John Russell, of Reform Bill fame, became Prime Minister, and Palmerston returned to the Foreign Office. Palmerston in fact now shone out as the most prominent member of the government, for Russell, 'a little fellow not weighing above eight stone', lacked his colleague's energy and forcefulness. Moreover, interest in domestic politics waned after 1846 and Britain paid more attention to events abroad. With Russell's schemes of further parliamentary reform coming to nothing, Palmerston increasingly occupied the limelight. He himself had never been greatly interested in domestic affairs, though he was a generous champion of Factory Acts for women and children. He was lukewarm about any further parliamentary reform, and in later years, when, as Prime Minister, he was asked what reforms he wished to introduce, he replied: 'Oh, there is really nothing to be done. We cannot go on adding to the Statute Book *ad infinitum*.'

The revolutions of 1848

In 1848 a storm broke over Europe. Revolution, starting in Paris in February, swept across the Continent. It was like 1830, only on a greater scale. Louis Philippe, 'the citizen king', too drab and unspectacular for French taste, was

France becomes a republic

expelled and a republic proclaimed for the second time in French history. Within a short time the President of the Republic was Louis Napoleon Bonaparte, nephew of the great Emperor.

As in 1830, the rising in France was a signal to the discontented throughout Europe. In Germany the nationalists and liberals were everywhere active, and obtained their first demands with little bloodshed. Most of the thirty or more rulers who controlled Germany granted constitutions to their subjects, and a National Assembly with delegates from all over Germany was set up at Frankfurt to pave the way to complete German unification. Unfortunately it had more than its fair share of professors, lawyers and writers, and was better at talking than acting; moreover, powerful forces in Prussia, Austria and Russia were soon working against it. *Revolution in Germany* *The Frankfurt National Assembly*

The crux of the situation lay in the Austrian Empire, ruled by the Habsburgs. Their chancellor was Count Metternich, the main architect of the system of repression that the despots had striven to maintain in Europe since 1815. Within a fortnight of the revolution in Paris, a popular rising in Vienna compelled him to flee—smuggled out, it is said, in a laundry cart. As if it were not enough that the Emperor had to promise a constitution to the Austrians, the subject peoples of the Habsburg Empire also rose in revolt to claim complete or partial independence—the Hungarians, the Italians of Northern Italy, and the Czechs. It seemed that Metternich's long-mouldering system had at last collapsed. *Revolution in the Austrian Empire* *Flight of Metternich*

The Italians were at first successful. From Milan and Venice, the capitals of the Austrian-ruled provinces of Lombardy and Venetia, they drove out the Austrian garrisons. This induced the strongest native Italian ruler, the King of Sardinia, who had granted a constitution to his people, to help his fellow Italians. He therefore invaded the Austrian provinces. This struggle for freedom was followed with the greatest sympathy in Britain, and Palmerston tried to negotiate for a withdrawal of the Austrians from North Italy and the establishment of a native North Italian kingdom under the King of Sardinia. His efforts were in vain. At Custozza the Austrians inflicted a heavy defeat on the Sardinian king, and soon they were able to reconquer all their dominions in Northern Italy. *The Italians* *Palmerston against Austrian rule in N. Italy* *The Italian movements fail*

The
Hungarians

Elsewhere, too, in the Austrian Empire the hopes of the revolutionaries were dashed. The Czechs were quickly crushed, and the Croats began to fight against the Hungarians. In Austria itself, a new emperor, Francis Joseph, consequently soon felt strong enough to cancel many of the concessions that had been granted. Hungary proved the toughest nut to crack. Here the Hungarians, under their

Kossuth

leader Kossuth, eventually proclaimed complete independence and by June 1849 were in control of their country. Their triumph did not last long. The Russian Tsar Nicholas I, who hated the idea of rebellion by subject peoples, eagerly answered Francis Joseph's appeal for help.

Russia
helps
Austria
to suppress
Hungary

In vain Palmerston protested against the intervention. Russian, Croat and Austrian troops converged on Hungary, and within a few months all resistance was at an end. Kossuth was able to escape to Turkey, whence Austria and Russia at once demanded his surrender, but backed by Palmerston the Turks refused. Later, the Hungarian leader came as an exile to Britain—and Palmerston ignored the protests of Austria and his own colleagues by entertaining him.

Collapse
of revolu-
tionary
movement
in Germany

With her own house once more under control, Austria soon threw her influence into re-establishing the old régime in Germany as well. Well aware of the attitude of Austria and Russia, and himself disliking anything of revolutionary origin, the King of Prussia refused the crown of a united Germany offered him by the Frankfurt National Assembly, and after that the Assembly soon collapsed. This complete triumph of the despots disappointed people in Britain, who were especially angered by the harsh way in which the Austrians had put down the risings in Hungary and Italy. In 1850 one of the chief Austrian commanders responsible,

General
'Hyena'

General Haynau, came to London, where he was soon known as 'Hyena'. He was mobbed and chased down a street by the workmen of Barclay's Brewery. Palmerston, who remarked privately that the general deserved a great deal worse, refused more than a perfunctory apology to Austria, and this he gave only on the insistence of Russell and Queen Victoria.

Palmerston was by this time very unpopular with the Court. In 1840 the Queen had married Prince Albert of Saxe-Coburg-Gotha, a German of irreproachable morals and some talents. Being connected with the royal families of Europe, the queen and her husband disliked Palmerston's brusque methods of dealing with the despots, and they also strongly disapproved of his habit of acting without consulting others—especially themselves. In 1850 the hopes of Palmerston's enemies rose sharply, for he treated the Greek government in a particularly high-handed way. He had had difficulties with the Greeks about non-payment of debts, and he now seized on an incident to teach them a lesson. Don Pacifico, a somewhat shady Portuguese Jew born at Gibraltar and only doubtfully a British subject, put in an exaggerated claim to the Greeks for loss of property during riots at Athens; when the Greeks refused to accept it, Palmerston went to the length of sending a fleet to Athens to back up Pacifico. This alarmed peace-lovers in England, and Cobden and Bright launched a great attack in Parliament on the Foreign Secretary. But by a brilliant speech in the Commons that started at 10 p.m. and lasted over four hours, Palmerston justified his policy to the satisfaction of the House. He ended with words which were long remembered: 'As the Roman, in days of old, held himself free from indignity when he could say *"Civis Romanus sum"*, so also a British subject, in whatever land he may be, shall feel confident that the watchful eye and the strong arm of England will protect him against injustice and wrong.'

If the 'Don Pacifico' incident shows Palmerston in some respects at his worst, his unceasing efforts to wipe out the slave-trade show him at his best. When the Portuguese refused to co-operate, he declared all Portuguese slave-ships to be pirates and the British Navy swept them from the seas. The U.S.A. could not be dealt with in so lordly a fashion, and the Americans obstructed for many years every attempt to bring the dreadful traffic to an end. But in 1850 Palmerston had another success when he induced Brazil to take no further part in the trade. Looking back later over

Marginal notes:
Marriage of Queen Victoria, 1840

Court opposition to Palmerston

The 'Don Pacifico' incident, 1850

Palmerston and the slave-trade

Brazil

his political life, this struck Palmerston as the action that gave him the 'greatest and purest pleasure'.

The Eastern Question again

During this second period of office Palmerston continued to keep a watchful eye over the Near East, for the Russian threat to Turkey remained a pressing problem. The Tsar had suggested to Aberdeen that Turkey was 'a sick man' and might eventually be partitioned, but Palmerston rejected this idea and continued to bolster up the Turks. This clash of Russian and British policies was soon to lead to the Crimean War.

Dismissal of Palmerston, 1851

Before this, however, Palmerston's enemies had at last secured his dismissal. In 1851 Louis Napoleon Bonaparte, whose term of office as President of the new French Republic was shortly due to expire, carried out a *coup d'état* to prolong his power. Palmerston welcomed this action without consulting either the Crown or the rest of the Cabinet— and Russell was stirred to dismiss him. But within three weeks Palmerston had his revenge. He attacked the government on another issue in the House of Commons and secured a majority against the ministers, with the result that Russell resigned (1852). As Palmerston wrote to his brother: 'I have had my tit-for-tat with John Russell, and I turned him out on Friday last.'

Defeat of Russell

Palmerston's later career, 1852–65

Within less than a year Palmerston was in office again, though this time only as Home Secretary. The government was a coalition of Whigs and Peelites, with Aberdeen as Prime Minister. It first of all blundered into the Crimean War, and then conducted it badly. The call went up for a strong man to succeed Aberdeen, clear up the muddle and make victory possible. The man was at hand. In 1855, at the age of seventy, Palmerston became Prime Minister—a position which he was to occupy, with only one brief five-month intermission, for the remaining ten years of his life.

CHAPTER TWENTY-TWO

THE GROWTH OF EMPIRE

1. North America, Australasia, South Africa

IN 1783 the newly-won independence of the thirteen American colonies seemed to spell the end of the British Empire. Britain had lost by far the most important part of her colonial territory and nearly all her settlers overseas. She still controlled several West Indian islands, various points in West Africa and Australia, and large stretches of India and North America, but all these together, in their existing state of development, seemed little compared with what had been lost. Yet a hundred years later Britain was the greatest imperial power in the world, controlling not only territories in which a few British officials ruled an alien people but also vast lands settled by millions of folk from British homes.

This rapid recovery began in the early nineteenth century. It was made possible by, among other things, the earlier work of explorers like Cook, the rising rate of emigration after Waterloo, and the British command of the seas, unchallenged after Trafalgar. This last point had special importance. During the Napoleonic wars, supremacy at sea brought Britain certain territories, such as Malta and Cape Colony, which had immense value as bases or supply centres for the Navy. The possession of these enabled Britain not only to maintain her Empire but eventually to extend it still further.

After the conclusion of peace in 1815 the tide of emigration from the United Kingdom began to flow with increasing strength. Over the first fifteen years the average total of emigrants was not great. Then the figures soared. In 1832 there were more than 100,000 emigrants, and after the potato failure of 1846 the average number for the next three years was 250,000. The discovery of gold in California (1849) and in Australia (1851) provided a further reason to venture overseas, and for 1850–54 the annual average was no less than 325,000.

A great number of these folk, especially in the years immediately after 1846, were Irish. In the early part of the century nearly all went to North America, and most of them to the U.S.A. A considerable number, however, did settle in British North America—the population of which increased between 1815 and 1865 from half a million to three and a half million. Of those who made this latter choice, a high proportion came from Ulster and western Scotland. There can still be seen on the Scottish west coast ruined villages whose entire population departed to find a better life on the far side of the Atlantic. By the middle of the century considerable numbers were also going to Australasia.

British North America, then, was the part of the Empire to attract most settlers in the generation after Waterloo. The Peace of Ghent which concluded the hostilities of 1812–14 between Britain and the U.S.A. left the boundaries of British North America unchanged. Thus it still consisted of six colonies, each quite distinct in government and way of life—Newfoundland, Nova Scotia, New Brunswick, Prince Edward Island, Lower Canada (the modern Quebec, mainly inhabited by settlers of French descent) and Upper Canada (the modern Ontario, mainly inhabited by the Loyalists who had left the newly formed U.S.A.). All these colonies were but thinly populated, and to the north and west of the Canadas there lay a great hinterland, known among white men only by the fur traders, and much of it unexplored even by them. The two great rivals of the fur trade were the North West Company operating from Montreal, and the Hudson's Bay Company operating from Fort York. After 1821 the Hudson's Bay Company, having forced its rival to amalgamate with it, reigned supreme in both north and west, controlling trade and administration alike.

British
North
America

Some years before this, Alexander Mackenzie, one of the

Exploration:
Mackenzie

greatest of Canadian explorers, had found the boundaries
of the continent both in the north and west. In 1789 he had
traced northwards the course of the river that now bears

'The Last of England'

From the famous picture by Ford Madox Brown, painted in 1852. Behind
the darkly brooding man and the sadly resigned woman with their baby
(concealed beneath the woman's cloak) may be seen other figures of the
emigrant ship—a child eating, an agitator cursing his country, a horrified
listener trying to restrain the agitator.

his name to its mouth in the Arctic Ocean—or, as he called
it 'The Frozen Ocean'. Later, working westward, he had
forced his way through the Rockies and at length reached

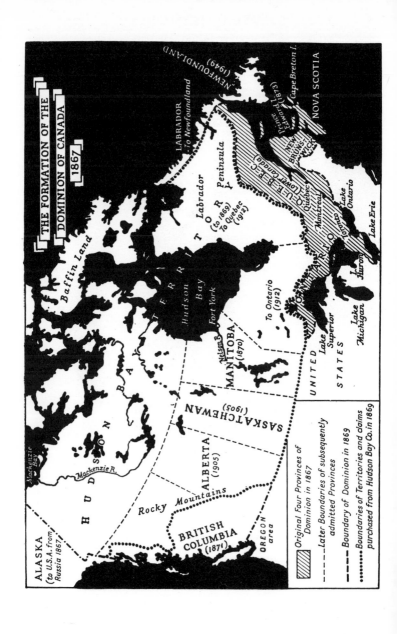

THE FORMATION OF THE
DOMINION OF CANADA
1867

ALASKA
(to U.S.A. from
Russia 1867)

Mackenzie Bay

Mackenzie R.

Baffin Land

H U D S O N   B A Y

T E R R I T O R Y

Rocky   Mountains

OREGON
area

BRITISH
COLUMBIA
(1871)

ALBERTA
(1905)

SASKATCHEWAN
(1905)

MANITOBA
(1870)

Nelson R.

Fort York

Hudson
Bay

To Ontario
(1912)

Labrador
(to 1869)
To Quebec
(1912)

LABRADOR
-to Newfoundland

Peninsula

NEWFOUNDLAND
(1949)

Cape Breton I.

NOVA SCOTIA

Prince Edward I. (1873)

NEW
BRUNS-
WICK

QUEBEC
(Lower Canada)

Quebec

Montreal

O N T A R I O
(Upper Canada)

Lake Ontario

Lake Erie

Lake Huron

Lake Michigan

Lake Superior

U N I T E D

S T A T E S

Original Four Provinces of
Dominion in 1867

Later Boundaries of subsequently
admitted Provinces

Boundary of Dominion in 1869

Boundaries of Territories and claims
purchased from Hudson Bay Co. in 1869

the Pacific north of Vancouver Island. Here he had daubed on the rocks words which were to become famous: 'Alexander Mackenzie, from Canada, by land, 22nd July 1793.' He was the first man to have crossed America north of Mexico from sea to sea. The Oregon Treaty of 1846 established the British claim to this part of the Pacific Coast, and here in 1858 was founded the colony of British Columbia, with which the earlier settlement on Vancouver Island was later joined.

During these years a change of great importance took place in the way British North America was governed— a change which marks the beginning of the development of the British Empire into the British Commonwealth of Nations. In 1837 rebellions took place in both Lower and Upper Canada, both provinces being dissatisfied for different reasons with their system of government. The risings were quickly put down, but the British government under Melbourne decided to send out Lord Durham of the Reform Bill as Governor-General to investigate matters. He and a few other Radicals, of whom the most important were Charles Buller and Gibbon Wakefield (both of whom accompanied him), were among the very few in Britain at this time interested in imperial affairs. The old idea of the Empire as a trading preserve for the mother country was breaking down with the advance of Free Trade, and the American War of Independence had convinced many that the colonies would inevitably demand independence. So there were plenty in Parliament (though by no means a majority) who thought at this period that the Empire was an unnecessary expense to Britain. They agreed with Disraeli that 'the wretched colonies' were 'millstones round our necks'.

Durham soon ran into trouble and resigned his position after five months. But his later report, published in 1839, was a masterly survey of the Canadian scene. He looked forward clearly to the eventual union of all the North American colonies, and suggested that as an immediate step the two Canadas should be combined into one province. This, however, was mainly to 'swamp' French influence in

Changes in government

Canadian rebellions, 1837

Lord Durham

The Durham Report, 1839

Lower Canada. He also proposed state-aided emigration and the construction of great railways.

The most important and the most radical reform that he suggested, however, was a greater measure of self-government for all the British North American colonies: in domestic affairs, at least, the wishes of their own representatives should be followed. Gradually the British government took this advice, and Lord Elgin was the first Governor-General of Canada to apply the new principles in full (1848). He chose his ministers from the majority in the Colonial Assembly (instead of from any source he pleased, as colonial governors normally did), and accepted measures passed by the Assembly even when he disagreed with them.

Responsible government, 1848

He also allowed his ministers to be responsible to the Assembly in the same way as British ministers are to Parliament, i.e. a hostile vote in the Assembly could bring about their resignation. By 1851 all the North American colonies except Newfoundland had attained this 'responsible' type of self-government.

Canadian railways

Meanwhile the railways were coming to Canada. The first line was opened in 1837, and the first great boom came in the 'fifties, when Stephenson's bridge was built across the St. Lawrence. Before long the railways were to open up for settlement the hinterland of the west and strengthen the links between the various colonies, with the result that

Canadian federation, 1867

by 1867 Canada, New Brunswick and Nova Scotia could unite to form the Dominion of Canada. This of course had self-government. From then onward the development of modern Canada was fast and continuous.

The West Indies

Of the other British American territories, the West Indies with their valuable products of sugar and rum were at the end of the eighteenth century far more highly prized than Canada. Moreover, the British possessions there increased during the Revolutionary and Napoleonic wars, when Trinidad, Tobago and St. Lucia were added to the older colonies—of which Jamaica and Barbados were the most important. As the nineteenth century wore on, however, the West Indian colonies encountered hard times. The end of the slave-trade, the freeing of the slaves, the coming of

Free Trade—all these confronted the planters with many problems. Unrefreshed by large-scale emigration from the United Kingdom—the hot climate and the lack of suitable work prevented this—the West Indies began a decline in prosperity which was halted only within the present century.

Apart from Canada, the most popular destination for emigrants within the Empire was Australasia. In New South Wales the British settlers soon fanned out from the original penal colony established at Sydney in 1788, and additional penal colonies were founded in Tasmania. After 1815 a steady trickle of free settlers also began to arrive in Australia. This became a broader flow in the 'thirties and 'forties, when the British Government started to give grants to emigrants and the time on the voyage dropped to 140 days (the first fleet to Australia had taken over eight months). In the 'fifties the clippers reduced the time of passage still further to ninety days, and after 1851 the discovery of gold turned the flow into a flood.[1] Between 1851 and 1861 the population increased from 405,000 to 1,145,000, but it was still sparsely scattered: Australia has an area of nearly three million square miles.

The arrival of the free settlers completely changed the status of Australia. In the 1820s, New South Wales and Tasmania were both made normal colonies, though for many years they were still required to receive convicts. Meanwhile the interior was being opened up. In 1813 explorers working through the coastal mountains of New South Wales discovered good land beyond in the valleys of the Darling and Murray. In 1830 Charles Sturt, with a few companions, crossing the mountains from New South Wales, launched a small boat on the Murrambidgee. Despite the natives and underwater snags he completed an expedition in which he rowed 1,700 miles along the Murrumbidgee, Murray and Darling. The secrets of the great river system of south-eastern Australia were at last revealed. Sturt had traced the streams to the point from

Marginal notes: Australia; Gold; Australian exploration; Sturt

[1] The first discoverer was a convict, who was promptly whipped on the supposition that he had stolen some gold and melted it down.

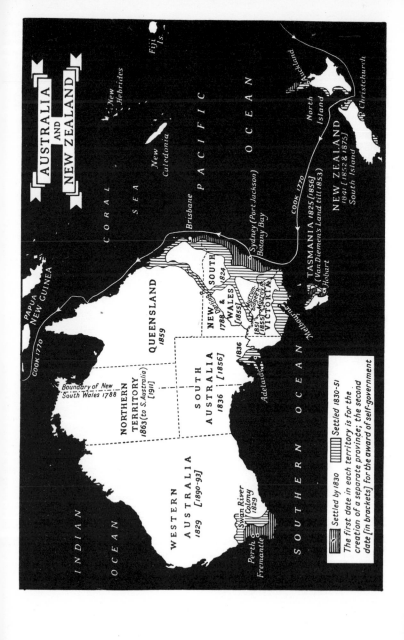

AUSTRALIA
AND
NEW ZEALAND

INDIAN OCEAN

PAPUA NEW GUINEA

COOK 1770

CORAL SEA

New Hebrides

New Caledonia

New Zealand

Auckland

North Island

COOK 1770

NEW ZEALAND
1841 [1852 & 1875]
South Island

Christchurch

P A C I F I C   O C E A N

Fiji Is.

Brisbane

Sydney (Port-Jackson)
Botany Bay

TASMANIA 1825 [1856]
(Van Diemen's Land till 1853)
Hobart

QUEENSLAND
1859

NEW SOUTH WALES
1788 & 1824

Murrum-bidgee
1851
1855
VICTORIA

Murray
Melbourne

Boundary of New
South Wales 1788

NORTHERN TERRITORY
1863 [to S. Australia]
[1911]

SOUTH AUSTRALIA
1836 [1856]

1836

Adelaide

WESTERN AUSTRALIA
1829 [1890-93]

Swan River
Colony 1829

Perth
Fremantle

S O U T H E R N   O C E A N

▨ Settled by 1830   ▥ Settled 1830-51

The first date in each territory is for the
creation of a separate province; the second
date [in brackets] for the award of self-government

which they all enter the sea together—but there was no broad estuary, only a lake whose exit to the sea he found after a three-day search amidst a maze of sand-bars.

These discoveries opened up great new districts and increased enormously the area devoted to sheep—an animal pioneered in Australia by John MacArthur, who by 1822 had produced Australian wool as fine as European. Sturt's discovery of the country at the mouth of the Murray also led to the foundation in 1836 of a new colony there— South Australia. The moving spirit in Britain behind this enterprise was Gibbon Wakefield—though he had no official position, as he had been in prison for abducting an heiress (he lured her from school by a forged letter and married her at Gretna Green). The pioneer settlers arrived to found the colony's first town and capital, Adelaide, in 1837.

Of the remaining Australian colonies, Western Australia, based on the Swan River, was founded in 1829. In the 1850s Victoria and Queensland were separated from New South Wales and made separate colonies. By stages all these territories except Western Australia acquired self-government on the Canadian model, most of them achieving it fully in 1855. Economic progress and exploration also continued, and in 1861 a party of four men completed the first complete crossing (south to north) of the island. By that year modern Australia was taking shape, though the colonies did not unite into a single Dominion until 1901.

The native inhabitants of Australia, the aborigines, were few and backward, but in New Zealand the first British settlers found a vigorous and warlike race already established —the Maoris. For long the white settlers were left to fend for themselves, and some thorough scoundrels found a happy hunting ground there. However, in 1838 Gibbon Wakefield and his brothers formed the New Zealand Company for the proper colonization of the islands. Its object was to sell land and use the proceeds to bring out carefully selected emigrants in orderly sequence. The beginning of this venture was opposed by the government out of consideration for the natives, but when the ministry heard that a French company was also preparing to colonize the islands it changed its tune. In 1840 the islands were declared to be officially annexed and a regular colonial administration was set up. Many difficulties followed, including disputes about land between the government, the Company, and the Maoris, but during the 1850s matters improved and New Zealand was given a large measure of self-government. Her European population at this time still numbered less than 50,000. As in Australia, gold and sheep quickly became important items in the economy; but settled conditions were a long time in arriving, and the last of the Maori wars did not end until 1870.

The only other imperial territory that attracted European settlers in the first half of the nineteenth century was South Africa. Here there was a confused situation involving three main parties. First, there were the warring African tribes, the nearest and most numerous of whom were the various Bantu groups (usually known as Kaffirs) who had been gradually moving south from central Africa. Secondly, there were the Boers, the original Dutch settlers who had remained when Cape Colony became formally recognized as British in 1814. Thirdly, there were the British settlers who from then on came out to the Cape. Of these, the first sizeable party, sent out by the government to strengthen the white inhabitants against Kaffir attacks and to relieve distress at home, arrived in 1820. They were established in the east of Cape Colony in a settlement named Albany. After many setbacks it throve, and the district still has a distinctly British character.

It was not long before many of the Boers became dissatisfied with British rule. The use of English instead of Dutch in the law courts was one grievance. The abolition of slavery in 1833, together with the small compensation received from the government, was another. Worst of all was the fact that when conflicts on the frontiers occurred between Boers and Kaffirs, the British government at home, advised by missionaries, often supported the latter. The clearest case of this came when the Governor of Cape Colony, Sir Benjamin d'Urban, annexed the territory of a

Margin notes:

Annexation, 1840

Responsible government in New Zealand

South Africa

Kaffirs, Boers and British

Albany settlement, 1820

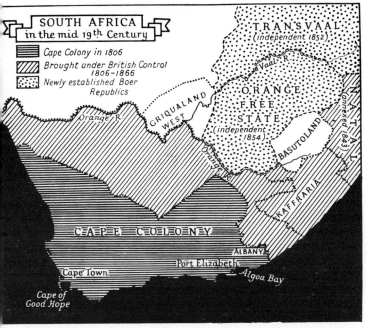

SOUTH AFRICA
in the mid 19th Century

▤ *Cape Colony in 1806*
▨ *Brought under British Control*
   1806–1866
▦ *Newly established Boer*
   Republics

T·R·A·N·S·V·A·A·L
(independent 1852)

Vaal R.

Orange R.

GRIQUALAND WEST

O·R·A·N·G·E
F·R·E·E
S·T·A·T·E
(independent
1854)

Orange R.

N·A·T·A·L
(annexed 1843)

BASUTOLAND

KAFFRARIA

C·A·P·E   C·O·L·O·N·Y

ALBANY

Port Elizabeth

Cape Town

Algoa Bay

Cape of
Good Hope

tribe which had raided the colony, only for the Colonial
Secretary at home to disallow the annexation. But even
more important than all these grievances was the fact that
many Boers were dissatisfied with their farms in the Colony,
and were aware that there was plenty of promising land to
be had beyond the frontiers.

All these things together caused the Great Trek, which *The Great
reached its height during 1836. With their goods and *c. 1836*
families in waggons drawn by a span of oxen, parties of
Boers crossed the Orange River (the boundary of Cape
Colony) and headed north-east to seek a new home in the
interior. In all, some 5,000 Boers, men, women and
children, left the Colony in this way during 1835–7. Some
moved into the area now known as Natal—only to move
out again when the British annexed this in 1843. Others
settled either between the Orange and the Vaal rivers or

else still farther north beyond the Vaal. These areas, too,
Britain after some hesitation annexed in 1848, only to
change policy again and to recognize first the virtual
independence of the Transvaal state, and then that of the
'Orange' Free State. This, however, was by no means the
end of the story. In the second half of the century, discoveries
of diamonds and gold were to lead to an attempted tightening of control over these Boer territories, and eventually to
the Boer War of 1899–1902.

Independence of Transvaal (1852) and Orange Free State (1854)

2. *India and the Far East*

India

Of British territories in which an alien population was in an
overwhelming majority the only one of great importance
until the closing years of the nineteenth century was India.
Clive had ensured the defeat of the French, but when he
finally left India in the 1760s the East India Company
controlled little more than the lower Ganges valley (Bengal)
and a few coastal areas. Fifty years later the Company,
subject since Pitt's India Act of 1784 to a government
Board of Control in London, was dominant throughout not
only the whole Ganges valley but also southern India. Two
great men helped to bring this about. During the rule of
Warren Hastings as the Company's Governor-General from
1773 to 1784, its influence and territory were preserved
against many dangers; but it was the Marquis Wellesley,
brother of the future Duke of Wellington and Governor-
General from 1797 to 1805, who made British supremacy a
fact. He removed the only two remaining sources of danger.
In 1799 at the great battle of Seringapatam he overthrew
Tipoo, ruler of Mysore, who had been intriguing with the
French. Then between 1801 and 1805 Wellesley and his
brother broke the power of the Maratha chieftains, whose
war-bands had raided far and wide in central India. Wellesley was recalled before the Marathas were finally subdued,
but the task was completed by his successor, the Marquess
of Hastings, in 1816–19.

Warren Hastings

Wellesley

Tipoo beaten at Seringapatam, 1799 Overthrow of the Marathas

Peace at last then came to most of India, and an Englishman travelling over central India in the 1820s was greeted

on all sides by '*Atul Raj*' (May your rule last for ever!).
By this time the whole of southern and central India was
ruled either directly by the Company's servants or by
Indian princes dependent on British advisers. Of India
proper, only the Punjab and Sind, in the north-west,
remained beyond British control.

Accordingly it was to the Indus Valley and the north-
west frontier that the British next turned their eyes. In 1839
the Governor-General, Lord Auckland, stirred by the same
distrust of Russia that Palmerson felt, dispatched a British
force to Afghanistan. It deposed a popular ruler and set *Afghanistan*
up a rival who had held the throne earlier, and who was
prepared to act on British orders. Within two years,
however, the Afghan tribes rose against this British puppet
and captured or massacred his troops: out of 15,000
combatants and non-combatants trying to evacuate the
country, one man alone reached Jallalabad (a Dr. Brydon,
whose dramatic arrival was a favourite subject of Victorian
prints). A punitive expedition then marched on Kabul, the
Afghan capital, and sacked it—but left the country still
unsubdued.

Almost immediately afterwards, in 1843, General Napier *Annexation of Sind, 1843*
was sent to conquer Sind, which had owned allegiance to
Afghanistan. *Punch* signalized his victory by inventing for
him a one-word despatch, 'Peccavi' (Latin for 'I have
sinned')—a pun made more pointed by his doubts about
the justice of the annexation. Two years later the Sikhs, the
great military power in the Punjab, encouraged by the
British disaster in Afghanistan, launched an all-out attack
on British India. After some of the hardest fighting ever *Defeat of Sikhs*
recorded there they were defeated. Kashmir was taken
from them and its predominantly Moslem people were
handed over to the rule of a Hindu prince in alliance with
the British. But again the Sikhs rose, and after a second *Annexation of Punjab, 1849*
defeat in 1849 the Punjab, too, was annexed. With posses-
sion of both the Punjab and Sind the Company now
controlled the valley of the Indus as well as that of the
Ganges, and northern India was as firmly in its grip as the
centre and the south.

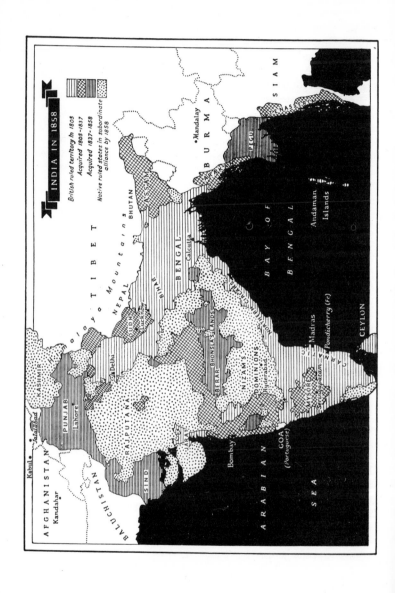

INDIA IN 1858

British ruled territory in 1805
Acquired 1805–1837
Acquired 1837–1858
Native ruled states in subordinate
alliance by 1858

AFGHANISTAN
Kabul•
Kandahar•
Jellalabad•

BALUCHISTAN

KASHMIR

PUNJAB
Lahore•

SIND

RAJPUTANA

•Delhi

OUDH
Lucknow•

NEPAL

TIBET

Himalaya Mountains

BHUTAN

BIHAR

BENGAL
Calcutta

BURMA

•Mandalay

ARAKAN

PEGU

SIAM

BERAR

NIZAM'S
DOMINIONS
Hyderabad•

BHONSLA'S LANDS

MALABAR

GOA
(Portuguese)

Bombay

MYSORE
Seringapatam•

Madras
Pondicherry (Fr.)

CEYLON

BAY
OF
BENGAL

Andaman
Islands

ARABIAN

SEA

The government of all this territory was an immense The task of task. In 1850 the native population numbered about government 200 million. To control them—to govern in annexed states and to keep an eye on the native rulers in unannexed states— the Company had fewer than 800 European officers. These, however, were usually men of great courage and energy. Most of them served as District Officers in charge of a territory that might be as large as Scotland. Sometimes the only European in all this area, they spent much of their time on horseback touring their district. To cover it might take them almost a year, and they had to be ready to deal with every kind of emergency. In addition to these officers, there were at centres like Calcutta and Bombay small numbers of clerks and a few 'quibbling quill-driving lawyers'—as 'Boy' Malcolm, one of the most active of the Company's officers, described them. After a district was annexed the first job to be done was to make a new tax assessment. Through the whole length of the territory boundaries would have to be discovered or laid down and then an assessment made. So for years a District Officer's men would be making entries like this: 'North: "the white rock where the vultures sit"; West: "the tall pine by Gopalu's cowshed"; South: "Bhim Sin's Ridge"; East: "Thorn bush Burn".' Thus were recorded the boundaries of a village.

Then there was the giving of justice. This was most Suppression difficult in cases where local practices were still quite of uncivilized uncivilized. Gradually, however, British ideas were intro- practices— duced. The Khonds, for instance, a primitive people living —human in Orissa, were accustomed to human sacrifice. Each sacrifice village used to buy its victims. They were well looked after and sometimes kept for years—until the day arrived that they knew could not be escaped. Then amidst barbarous rites they were killed. A District Officer managed to end this custom without a war. He himself rescued over a thousand of these captives, all awaiting death.

In the more civilized areas, too, there were practices which the British sought to stamp out. Among them were slavery (which was made illegal in 1843), the throwing of —slavery

The Ganges Canal in 1863

From a water colour by William Simpson. The (upper) Ganges Canal, here seen at Roorkee was one of the

children to the crocodiles in the Ganges, the drowning of
the aged, and suttee—the practice by which the widows of —suttee
high-caste Hindus were burnt alive on the funeral pyre of
their husbands. The Thugs, too, were gradually suppressed. —the Thugs
They were hereditary gangs of killers, some known to have
notched a thousand murders in a single season. Their
motives were professedly religious. They never killed except
by a handkerchief, in one corner of which was knotted a
silver coin consecrated to their goddess Kali. Their victims
were supposed to be sacrifices to her. Naturally the mur-
derers relieved the body of its valuables afterwards.

Side by side with the suppression of abominable practices, Bentinck
went the introduction of Western ideas and inventions. The (1828–35)
Governor-Generalship of Lord William Cavendish Bentinck,
which saw the drive against suttee and the Thugs, saw also
important developments in the education of higher-class
Indians (in English), the beginning of a unified system of
law, and the foundation of Calcutta Medical College. By
the India Act of 1833, too, the East India Company, which
had lost its monopoly of trade with India twenty years
earlier, was forbidden to engage in trade at all, and was Company
confined to purely political and administrative functions. forbidden
It was during the rule of Lord Dalhousie, however, that Dalhousie
westernization really began in earnest. Apart from much and
work on roads, canals and harbours, he mapped out the westerniza-
plan for India's railways—the first piece of line, from 1848–56
Bombay to Thana, being opened in 1853. The electric
telegraph was also introduced. Engineering colleges, too,
were founded, new mines opened up, and a new scheme
of education laid down. A cheap postage system was
instituted for all India. Not content with all this, Dalhousie
also annexed to the Company's territory a number of
states and enforced a rule that on the death of a native
ruler without an heir (and he was now never allowed to
adopt one), his family's rule would lapse, and his territory The
pass to the Company. But, all together, these changes, doctrine
though on the whole beneficial, had an unsettling effect on of lapse
the Indian people. While they were not the immediate
cause of the great revolt of the Company's native troops in

The Mutiny, 1857—the Indian Mutiny—they contributed greatly to the
1857
state of unrest which made the Mutiny possible. And with
the suppression of the Mutiny there opens another long
chapter in Indian history—a chapter which begins in 1858
with the abolition of the Company and the assumption of
direct rule by the Crown, and ends after the Second World
War with the partition of India into India and Pakistan,
and the attainment by these states of complete independence
within the Commonwealth.

British influence in the East during the early nineteenth
century was not confined to India. From there it extended
both westwards and eastwards across the neighbouring

Protectorate seas. To the west across the Arabian Sea the ruler of Aden
of Aden, was forced to grant Britain a protectorate over this valuable
1839
port—which was in a strategic position on the new Egypt-
to-India steamship route. To the east across the Bay of
Bengal the first Burmese War, waged in 1824–6 after the

Burma Burmese had caused trouble on the frontiers, gave Britain
the entire coast of northern Burma and so safeguarded the
approaches to India from that direction.

Further east still, the East India Company had long
traded with China for tea. On this voyage the Malay Penin-

Penang, sula was a half-way house, so in 1786 the Company pur-
1786
chased the almost uninhabited island of Penang, off the

Raffles and west coast. Thirty-three years later Sir Stamford Raffles,
Singapore, then in charge of the Company's interests in this area,
1819
persuaded the Company also to purchase the swampy and
almost uninhabited island of Singapore, at the foot of the
peninsula. He afterwards administered it so efficiently that
within four years it had an annual trade worth £2,500,000.
Both from the commercial and from the strategical point
of view, it was soon a place of the greatest value.

China With China itself, British relations during the first half of
the nineteenth century became increasingly difficult. The
Chinese Emperor, the 'Son of Heaven', regarded all
Europeans as barbarians, and was anxious to keep them out
of his empire. While the East India Company alone was
trading with China, any quarrels were not pressed to the
point of armed conflict; but when the Company's monopoly

was thrown open, difficulties multiplied. In 1839 matters came to a head. The Chinese were trying to stop the importation of opium and they prevailed upon the British in Canton to hand over their illegal stocks. A dispute about the right of the Chinese to try British merchants then followed. The Chinese attacked a British ship and forbade all trade with Britain, and Palmerston put in a number of demands which were refused. War then broke out, the British captured Canton and various other towns, and finally the Chinese accepted terms which met the British requirements. Shanghai, Canton and three other ports were to be open to European trade under reasonable tariffs, the confiscated opium was to be paid for, and the almost barren island of Hong Kong was ceded to Britain. Before long it was to become one of the greatest centres in the Far East not only for British but for international trade. *War, 1839-42* *Trade ensured and Hong Kong acquired, 1842*

All told, we thus see that although British governments in the early nineteenth century had no intention of building up a great colonial empire, one was nevertheless coming into existence. British statesmen might think that colonies were unrewarding and expensive: that they cost the mother country a great deal, gave very little in return, and then, like the United States, broke away. Economists might regard them as unnecessary in a world of increasing free trade. But British folk were nevertheless emigrating by the thousand to lands which had to be governed and protected; the East India Company, to preserve and administer its territories, found it necessary to acquire still more; and even British statesmen who disliked colonies usually had a keen eye for naval vantage points. So it came about that, despite remarkably little conscious effort on the part of the government, an extensive empire again developed—an empire of which the parts populated by people of British descent were, by the mid-nineteenth century, already assured of the right to govern themselves.

CHAPTER TWENTY-THREE

SCIENCE AND INDUSTRY IN THE EARLY NINETEENTH CENTURY

1. Science

The new chemistry

IN Chapter VIII we saw how among the important developments of the eighteenth century was a great advance in the study of chemistry. This 'chemical revolution' yielded a richer and richer harvest during the nineteenth century.

Dalton's atomic theory

John Dalton (1766–1844), the son of a poor weaver from Cumberland, carried chemistry forward by a big step when he propounded his atomic theory. He said that matter was made up of particles which could not be split—atoms—and that an element was a substance in which all the atoms were identical. Atoms of different elements, however, varied at least in weight. He proceeded to try to discover the weights of the atoms of the various elements—of which he recognized twenty—using as his basis the weight of the hydrogen atom, which he found to be the lightest. Dalton thus put forward one of the basic ideas of chemistry—that matter consists of atoms, and that to understand the formation of chemical compounds from different elements it is necessary to sort out the molecule of the compound (the smallest unit in which it can exist) into its component atoms. Thus a molecule of water consists of two atoms of hydrogen (H) and one of oxygen (O) and the chemical composition of water is shown by the formula H_2O. The atomic theory has proved very fruitful, and with fresh discoveries the list of elements now runs to over ninety instead of Dalton's original twenty. In the twentieth century the invention of techniques for splitting the atom has of course resulted in immense new possibilities of power, both for peace and for destruction.

Dalton was a Quaker, and he dressed in the old-fashioned way of that sect—in knee-breeches, dark grey stockings, and buckled shoes. He had few friends and devoted his entire life to science, earning his living by teaching. When asked late in life why he had not married, he replied, 'I never had time.' He lived his later life in Manchester and his only amusement was to go once a week to The Dog and Partridge to play a game of bowls.

Drawn & Etched by J. Stephenson.

John Dalton
From a contemporary engraving by G. Stephenson.

Less eccentric were two other famous British scientists of this period. Both were closely connected with the Royal Institution, which had been founded in 1799 in London to promote scientific development and interest in science. Sir Humphry Davy (1788–1829) became a lecturer there in 1801 and shortly afterwards the Director of the laboratory and Professor of Chemistry. His strikingly phrased lectures attracted many in the fashionable world—not surprisingly,

Royal Institution, 1799

Davy

A Chemical Lecture, 1810

A lecture at the Surrey Institution, satirically depicted by Rowlandson. Such lectures were by then a fashion of the day.

when Coleridge could declare that 'had Davy not been the first chemist of his age, he could have been the first poet'. His invention of the miners' safety-lamp has already been mentioned, but his chief claim to scientific fame lies in his discovery of new elements, particularly the metals potassium and sodium. He separated these from their compounds by the new method of electrolysis—i.e. by passing an electric current through the compounds. This was possible because an Italian scientist, Count Alessandro Volta, had invented in 1799 a battery which produced a continuous electric current. Davy built up huge batteries, some with over a thousand cells. These he used for his chemical experiments and also to produce a brilliant arc-light at a lecture—the first demonstration of electric lighting. Electric lighting, however, had no future as long as the only source was expensive and cumbersome batteries.

New elements

Electrolysis

One of Davy's most important discoveries was Michael Faraday (1791–1867). The son of a blacksmith and born in a poor part of south London, Faraday was apprenticed to a bookbinder. His introduction to the world of science came by good fortune. One of the bookbinder's customers took him to some lectures by Davy at the Royal Institution. He wrote up notes on these lectures with great care and sent them to Davy, who was impressed and found him a job at the Institution as a laboratory assistant. Once established in a scientific life, Faraday soon made his mark —to such effect that he eventually became, like Davy, the Institution's Professor of Chemistry.

Faraday's most important work, however, was in physics. Magnetism and electricity were the subjects that most fascinated him. The first person to prove a connection between magnetism and electricity was a Dane, Oersted: he found in 1820 that when an electric current was passed along a wire, the needle of a compass lying close to the wire was deflected. Five years later a Lancashire shoemaker, William Sturgeon, constructed an electro-magnet. He surrounded a core of iron with a coil of copper wire, and passed an electric current through the coil. It magnetized the iron for so long as the current was maintained. Thus it was shown that electricity had a magnetic effect. Faraday, meanwhile, was trying to achieve the opposite—to produce an electrical effect from a magnet. For years he puzzled over the problem, carrying round in his pocket a magnet and an electrical conductor. In 1831 he triumphed. The secret was that the conductor (e.g. a piece of wire) and the magnet had to move in a special relation to one another. Faraday fitted a large copper disc edgeways between the poles of a magnet and rotated it. Electricity was generated —and a metal strip that scraped the side of the disc conducted away the electricity. Thus was made the first generator.

From this invention flowed, during the later nineteenth century, great developments in electric power, which in the twentieth century was for most purposes to supersede steam. The great generating stations which provide our

Michael Faraday at the Royal Institution

From a water-colour of Faraday in his laboratory, painted by Harriet Moore
in 1852.

electric light and power today, and the dynamos on which
the electrical system of our cars depends, are alike based on
the same principle as Faraday's original generator. Faraday
himself went on to show that the electricity derived from
friction, a battery, and his generator was, contrary to
common belief, the same. All this, however, was only a
part of his work at the Royal Institution—where he
remained all his life until health failed him. It was perhaps
typical of his modesty that he belonged to a small and
obscure Nonconformist sect—which on one occasion
suspended him when, commanded to Windsor to dine with
the Queen, he travelled on a Sunday and missed a service.

Other important work was done in physics at this time by J. P. Joule (1818–89), the son of a Manchester brewer and a pupil of Dalton. Many scientists in the first half of the nineteenth century were beginning to believe that heat, motion, electricity and magnetism could all be converted into one another—in fact, that they were all aspects of one thing, energy, which they defined as the capacity for doing work. Joule conclusively demonstrated that heat at least was a form of energy. He measured the amount of heat liberated by certain mechanical work, and then in 1843 propounded his law of the conservation of energy—that energy cannot be lost or gained, but only changed into another form.

J. P. Joule and the conservation of energy

In the end these discoveries in physics have had incalculable effects, but practical results were slow in coming. In the 1840s metal-plating began to be done by electrolysis, and various forms of electrical telegraph, including those of the American Samuel Morse and the British inventors Wheatstone and Cooke, were slowly introduced. It was not, however, until the 1870s that an economic electrical generator was produced, and that the modern triumphs of electricity became possible.

Practical applications of physics in the 1840s: Electrolysis and the electric telegraph

The new chemistry brought quicker results. Even before the nineteenth century it had made balloons possible. These were filled either with hot air or with hydrogen, the pioneers being two Frenchmen, the brothers Montgolfier. As early as 1784, flights were made in England, and the next year saw the first Channel-crossing.

Practical applications of chemistry: Balloons

Chemistry brought, as we shall see, not only many changes to industry but also a great boon to mankind— the possibility of an anaesthetic. Sir Humphry Davy had discovered the anaesthetic effects of nitrous oxide or 'laughing-gas', and later Faraday found similar properties in ether. These discoveries, however, were at first put to no practical use in England, and it was in America that ether was first employed to achieve painless surgery. In Britain the first surgeon to experiment with it was Robert Liston: in 1846, with the help of ether, he amputated a man's leg at the thigh in twenty-five seconds. The best known of the

Anaesthetics

Simpson and chloroform, 1847

British pioneers, however, was J. Y. Simpson, a professor at Edinburgh, who used ether as an anaesthetic in 1847. In the same year he experimented with another gas, chloroform, which he found more effective. The practice was gradually spread by Simpson, who fought with un-flagging zeal all those who ridiculed or denounced it. The opposition to anaesthetics seems extraordinary to us; but new ideas are rarely accepted at once, and in the nineteenth century they had to surmount not merely practical but also religious objections.

Lack of great medical discoveries

In general, medicine and biology progressed only slowly in the first half of the nineteenth century. It was German chemists who discovered that all living bodies are con-structed from cells; and they were the pioneers in both organic chemistry and biochemistry. Not until the second half of the century did the discovery of bacteria by the Frenchman Louis Pasteur result in new and powerful weapons, such as antiseptics, in the fight against disease.

Geology:

In another field of enquiry, many scientists at this time were investigating the early history of the earth and of life upon it. They studied its structure, and in particular the rocks and the fossils embedded in them. In 1830–33 Sir Charles Lyell published his *Principles of Geology*. He suggested

Lyell and the creation of the earth

that the earth must have been created a very long time ago —a thought disturbing to the Victorians, who mostly accepted at this time a date for the earth's creation (4004 B.C.) which James Ussher, a seventeenth-century Irish archbishop, had calculated from the Bible. To some extent Lyell prepared the way for the later and far more revolutionary theories of evolution put forward by Charles Darwin.

2. *Applications of Science to Industry*

As the nineteenth century wore on, the progress of industry began to depend more and more on the work of the scientist. Even before 1800, as already recounted in Chapters VIII–X, there was the steam-engine, with its applications in mines and mills, forges and factories. Soon

afterwards there were the further applications of the locomotive and the steamship, with their revolutionary effect
on transport. In the same way a growing chemical industry
began to centre round new methods of producing alkalis Alkali
and new methods of using coal. Alkalis had long been production
necessary for certain industries, particularly for bleaching
and the manufacture of soap and glass. In the eighteenth

Burning Kelp (1778)
From a contemporary engraving by S. H. Grimm.

century there were various methods of obtaining alkali,
notably from burnt timber, peat, fern, and kelp. The
number of Scotsmen collecting and burning kelp or seaweed
was estimated during the Napoleonic Wars to be as high as
80,000, of which 20,000 followed the trade in the Orkneys
alone. After 1815 this time-honoured occupation became
unnecessary, for chemists discovered a method of producing
a synthetic alkali that was much more effective. The best
kelp usually contained no more than five per cent alkali.
Synthetic alkali seems first to have been successfully
produced in the 1790s at Southwark and Newcastle, when
a reaction of common salt with sulphuric acid gave sodium
sulphate, from which by a further process was made sodium
carbonate—a strong alkali. The centres of the new industry

became Tyneside, Glasgow (where the great Tennant works were established), and the Mersey. The process was much boosted in 1825 when the government removed the heavy salt duty.

Alkalis for soap production

Cheap alkali from this new process led between 1805 and 1845 to a threefold expansion in the production of soap. In the same way the enormous expansion of the textile industry depended partly on cheaper and quicker methods of bleaching, for which alkalis and acids were needed. In

Alkalis for textile-bleaching

the eighteenth century sulphuric acid was substituted for sour milk in the souring process (a part of the bleaching), and did the work in a fraction of the time. A still greater advance was made with the introduction of chlorine, discovered in 1774 by the Swedish chemist Scheele and later named by Davy. The idea originated in France, and James Watt was one of the pioneers in this country. By 1799 Tennants were producing an alkaline powder, chloride of lime, that enormously eased the problem of bleaching. In 1840 one factory was bleaching 1,400 pieces of cotton daily. A century earlier the process might have taken months.

Matches were another result of the new chemical knowledge. The early ones were either made from phosphorus, which was poisonous, or else were tiresome to light, the match-head having to be brought into contact with sulphuric acid. The first non-phosphorus friction matches seem to have been produced in 1827. These early matches, often called 'lucifers', were struck by being drawn across glass-paper. All of them were a great improvement on the old method of securing a light from a flint and tinder-box.

The expansion of the coal and iron industries has already been referred to in Chapter X. New uses were soon discovered for coal, apart from domestic heating and the

Coal-gas

driving of steam-engines. The use of coal-gas for lighting has already been mentioned. During the first half of the nineteenth century gas-works were built all over the country, and by 1818 the Edinburgh gas-works had already twenty miles of main. Before this, Lord Dundonald, an erratic Scottish nobleman and scientist, had succeeded in

Coal-tar

producing tar from coal on a commercial scale (1782).

Maudslay's Screw-turning Lathe (*c.* 1800)

From the original in the Science Museum, South Kensington.

In addition to all this there was great progress in the Mechanical
mechanical engineering industry. The beginnings of this engineering
industry in the work of Watt, Boulton, Murdock, Wilkinson
and Bramah have already been described. One of Bramah's
workmen, and his fellow-inventor of the hydraulic press,
was Henry Maudslay (d. 1831), who in turn invented a Maudslay
screw-cutting lathe and the slide-rest. Thenceforward screws
could be cut to a standard size, turning on the lathe became much more accurate, and a wide range of machine-
tools became possible. The advance towards precision may
be seen from the fact that Maudslay invented a gauge
which would measure one ten-thousandth of an inch. And in
Maudslay's works in London were trained two of the next
generation of engineers—both men who eventually built up
works of their own and amassed vast fortunes. One was
James Nasmyth, who invented among other things the Nasmyth
steam-hammer, the steam pile-driver, and a nut-shaping
machine. The other was (Sir) Joseph Whitworth, who by Whitworth
1833 was running his own business as a tool-maker in
Manchester. His ruling passions were precision and stan-
dardization. He produced true plane surfaces in metal—

including an iron billiard-table for his own house—and devoted much effort to securing uniform screw-threads and standard gauges. Among other things, he developed Maudslay's device to the point where it could measure one two-millionth of an inch. In the Great Exhibition of

Nasmyth's Steam Hammer (1840)

From a model in the Science Museum.

1851 his show of machine-tools was far ahead of that of any other competitor.

It is impossible to trace all the links between scientific and industrial development, even in a fairly uncomplicated period like the early nineteenth century. Enough, however, has perhaps been said to show that the results of scientific invention and discovery were often quickly applied to industry. Because of this a far greater range and volume of goods could be produced, and great new public works could be undertaken. Steam-excavators and pile-drivers, for instance, speeded the construction of new docks—which in turn, like the railways and the steamships, encouraged the growth of trade. From one cause and another, Britain's industrial and commercial wealth was steadily increasing, as may be seen from the fact that between 1820 and 1850 the volume of British exports doubled. In this development, which was later to bring greatly improved conditions of life to the British people, science was already playing a major part.

CHAPTER TWENTY-FOUR

LIFE IN THE MID-NINETEENTH CENTURY (I)

1. *Town and Country*

Legacy of
Industrial
Revolution

THE Industrial Revolution caused profound changes in the everyday life of the British people, and by 1850 many of its effects were plain. To begin with, the population of Great Britain in 1851 was treble what it had been in 1714: 21 millions compared with 6½ millions. Such an increase, while primarily due to improved medical knowledge and sanitation, could not have been supported without great progress in industry and agriculture. Very noticeable, too, was the immense growth in the number and size of the towns—in which more people now lived than in the country. And almost equally obvious was the growth of the middle classes, those products of the town, who had increased even faster than the population as a whole.

Population

Towns

Other marks of the Industrial Revolution were equally clear. The railway companies were gradually pushing their lines into every corner of the British Isles. Gas-lighting brightened the streets of most towns, even if oil lamps and candles still sufficed for the home. Iron was taking on new domestic uses—among other things for the ranges for heating and cooking with which most kitchens were now being equipped. In short, the material wealth arising from the Industrial Revolution was already being enjoyed by the middle classes and the skilled workmen. Not until after 1850, however, would this new wealth greatly benefit the ordinary working man.

Railways, etc.

Wealth

Apart from the effects of the Industrial Revolution, the most striking change from eighteenth-century life was a new seriousness. This sprang from the religious revival begun by

The new seriousness

Wesley, which had gradually spread throughout the land. By 1851 family prayers had been revived and a strict Sunday routine established in many houses. The serious outlook extended beyond religion to every aspect of life, including business affairs. Great stress was placed on hard work and eagerness to acquire knowledge. By cultivating these qualities men would ensure not merely that they themselves did well, but also that material progress would continue, and that eventually peace and prosperity would reign throughout the world. This belief in self-improvement and progress was the key-note of the mid-nineteenth-century prophets—men like Samuel Smiles, the author of *Self-Help* (1859), and Martin Tupper, the author of *Proverbial Philosophy* (1838 onwards), both works of immense popularity.[1]

Town and country, rich and poor, were all affected by the new means of transport. When Tom Brown set off for school he went by coach, starting from Islington at 3 a.m. and riding outside. The party stopped at an inn for breakfast, and Tom was offered pigeon pie, ham, beef, kidneys, steak, bacon and eggs, buttered toast and muffins. This was in the late 'thirties, the last days of the great coaching age. Coaches, it was soon discovered, could not compete with the railways for either speed, comfort or economy, and by 1850 most of the famous services had been withdrawn. Horse-drawn vehicles of various kinds, however—gigs, cabs, broughams, landaus, carts and the rest—still bore the brunt of all the local work. Moreover, there was an important development in horse-drawn public transport: the first omnibus had been introduced into England in 1829, and by 1837 there were already four hundred in London. *Transport*

Another change which was a wonderful boon to the whole public was the reform of the postal service. The old *The postal service*

[1] Smiles was also the biographer of the early engineers, whose lives were striking examples of what can be achieved by determination and hard work. Tupper extolled these and other virtues in verse—it would be too kind to call it poetry—and for over twenty-five years found the Victorian public eager to lap up fresh instalments of his moral reflections.

A Steam Omnibus of 1833

Hancock's 'Enterprise' ran between Paddington and the City. Steam vehicles c
this kind were a promising development, but they were heavy and caused damag
to the roads. They were therefore discouraged by high rates of toll and later (i
1865) by the 'Red Flag' Act: every mechanically propelled vehicle on the road
had to be attended by three men, one of whom had to precede it on foot bearing
a red flag.

system, still in force at the beginning of Victoria's reign,
was astonishingly inefficient. Postage rates differed according to mileage and were very expensive—to send a
letter from London to Holyhead, for instance, cost a
shilling. Moreover, the postage was paid by the receiver,
not the sender, with the result that the postman took a very
long time on his round. Poor people, too, often had to
refuse letters, even from their own children, when the cost
might easily amount to half a day's wages. Nor were
richer people unaffected—Sir Walter Scott once had to pay
£5 on a letter delivered from America. Because of this high
cost of long-distance postage, some people defeated the
system by employing a code in the address: the recipient

took the letter from the postman, looked at it, then handed it back without opening it! Much more widespread, however, was the abuse of franking. M.P.s and civil servants were entitled to have their correspondence officially franked and sent free, and all too often they used this privilege for their friends' letters too, and even for the entire business correspondence of firms. The total effect of these various factors was that in 1830 only a quarter of the mail in Great Britain paid any postage at all.

'Penny Blacks'

The first postage stamp, introduced in 1840. There was as yet no perforation between the stamps.

Fortunately there was someone quite outside the Post Office who had better ideas. In 1836 Rowland Hill produced his famous plan for reform. He suggested that a penny should be the standard postal rate for any place in Great Britain, and that the penny should be paid by the sender. The official in charge of the Post Office denounced Hill's scheme as 'fallacious, preposterous and utterly unsupported by facts'. The government, however, accepted the scheme and the penny post came into operation in 1840. It was soon found that the easiest way of prepaying the postage was by an adhesive stamp, and the first stamp was isused that same year—the famous 'penny black'. Franking was abolished. Moreover, Hill's scheme paid handsomely—so inefficient was the old system, and so popular the new. *Rowland Hill and the penny post, 1840*

In the countryside, the coming of the railways and the steady progress of enclosure were the most obvious points of difference from the late eighteenth century. The big house still remained the centre of local life—as can be seen from *The countryside: The great country houses*

Trollope's novels—and the service quarters in such a house as Stowe were the size of a small village. An American, a guest of the Duke of Richmond at Gordon Castle, found 'the whole visible horizon fenced in for the enjoyment of the household' and felt as if he 'had been spirited into some castle of felicity and had not come by the royal mail coach at all'. Responsibility as well as rights, however, were generally recognized, and in most areas the gentry made a point of visiting the poor and the sick and trying to relieve their needs.

There were a few improvements in material comfort in these great houses. Coal was now used on a large scale for heating; in fact some mansions even had a miniature railway from the coal-store into the house. Conversely, ice-pits were built so that guests might enjoy ices in the summer. One thing that we should now consider a necessity was still usually lacking in the houses of even the greatest—a fitted bath. Instead there were mobile bath-tubs and their use was growing steadily more frequent—at the beginning of the nineteenth century the Duke of Wellington was considered distinctly odd for having a bath every day. The great houses were of course very expensive to run, and it was said that Cassiobury cost over £10,000 a year.

Land-ownership
While the great landowners flourished during the early Victorian age, the smaller owners—the squires and the yeomen—declined. When the first accurate surveys of land-ownership were made in mid-Victorian days, it was discovered that only about fifteen per cent of the cultivated land of England was worked by direct owners. The remaining eighty-five per cent was worked by tenants. And just as it was the big landowner who flourished, so also it was the big tenant-farmer. The census of 1851 showed that over a third of the farmed land of England and Wales was laid out in farms of 200 to 500 acres, and nearly a sixth in farms over 500 acres.

The new-style tenant farmer
The larger tenant-farmer was thus very important by 1851, and often in his desire for self-advancement he adopted the ways of the gentry. Here is a contemporary satire directed against him:

Old style	*New style*
Man, to the plough;	Man, Tally Ho;
Wife, to the cow;	Miss, piano;
Girl, to the yarn;	Wife, silk and satin;
Boy, to the barn;	Boy, Greek and Latin;
And your rent will be netted.	And you'all all be gazetted.

On the other hand, the 1851 census also showed that nearly a half of the tenant-farmers—those with small-holdings—hired no labour and did the job entirely themselves.

Farming methods were changing, but only slowly, and there was still little mechanization. By 1851 the steam threshing-machine was widely used, but reapers were hardly known. Most ploughs were by now made of iron, yet old wooden ones drawn by teams of bullocks were used for most of the century in backward counties like Sussex. In the village the blacksmith and the wheelwright still flourished. For the ordinary labourer, paid a weekly wage by a farmer, life was much the same. He might go to chapel rather than church. He would find it easier to get an allotment, for these were being organized all over the country. He might by 1850 be a little better off than in 1800, and certainly would be if he lived in the North. In 1850 the average wage in the West Riding was twice that in Gloucestershire, fourteen to seven shillings. For in the North the draw of the many towns was felt throughout the countryside, and agricultural wages had to be fairly high to hold men on the farms. *Farming methods*

The labourer

Like the new industrial towns, London with its population of two and a half million in 1851 was still growing fast. Close building by now reached to Pentonville and Hackney on the north, Poplar on the east, Dulwich on the south, and Kensington on the west. The population of the City, on the other hand, was declining, for here were being erected the great offices of the banking and insurance firms that grew with Britain's ever-expanding trade, and that were to help make London the financial capital of the world. Those who worked in these offices were now living farther *London*

Extent

The Hub of the City, 1851

and farther afield, a habit vastly extended by the coming of the railways. In 1836 the first suburban line was opened with the completion of the London and Greenwich railway. By 1850 Euston, Paddington, Liverpool Street, Fenchurch Street, King's Cross and Waterloo were all built, and were handling suburban as well as main-line traffic.

In many of the newly built-up parts of London, such as Shoreditch and Euston, the houses were mainly jerry-built, squalid and mean. Equally noticeable, however, were the districts covered by the large, solid houses of the middle class—houses built in great numbers during the prosperous 'fifties. To realize the numbers and wealth of this class one must wander through Paddington, Bayswater, Belgravia, Pimlico, Camberwell and Dulwich. Here one will still find long terraces of four- or five-floored houses, each complete with a classical portico, or farther out, at Dulwich for instance, large detached villas often the size of a small block of flats. The typical middle-class house in a terrace had four or five floors. The bottom floor, often a basement, with windows looking on to a small excavated 'area', comprised a kitchen and scullery, a pantry, and a servants' sitting-room. The ground floor usually boasted two rooms— a dining-room and a study—and the first floor was often given over to a single large room, the drawing-room. The second floor might contain the best bedrooms, and above this there were one or two floors for the servants and children. Thousands of these houses still stand, nowadays nearly all split up into flats and with their stucco flaking away—faded monuments to Victorian prosperity.

Middle-class houses

The upper-middle-class house of this kind was normally run on a standard routine. The day started with a family breakfast, prefaced in some houses by prayers and in almost all houses by 'grace',[1] and then Father went off to business. Luncheon and afternoon tea followed, and between 7 and 8 p.m. came dinner, over which Father again presided. The less fashionable, however, might still dine between 12 and 2 p.m. At most meals, and certainly dinner, the family would be waited upon by servants. When visitors came,

The upper-middle-class routine

[1] A brief formula of thanksgiving for food.

dinner was a very formal affair; at the end, the womenfolk retired and the gentlemen sat on over the port, to join the ladies later in the drawing-room. Still later, in a big house, the men might retire to the smoking-room, for it was not considered polite to smoke in the presence of ladies or, in big houses, to smoke in the drawing-room. For the ladies of this type of household, life was probably becoming duller than before, since the idea was gaining ground that a 'lady' must do nothing which could be regarded as 'work'. 'Ladies' might talk, write letters, do embroidery, practise 'accomplishments' such as painting in water-colours or playing the pianoforte, go for carriage drives, and take part in the complicated ritual of calling on one another. But they hardly ever occupied a paid position—except that poor gentlewomen sometimes became governesses; and by now all the housework in such houses was left to the servants, of whom there were over a million in Britain in 1851. The possession of at least one servant, indeed, was that which marked out the lower-middle-class home from the upper-working-class home. Mrs. Beeton, the famous writer on household management, reckoned that on an income of £500 a year it would be possible to keep a cook and a housemaid; and for an upper-middle-class house three or four servants was a minimum.

Club life   If the London merchant or professional man wished to escape from his home, he might find relaxation in one of the growing number of clubs scattered around St. James's Street and Pall Mall. Many of these, such as the Athenaeum and the Reform, were built rather like palaces. The Victorian club was very different in atmosphere from White's or Brooks's under the Regency. Gone were the days of heavy gambling. Money was spent lavishly on buildings, but inside all was respectable and serious. Within the palatial interiors, nowadays distinguished mainly by their shabby paintwork and worn-out furniture, well-off London citizens ate ample meals, drank wine, read the journals, and discussed the questions of the day. Such discussion played a greater part in club life then than now: for in 1851 the working class had no vote and the opinions of the

An Early Victorian Sampler

A sampler was a piece of embroidery worked by a girl as a specimen of proficiency; frequently it was framed or hung on a wall. This one, preserved in the Victoria & Albert Museum, was worked by Mary Pether in 1839.

wealthier middle class carried proportionately greater weight.

We have so far glanced only at prosperous aspects of life The slums in London. The capital, however, also had a very seamy side. Even in the West End there was little proper drainage, and the Serpentine, used in place of sewers, was in a loathsome state. Many of the slum quarters were as bad as they had been in the eighteenth century, or even worse. One investigator in 1849, for instance, discovered a court or alley twenty-two feet wide surrounded by twenty-six houses in which lived nearly a thousand people. Frequently such warrens were created by speculators running up jerry-built houses in the garden of a larger house, and so creating an enclosed and airless court. In *Bleak House*, Dickens depicts with all his skill Tom-all-Alone's, a notorious slum that then existed in Southwark. There were many others, not only south of the river and in the East End, but in Westminster and around Oxford Street.

A London Slum in 1851

The engraving is of Duke Street, Southwark.

London low life

The London working man made his living in many ways apart from the standard trades and occupations. The streets were full of costermongers with their carts and donkeys—creatures usually treated with much care by their owners, who often shared their lunch with them. Then there were the many street salesmen and performers. The latter included all sorts—singers, pavement artists, Punch and Judy men, acrobats, sword-swallowers, fire-eaters, men with dancing bears, exhibitors of monstrosities, and scores of others. Perhaps the most curious and certainly the most repulsive of the low-life characters were the 'toshers', who made a living by entering the sewers at low tide, braving the rats, and collecting anything of value they could find.

The Directors of the Bank of England were surprised in 1836 to receive a letter from a man offering to meet them in their strong-room. They fixed a time and he duly emerged from the middle of the floor just where their gold bars were stored. He had found his way down an old sewer.

In the largest towns outside London conditions were very similar, vile slums jostling close to areas of great wealth and respectability. The centres of towns like Manchester, Liverpool and Birmingham were by now filled with imposing new buildings—banks, town halls, offices, clubs, and the like. These towns, too, had prosperous residential districts, especially Liverpool, which was a great commercial as well as an industrial centre. Here life was similar to that in London. The tall mansions of the merchants were still close to the centre, but already there was a rash of suburban villas out beyond the Mersey estuary at Waterloo, where many of the merchants' families spent the summer. In Manchester, too, a great new housing estate— Victoria Park—had appeared a couple of miles south of the town centre: protected by private roads and toll gates, it was entirely for the prosperous.[1] *Provincial towns*

In industrial and factory towns the routine of the wealthy was different from in London. The Gotts, the great wool manufacturers of Leeds, were at the mill by 6 a.m. and dined when they finished work at about 4 or 5 p.m. In Manchester all but a few dined at 1 p.m., the heads of business not usually returning till 3 p.m. Mancunians then had tea at 5 p.m.; supper followed after 9 p.m., an hour which in this part of the world was not considered too late for hot meat washed down by strong tea.

By 1850 the lot of the town wage-earners had not greatly improved. It was only about then that their earnings started to rise appreciably and to continue to rise. Their houses, especially in the mushroom towns of the North, were often a disgrace. In Bradford and Manchester (where *Housing in the new towns*

---

[1] Its fine large residences have long since become flats and boarding-houses. By the 1880s, wealthy Manchester was moving out another two miles—to West Didsbury; and since 1918 most of it has gone farther still—to Alderley Edge and beyond.

the walls of some of the houses were only half a brick thick) most of the dwellings were run up in small batches by speculators whose only concern was their pockets. Rarely did anyone make a serious attempt at improvement or control—though there were honourable exceptions. Efforts to make houses airier were for long discouraged by the window tax, which was not repealed till 1851; but much the worst evils were the lack of sanitation, drains, and a good water-supply. Working-class accommodation was built with no more than one closet to two, four, or even a whole terrace of houses; and in areas where there was piped water the company often turned it on for only a quarter of an hour a day. In any case everyone left the taps on, so that much even of this small supply was wasted. These were the conditions that were responsible for so much disease, including the cholera which plagued Britain from 1830 to 1870.

Social criticism by writers Writers like Charles Dickens and Thomas Hood did much to awake the public conscience on such matters. In 'The Song of the Shirt', which appeared in the 1843 Christmas number of *Punch*, Hood told of the hardships of one unfortunate group—the seamstresses:

> With fingers weary and worn,
>   With eyelids heavy and red,
> A woman sat, in unwomanly rags,
>   Plying her needle and thread—
>   Stitch! stitch! stitch!
> In poverty, hunger and dirt
>   And still with a voice of dolorous pitch
> She sang the Song of the Shirt
>   Work—Work—Work
> While the cock is crowing aloof;
>   And Work—work—work
> Till the stars shine through the roof. . . .

The relief of distress To offset some of this grimness, in the industrial areas Friendly Societies were very active—clubs in which men joined together partly to help each other in need and partly to find company and entertainment. Outside these and the workhouses, however, the relief of distress still

Mr. Punch's Industrial Exhibition

John Leech, the famous cartoonist, depicts Mr Punch showing the Prince Consort industrial exhibits of a different kind from those seen in the great exhibition—the sweated and starving workers of the tailoring and other trades.

depended largely on private charity rather than on organized or official help. Sometimes this charity was provided by individuals, like the squire in the country districts, and sometimes by the establishment of some institution or fund from voluntary contributions. During the first half of the nineteenth century a large number of hospitals, orphanages, almshouses, schools, and refuges for the homeless were built in this way.

2. *Recreation*

The air of seriousness and formality associated with the Victorians was also seen in their clothes. The frock-coat and morning dress, both in black cloth, with top hats, were by

Waiting for an Execution at Newgate, 1848

Public executions remained a popular spectacle until their abolition in 1866.

1851 the normal dress for the professional and business classes. Even working men often wore bowler hats. The most distinctive feature of the ladies' dress was the vast bell-like skirt that reached to the ground. Layers of starched clothing were worn underneath to keep the skirts out, until a Frenchman invented the crinoline—a light framework of steel wires which supported the skirt. It needed skill and practice to sit down gracefully in one of these contraptions.

Recreation   The Victorians did relax on occasion, though they had far less leisure than ourselves in which to do so. By 1850 many offices in centres like Manchester and London no

Saturday   longer worked on a Saturday afternoon, and the Factory
afternoon   Act of 1852 brought in a 2 p.m. close-down on Saturdays for the cotton-mills. But there were not many opportunities as yet for recreation in the big provincial towns, which often had no open spaces. However, in 1846 Manchester

Parks   opened three parks and other towns imitated these examples in the 'fifties. In addition cheap day and half-day excursions Excursions offered by the railways soon enabled many thousands of town-dwellers to take an occasional trip to sea or country. For the evening, apart from the parks, there were the Mechanics' Institutes, with their lectures and small libraries. Mechanics' Institutes These, however, for the most part appealed only to the studious minority of the lower middle and working classes. In 1852 Manchester opened the first free public library in England, and from this great developments were to come. Theatrical entertainments in the provinces were few and poor, and public concerts irregular. Much the most popular form of diversion for the working man still remained drinking in the 'pubs'. Nor was there much more provision of entertainment for the better-off: work and the home were the gospel of Victorian England.

For the Londoner, however, there was a wider range of Recreation in London choice in the evening—the pleasure gardens (though their great days were coming to an end), the Zoo (founded in

'To Brighton and Back for 3s. 6d.'

From a picture by C. Rossiter, painted in 1859, illustrating the joys of the new railway excursions.

1828), the circus, the theatre, the music-hall. For those who could afford it, both in London and in the provinces an annual holiday, usually at the sea, was becoming a custom. Resorts were therefore growing rapidly. Margate, easily reached by paddle-steamer, was jolly but rather vulgar. Folkestone was respectable. In the North, Blackpool began to cater for the needs of Lancashire, Scarborough for those of Yorkshire. In addition, well-off people of venturesome disposition could now, thanks to the growth of railways on the Continent, take a holiday abroad without too much difficulty.

The age of popular sport had not yet arrived, but games were already being more widely played, especially in schools and universities. Dr. Arnold of Rugby made games a part of the curriculum of the public schools, and thence the practice spread to the universities. Games were a convenient form of exercise, too, for the townsman. Street football of the 'all-in' variety played by mobs died out about 1830, except in a few special places, but both the modern types of football were being developed at schools during the 1840s and 1850s. Standard rules began to follow in the 1860s. Cricket, of course, had long been a popular game, with rules dating from the mid-eighteenth century; bats of the modern shape and over-arm bowling came in under George IV. Athletics in 1851 was still largely confined to schools, and golf remained something only for Scotsmen. The first Oxford and Cambridge boat race, however, had been held in 1829. In 1843, Oxford rowing with seven oars beat the Cambridge eight, and in the jubilations that followed the toll-gate on Henley bridge was thrown into the river. The fixture became annual in 1856. Most of the crueller sports, such as prize-fighting without gloves and cock-fighting, were by 1851 in decline; two of the worst, bull-baiting and bear-baiting, had been legally forbidden since the 1830s. Horse-racing, hunting and shooting were all popular pastimes among the upper classes, and all were becoming more elaborately organized and expensive. Apart from hunting and archery, the only sport that ladies could take part in was croquet, first played in England in

Seaside holidays

Sport

1852. The crinoline, males sometimes complained, made a useful cover for moving the ball with the foot into a better position.

3. *Wales, Scotland, Ireland*

Thus far we have referred only to England. But the Indus- Wales trial Revolution came to Wales, too, and brought with it vast changes to the southern valleys, where there was an extensive coalfield. New industrial towns sprang up, and became big within a few years—towns such as Merthyr Tydfil, the centre of the Welsh iron industry, and Swansea and Cardiff, where the canals and railways of the coalfield came down to the sea. In 1851, Merthyr Tydfil, a mere village a hundred years earlier, was the largest town in Wales; while Cardiff, with less than 2,000 inhabitants in 1800, had over 30,000 by 1860. So the valleys of South Wales, once green, became full of pit-heads, slag-heaps, and long lines of dreary houses. Thousands of new workers poured in: between 1801 and 1831 the population of Glamorgan rose faster than that of any English county except Lancashire and the West Riding. The result is that today as many people live in Glamorgan as in the rest of Wales. Outside this industrial belt, however, Wales remained a land of small tenant farms.

There was an equally rapid transformation in the life of Scotland Scotland. The whole of the central belt became a hive of industry, the chief concerns being connected with cotton, coal, and iron. By 1851, Glasgow, with a population of 329,000, was the third-largest town in Britain; and the population of Lanarkshire in the first half of the nineteenth century grew faster than that of any English county. As more and more folk thronged into the Clydeside area the conditions in Glasgow became appalling. Prosperous merchants quickly moved into spacious houses away from the centre, but their tall old houses were taken over, extra dwellings pushed in wherever possible, and the whole converted into tenements for the poor. These were the notorious Glasgow wynds. Conditions were at their worst after 1846, when the potato blight brought thousands of **hunger-stricken** families into Glasgow from both Ireland **and** western Scotland. As late as 1861, 100,000 Glasgow **people** were living in one-roomed dwellings.

The north and west of Scotland were little touched by the Industrial Revolution. The population increased as in Ireland, perhaps owing to the potato, then after 1846 it dwindled, with the result that in some counties, such as Argyll, it was lower in 1900 than in 1800. Poverty and famine, more than the evictions by landlords, were responsible for this decline. In the countryside, families still lived in two-roomed cottages with the well-known arrangement of 'but' and 'ben'—the outer and inner room. Many of the cottages for the labourers had only one room, and in the north they were often made of turf.

Ireland   Except around Belfast, where the population increased from 20,000 to 100,000 in the first half of the nineteenth century on a flourishing trade in linen, cotton and shipping, the Industrial Revolution had hardly touched Ireland by 1850. However, Ireland lost by this, for if she had none of the new industrial slums, she also had none of the new industrial wealth. Her peasantry still lived in appalling poverty, often in cabins with mud walls roofed with straw or sods of turf. Increase in the food supply from the cultivation of potatoes was offset by a rapidly growing population. The holdings of the peasants, who were mainly smallholders, became more and more minute. By mid-century half of them held less than five acres, while the average farm in England and Wales in 1851 was calculated to cover 111 acres. With so little land the Irish were never far from the starvation line, and the potato-blight of 1846 brought disaster from which the country was long in recovering. It was not helped to do so by the attitude of its ruling classes; for after the Act of Union of 1800 the great landlords looked still more closely towards England. Their estates might be in Ireland, but they themselves were usually elsewhere. Agents, not aristocrats, had the last word with the Irish peasant.

CHAPTER TWENTY-FIVE

LIFE IN THE MID-NINETEENTH
CENTURY (II)

1. *Religion*

ENTION has already been made of that more serious The
attitude to religion which largely followed from the Evangelicals
work of John Wesley. In the nineteenth century the
first great group of men who approached Christianity in
this spirit were known as Evangelicals. Their influence
steadily increased in the Church of England after 1800.
They believed in an austere life, in works of charity, and
in the importance of personal faith, the Bible (especially
the Gospels, or 'evangel', of the New Testament—hence
their name), and the individual conscience. They attached
much less importance to priestly ministrations and the
sacraments. Two of the best known of the Evangelicals—
both laymen—were Wilberforce and Shaftesbury.

There were, however, still old-fashioned clergy of the less
enthusiastic sort who lived a spacious and magnificent life.
Hugh Percy, Bishop of Carlisle, spent £40,000 on restoring
Rose Castle and drove in person the four horses of his
mail-coach. Howley, the Archbishop of Canterbury, also
lived in great state. He drove to the House of Lords in a
coach flanked by outriders, and his guests were attended
by thirty flunkeys in livery and fifteen other servants. In
1848 he was succeeded by Charles Sumner, who, unlike his
predecessor, was an Evangelical. Sumner rose early, lit his
own fire, and walked to the House of Lords with an umbrella
under his arm.

The Evangelicals joined with the Whigs and the Radicals Church
in thinking that the Church needed reform. After the reform
triumph of the Reform Bill of 1832 the demand for a similar
reform of the Church became overwhelming. The Whigs

The Church of Ireland started with the Church of Ireland, a large organization with no fewer than twenty-two bishops. To this Church only a small portion of the Irish belonged, but all of them —including the Roman Catholics—had to pay taxes towards its upkeep. The Irish Church Act of 1833 abolished ten of the bishoprics and effected other economies. This made it possible to abolish the unpopular Church rate, though the Irish had to continue to pay tithe.

The future of the Church of England also came under debate. Many of the Radicals were hostile to it, partly because the bishops, one and all, had used their votes against the Reform Bill. The Radicals wished to disestablish the Church, i.e. to deprive it of its position as the official Church of England, and of the revenue which followed from this. The Evangelicals, on the other hand, wished only to rid the church of its more glaring abuses, such as non-residence and pluralism (the holding of more than one living), and to use the resulting savings to increase the Church's work in the new industrial areas. It was largely the proposals of the Evangelicals that Parliament adopted.

The Ecclesiastical Commission In 1836 the Ecclesiastical Commission was set up permanently to administer Church property and to ensure a fairer distribution of Church revenues. The income of the Bishop of Durham, for instance, recently swollen to £20,000 a year from the ever more profitable leasing of coal-mining rights, was reduced to £7,000 a year, and two new bishoprics, those of Ripon and Manchester, were created in big new centres of population. In 1838 pluralism was severely restricted. These reforms, together with the work of great voluntary organizations such as the Church Building Society, largely silenced the Radical criticism of the Church.

The Oxford Movement The strongest opposition to these measures came not from those who simply defended the old arrangements but from those who regarded the Church as too sacred to be controlled by the State. Alarmed by the abolition of the ten Irish bishoprics, a group of clergy at Oxford decided to start a campaign against state regulation of Church matters. The first blow was struck by John Keble, a fellow of Oriel

College, who denounced the Irish Church Act in a sermon in 1833. Keble and his friends decided to broadcast their views by publishing a series of *Tracts for the Times*. Despite a poor start—for tracts are never very inviting reading—they had a wide sale. Their authors became known as the Tractarians, and their movement as the Oxford Movement. Besides Keble, the main leaders were Hurrell Froude, Edward Pusey, and John Henry Newman. All were clergy of the Church of England, and all were or had been fellows of Oriel. Newman was the real force behind the Tracts. He was the most brilliant (and the most unstable) of the Tractarians. All these men, and particularly Newman, emphasized the authority of the Church and the clergy in religious questions, and played down the authority of the Bible and the individual conscience. In other words, the Tractarians were of High Church views, while the Evangelicals were Low Church.

Tracts for the Times

The movement at first gained some support, especially in Oxford, but it suffered a great reverse in 1845 when Newman became a Roman Catholic. As a result, the Tractarians lost much sympathy, but Pusey and Keble rallied their forces and finally secured a lasting effect on the Church of England. They introduced practices now generally accepted, e.g. weekly communion services—many members had previously attended communion only once or twice a year—and a greater degree of ceremonial in all services. They also ceaselessly asserted that the Church of England is a Catholic Church, i.e. a Church descended by continuous tradition from the Early Church—for which reasons they also came to be known as Anglo-Catholics. Their comparative success was remarkable, for their attempts to increase the authority of Church and clergy were unlikely to be widely popular in a country then as strongly Protestant as England. They were aided to some extent by the contemporary revival of interest in the Middle Ages—a period when the authority of the Church had been at its height.

Newman

After the Church of England, the largest section was that of the various Noncomformists. Among these the Wesleyans

The Non-conformists

or Methodists increased in numbers until 1846, when they had about 350,000 members. Then there was a decline, largely due to an internal quarrel which led to a split. There had been earlier schisms as well, and the various malcontents united to form another group—the United Methodist Free Churches. By mid-century the Baptists, too, had ceased to make much progress, though they were 100,000 strong at this period. For the other big Nonconformist body, the Congregationalists, there are no figures. They were a union formed by independent congregations, some dating back to the days of Cromwell, and had little central organization.

Scotland In Scotland the established Church was, as it is today, the Presbyterian Church. The Church of Scotland, like the Church of England, was fired at this time by a new enthusiasm—a revival which owed much to Thomas Chalmers, Professor of Divinity at Edinburgh from 1828 to 1847. Many Presbyterians thought that congregations should have a greater say in the appointment of their ministers, a decision at that time in the hands of the patron. The government would not accept this view and defended the Presbyterians split rights of the patron. As a result many of the reformers left the Church and founded the Free Church of Scotland (1843). Within four years they had raised over £1 million and built over 600 churches—a remarkable feat.

Roman Catholics Throughout Great Britain, freedom of worship had been officially accorded to Roman Catholics in 1791, and equality of political and civic rights followed by the Catholic Emancipation measure of 1829. All this helped to bring about a Roman Catholic revival, and by 1850 there were more Roman Catholics in Britain than Baptists. Their greatest success was the conversion of Newman and of some other Tractarians who went over to Rome. The bulk of their new members, however, came from Irish immigrants.

Missionary work Meanwhile the Evangelicals had entered upon missionary work, a field previously neglected by the British. Many lives and much money were devoted to this activity, which was organized largely through voluntary societies. An Evangelical society—the London Missionary Society— led the way in the 1790s, and societies of other groups followed. Among the places which soon attracted missionaries, including many who qualified as doctors, were India, Africa, China, and the islands of the Pacific. The Church Missionary Society, for example, took the leading part in the conversion of the Maoris.

After 1850 an even greater effort was put into the mission field, especially in Africa, to which the London Missionary Society had already directed a Scots missionary who was to open up much of the unknown interior—Dr. David Livingstone. Thus, overseas as well as at home, the Evangelicals sought to spread the Christian faith and to promote the serious, dedicated life.

2. Education

Still vitally linked with religion throughout the whole of the early nineteenth century was education. There were no state schools, even by 1851, and almost all the schools which existed had some sort of religious foundation or connection.

In 1833, however, the State began to offer a tiny grant (£20,000 a year) for school-building to two of the chief religious organizations that were running schools. From this small beginning, state interest in primary education gradually increased: a special committee of the Privy Council was set up to administer the grant (which grew rapidly), and an apprenticeship scheme was started for 'pupil-teachers'. By 1851 there were nearly a million children at Church of England schools—mainly primary ones—and some hundreds of thousands at non-denominational or Nonconformist schools. Even so, many children were still going entirely uneducated—at least a third, over the country as a whole, still did not attend school of any kind.

In secondary education the greatest change during this period was seen in the public schools. During the eighteenth century many of these had been centres of idleness and vice to which sensible parents were reluctant to send their sons. Now reform set in. It was largely the work of a few individuals who took education seriously. The pioneer was Samuel Butler, who was appointed headmaster of Shrewsbury in 1798, when it had only three pupils left, and who

[marginal notes:] Education (primary)

State interest begins, 1833

Secondary education

The public schools

	ELLEN	ALICE		FANNY	HENRY
	To be called ¼ to 7.	To be called ¼ to 7.	**7**	To be called ¼ to 7.	To be called ¼ past 7.
	Rise	Rise		Rise	Rise
	Hymn, text, Collect.	Hymn, text, collect.	**8**	Hymn, text, collect.	
		Family		prayers	
		BREAK ·		· FAST ·	— · NER —
	Practise	Write Copy	**9**	Learn lessons	Write copy.
		Learn lessons.			
	Write copy		**10**	Write copy	
	Learn lessons	Practise.		Draw	
	Read Bible	and answer	**11**	questions thereon	with mamma
	Say lessons	Say lessons		Say lessons	
	General reading	& conversation		with mamma	
	Solfeggio	Solfeggio	**12**	Solfeggio	Solfeggio
	Draw	Draw		Practise	
	Gymnastics	Gymnastics.	**1**	Gymnastics	
			2		
		DIN ·		NER	
	New tune or song	Work	**3**	Exercises or Ciphering	
	Needle work.	New tune or song	**4**	New tune or song	
	Exercises Ciphering.	Exercises Ciphering.		Needle work	
			5		
	Walk	to	**6**	meet	me
	TEA.	TEA.	**7**	TEA	
			8		Go to bed
	Go to bed	Go to bed		Go to bed	

An Early Victorian Timetable

This timetable was drawn up by a Victorian father round about 1860 for the education of his children at home.

Arnold of Rugby

transformed it into a great centre of classical scholarship. Even more influential was Dr. Thomas Arnold, who became headmaster of Rugby in 1828. Not only did he insist on a high standard of work, he also strove above all to implant in his pupils the desire to live a truly Christian life. His example was followed by others, and such became the prestige of the public schools that the sons of the upper and wealthier middle classes flocked to them. To meet this increasing demand many new public schools—such as Marlborough, Radley, Lancing and Bradfield—were founded between 1840 and 1860.

During the first half of the nineteenth century most of the old grammar schools were still in poor shape. Many of them had been founded under Elizabeth I to teach only Latin and Greek grammar, and until an act of 1840 permitted variations they were confined to this original narrow curriculum. A wider choice of studies was to be had at the numerous private schools—good, bad and indifferent; but in some of the new towns there were still no secondary schools at all, either grammar or private. *The grammar and private schools*

The educational picture was brighter, however, in the universities, where old abuses were now disappearing. At Oxford and Cambridge standards of industry, both of tutors and students, greatly improved during the early nineteenth century, and it also became possible to take a degree in many new subjects, including history and natural science. Written examinations, too, began to replace the more haphazard methods of oral disputation. Both universities, however, still remained completely Anglican institutions, with all academic positions reserved to Church of England clergy. At Oxford, Nonconformists were not even admitted as students: at Cambridge they could enter, but not sit for degrees. Not until the later 'fifties were religious tests of this kind to be abolished. *The universities* / *Oxford and Cambridge*

After 1828, however, Oxford and Cambridge no longer had a monopoly of university education in England. In that year, University College (London) was opened as a non-sectarian centre for university studies, though without power to grant degrees. In opposition to this 'godless institution in Gower Street', King's College (London) was then quickly founded in the Anglican interest, and in 1836 the two colleges were linked together in the University of London—to which other colleges were later admitted. Outside London, too, a university was established in 1832 at Durham, but mainly for theological studies. Meanwhile the four Scottish universities, which still accepted students *London University, 1836* / *Scottish universities*

University College (London University) in 1857

at the age of fifteen or sixteen, continued to provide good education, and often brilliant lectures, at low cost. The benefits of this were felt throughout Scotland, not least in the better supply of suitably qualified teachers for secondary schools.

Outside Scotland, in 1851 only the upper and wealthier middle classes had much chance of securing higher education. The working man might find a good course of evening lectures on some scientific topic at the local Mechanics' Institute—if one existed—but as he had not enjoyed a secondary education it might well be above his head. He was hardly more 'educationally under-privileged', however, than the entire female sex of the country. In 1851 it would be long before any university opened its doors to women. Nevertheless, there was at least one ray of hope: certain newly-founded girls' schools, notably Queen's College and the North London Collegiate School, were now approaching secondary education in a serious spirit, comparable with that of the best public schools for boys. Not for many years yet, however, outside a few restricted circles, would Jill be regarded as a possible academic rival to Jack.

Education for women

CHAPTER TWENTY-SIX

THE ARTS, 1830–50

1. *Literature*

B Y 1850 many things had combined to produce a growing belief that Britain and the world were moving into a great era of progress. This conviction was by no means held by all the great mid-nineteenth-century writers. Alfred Tennyson (1809–92), however, the out-standing poet of the time, usually found himself in sympathy with the general outlook of the day. Poetry: Tennyson

The son of a Lincolnshire parson, Tennyson published his first verses at the age of eighteen. By the 1840s he was regarded as the foremost poet of the day, and in 1850, on the death of Wordsworth, he was appointed Poet Laureate. Soon afterwards, comfortably off at last from the sale of his poems, he retired to the Isle of Wight—whence he was later driven away by sightseers. A few years before his death he was made a peer—the first and thus far the last British poet to have been accorded this honour.

Almost everyone who can enjoy poetry at all has enjoyed Tennyson at some time in his life. He had a wonderful command over sound, and much of his poetry is exquisitely musical. A good deal less appealing to us nowadays than the word-magic of *The Lotos-Eaters* or the lyrics from *The Princess* are his many 'popular' poems of Victorian life, including the well-known *Charge of the Light Brigade* (1854). (This, however, was recited by soldiers in the Crimea: it would be hard to think of a present-day poet whom soldiers wished to recite.)

As for Tennyson's fashionable views on progress, these are well seen in the speaker's vision in *Locksley Hall* (1842), where aeroplanes, bombing and world war all lead up to final peace:

> Till the war drums throbb'd no longer, and the battle
> flags were furled,

In the Parliament of man, the Federation of the world.
There the common sense of most shall hold a fretful realm
in awe,
And the kindly earth shall slumber, wrapt in universal
law.

This poem also contains those famous lines so typical of the
great confidence of the Victorians:

Not in vain the distance beacons. Forward, forward,
let us range,
Let the great world spin for ever down the ringing
grooves of change—

composed, so Tennyson said, on the first railway journey he
ever made. There are also many poems in which Tennyson
reflects popular patriotic impulses of the moment, even to
the extent of glorifying war (in a just cause) as preferable to
the selfish money-making of peace. Tennyson, however, was
not so complacent as to accept all the opinions of his day.
Especially notable in this respect is *In Memoriam* (1850), his
broodings over many years inspired by the death of his friend
Arthur Hallam. This fine poem shows a deep concern with
fundamental questions of life and death, God and the
Universe—problems that already perplexed Tennyson, and
that were to perplex the later Victorians still more.

Browning   A good deal more difficult to read than Tennyson is the
other major poet of this time, Robert Browning (1812–89).
The son of a cultured and comfortably-off bank official, he
was brought up at Camberwell. He published his first work
in 1833, but it was long before he became well known.
Indeed, for many years his reputation as a poet was
surpassed by that of his wife, Elizabeth Barrett Browning,
whom he rescued from an invalid's couch and paternal
domination. Most of Browning's poems were about people,
for the human mind was his chief concern, and he delighted
to present in the form of dramatic monologues studies of
unusual and interesting men and women. For his subjects
he ranged far and wide, drawing characters like *Rabbi Ben
Ezra* and *Fra Lippo Lippi* from many different countries in
different ages. Compared with Tennyson's, Browning's
poems are rugged and unmusical, but they show a deeper

Alfred Tennyson
aged about 30—from a portrait by
Samuel Laurence.

Robert Browning
Aged about 47—from a chalk study by
Field Talfourd.

understanding of human character and conduct and have a
greater vigour and sense of joy.

Other poets of the early Victorian period were Thomas Minor poets
Hood (1799–1845), whose verses ran either to humour
(with many puns) or to pathos; the farm-worker's son,
John Clare (d. 1864), who wrote tender poetry of the
English countryside but whose mind became deranged;
and the Reverend Richard Barham (d. 1845), the author
of the high-spirited *Ingoldsby Legends*, including the immortal
Jackdaw of Rheims.

In addition to the poets of this period there were also a Novelists
number of famous novelists. Outstanding among these was
Charles Dickens (1812–70). His father was a clerk in the Dickens
Navy Pay Office. Working at Portsmouth when Charles was
born, he moved first to London, then to Chatham, and
finally back to London. Young Charles, of course, accompanied him.

Then came a crash in the family fortunes. Dickens's
father, though receiving a reasonable salary, was badly in
debt, and in 1822 was sent to the Debtors' Prison in Southwark, the Marshalsea. This improvident parent Dickens

afterwards portrayed as Mr. Micawber, a man constitutionally incapable of profiting from his own advice to David Copperfield: 'Annual income twenty pounds, annual expenditure, nineteen, nineteen-six, result happiness. Annual income twenty pounds, annual expenditure twenty pounds ought and six, result misery'. Charles himself did not enter the Marshalsea with the rest of the family. Though only ten, he went out to work—work which was a misery to him. It was at a warehouse where he toiled publicly in the window, tying up and labelling pots of blacking. His suffering during this period he described in the early chapters of *David Copperfield*—though the blacking factory is disguised as a bottling firm.

A revival of the family fortunes next enabled Dickens to go to school again for two years. Then at the age of fourteen he set out on his career. He began as a lawyer's clerk, but after learning shorthand became a reporter in the Law Courts. By the age of nineteen he had progressed to the Press Gallery of the House of Commons. His first fictional publications were a number of sketches of London life written under the pseudonym Boz, and illustrated by George Cruikshank. These were sufficiently promising for the publishers to ask him to write the stories for an illustrated series about a club of sportsmen doomed to suffer perpetual disasters. This was the origin of the *Pickwick Papers*, the first number of which appeared in the spring of 1836. Interest was moderate until the character of Sam Weller appeared, after which the circulation rose by leaps and bounds. By the end of the year Dickens's name was made, and he resigned his post as a parliamentary reporter to become a full-time author.

The *Pickwick Papers* are the journals of an imaginary club presided over by Mr. Pickwick—rotund and rubicund, good-natured and guileless. In the adventures of its members Dickens showed high-spirited imagination, a wide knowledge of everyday life, a remarkable talent for depicting character and places, and a great sense of fun. To these qualities as a novelist he later added considerable power as a story-teller (though his plots were often ramshackle),

The Trial in the 'Pickwick Papers'

ne of the many immortal scenes in Dickens. Sergeant Buzzfuzz is declaiming on
half of his client Mrs. Bardell (*large, in front row*) in her action for breach of
omise against the guileless Mr. Pickwick (showing consternation, *left of front row*).

together with a liking for death-bed and other pathetic scenes. With few exceptions all his writings are novels, and many first appeared in separate monthly or weekly numbers. For the most part they are great, sprawling affairs, often better for the excellence of their parts than for their shape as a whole. There is immense variety in their subject-matter, for which Dickens drew freely on his own experiences—such as the law in *Bleak House*, the Thames and its mud-flats in two novels written in the 1860s, *Great Expectations* and *Our Mutual Friend*. Again and again there are scenes from the teeming life of London that he knew so well. There is usually, too, a strong moral message in Dickens's novels, and often scathing criticism of institutions of the time. *Oliver Twist* (1837), for instance, showed up the brutality of work-house conditions, *Nicholas Nickleby* (1838) the harshness, inefficiency and squalor of many small private boarding-schools, *Bleak House* (1852) the cruel delays of government departments and the Chancery Courts, *Hard Times* (1854) the inhumanity and greed of some of the northern industrialists.

Thackeray   The background of William Makepeace Thackeray (1811–63) was very different from that of Charles Dickens. He was born near Calcutta, the son of an officer of the East India Company who had considerable means. His father died when he was four and Thackeray soon returned to England, where he was educated at Charterhouse and Cambridge. Like Dickens, however, he entered the ranks of authorship through journalism. In 1833 he bought a paper and through this and gambling lost most of his money. However, he was soon earning a living both by writing and drawing for magazines. His great works are his novels, particularly *Vanity Fair*, published in 1848, and *The History of Henry Esmond, Esq.*, a historical novel, published in 1852. By many people the former, with the calculating Becky Sharp, is reckoned the finest novel in the English language. In general, *Vanity Fair*, 'a novel without a hero', is a satire on the greed and selfishness of the upper middle classes of the day, especially those like Jos. Sedley, who had made their fortune in India. Thus both Dickens and Thackeray reflect the outcome of the Industrial Revolution, Thackeray in his picture of the upper middle classes who depended so much on the expansion of trade, Dickens in his scenes drawn from every aspect of life in the new Britain.

The other great novelists of this period, the Brontë sisters, were cut off from the ordinary life of the day. They lived in a gaunt stone parsonage flanked on two sides by a graveyard at the top of a remote place called Haworth, on the edge of the Yorkshire moors. Here their father, the Reverend Patrick Brontë, was parson. Four of his six children survived childhood: Charlotte, Branwell (the only boy), Emily and Anne, all born between 1816 and 1820. Their mother, not surprisingly, died in 1821, and an aunt came to look after them. The children spent most of their time at Haworth, rarely going to school. Later, however, Charlotte and Anne were away for considerable periods as governesses. Their first work was published at their own expense in 1846, a collection of poems by the three sisters, but announced as by Currer, Ellis and Acton Bell— pseudonyms intended to disguise female authorship. In the first two years only two copies were sold.

By this time the family was again together, for Branwell too had come home, dismissed by his employer, and was giving himself more and more to drink. Deeply grieved but undeterred, the sisters pressed on with their literary work. Their persistence was soon rewarded. During 1847 they each persuaded a publisher to accept a novel. Charlotte's book, *Jane Eyre*, with its unusual heroine, a quiet-looking governess who nourishes deep feelings for her married employer, was an immediate success; Emily's *Wuthering Heights* made only a slow start. Anne's novel, *Agnes Gray*, was of altogether lesser note. But very soon after the excitement of this treble publication, tragedy smote the family. Branwell, his health wrecked by drink and opium, died in September 1848. His funeral was the last occasion on which Emily left the house; she died in that December of consumption. In the following year Anne died of the same disease, with which the parsonage by then must have been riddled.

The
Brontës

The Brontë Sisters

Anne, Emily and Charlotte, painted by their brother Bramwell.

Charlotte fought on, writing *Shirley*, a novel of the machine-breaking days, and *Villette*, incorporating her experience as a teacher abroad. She married in 1854 but died the year afterwards.

The Brontës' books have never been forgotten. *Jane Eyre* is a great story vividly told and still widely read: in its insight into the romantic side of the female heart it was probably more skilful than anything previously written.

Wuthering Heights came into its own much more slowly. A story of revenge and deep romantic passion, it draws its life from the Yorkshire moors and the intensity of feeling of its characters, so that the book has a quite exceptional originality, power and beauty.

In addition to these great names, there were also many lesser novelists of merit writing during the years 1830-50. Of these the foremost were possibly Captain Frederick Marryat, with his stories of the old Navy, and Benjamin Disraeli, the later Prime Minister. Disraeli's *Coningsby* (1844) is probably the best 'political' novel ever written, while his *Sybil, or The Two Nations* brought out sharply the contrasts between rich and poor, the old aristocracy and the new world of industry. More popular at the time than either of these writers was Bulwer Lytton (later Lord Lytton), with his historical romances such as *The Last Days of Pompeii* (1834). The younger novelists at the end of our period included the Reverend Charles Kingsley, a leader of the new Christian Socialist movement: his *Yeast* and *Alton Locke* contained much criticism of contemporary society. Anthony Trollope, too, had begun writing, but his first success— *The Warden*—was not to come till 1855. Another younger writer was Elizabeth Gaskell, whose *Mary Barton* (1848) gave a vivid impression of social conditions in the Manchester area.

Outside fiction, there were many important writers in the fields of biography, the essay, history, and social enquiry. Among these, two or three were outstanding. Thomas Babington (later Lord) Macaulay, whose father had been prominent in the campaign against the slave-trade, suddenly achieved fame in 1825 with an essay on Milton. By 1830 he was in the House of Commons for a pocket borough, and well on the way to a successful political career. A strong Whig, he gave valuable support to the Reform Bill, and later did great work for educational and legal progress in India. Out of office with the return to power of the Conservatives in 1841, he began to concentrate more on his writing, and soon published his collected essays and his *Lays of Ancient Rome*. Then followed by far his

Lesser novelists

Other writers

Macaulay

greatest work—his *History of England*, the first two volumes of which appeared in 1848. It is one of the most readable, if prejudiced, great histories ever written, but unfortunately its author died when he had covered in full detail only the reigns of James II and William III. As a historian Macaulay was much helped by his wonderful memory: at a very early age he could recite by heart the whole of *Paradise Lost*!

Carlyle   Very different from Macaulay and much more complex in style was Thomas Carlyle (d. 1881). The son of a Scottish stonemason, he combined historical writing with social criticism and prophecy. His *French Revolution* (1837) contains some splendidly vivid, exclamatory writing—of which one may quickly tire—and his *Letters and Speeches of Oliver Cromwell* (1845) is a masterpiece of interpretation which for the first time brought out the true greatness of the Puritan leader. In his own personal philosophy, Carlyle ran completely contrary to the fashionable views of the time: he was pessimistic, grimly ironic, and, though a Radical, savagely critical of *laissez faire*. He demanded, not democracy, but strong, intelligent, and moral government.

Ruskin   A disciple of Carlyle, and a rising young writer in 1851, was John Ruskin, the son of a wealthy and highly cultured wine-merchant. A wayward genius dominated by his mother—she even took lodgings in Oxford to keep an eye on him while he was at the University—he first made his name by his defence of Turner in *Modern Painters* (1843 onward). Before long he was the foremost British writer not only on painting but also on architecture. From 1860, however, he concentrated less on art than on the evils of contemporary society, to the reform of which in a vaguely socialist direction he devoted his remaining years and his private fortune.

2. *Painting, Architecture, Music*

Painting   The early years of Queen Victoria's reign produced a great wealth of literature. They gave birth to no such riches in painting, apart from the later work of Turner.[1] Much the

[1] See page 226.

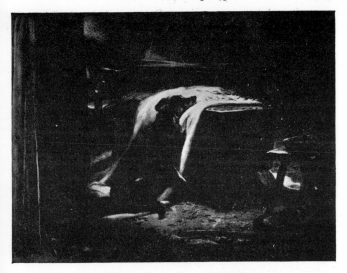

The Old Shepherd's Chief Mourner

This is typical of the 'human' or sentimental appeal with which Landseer
in middle and later life invested the animals of his pictures.

most popular of the artists of this period was Sir Edwin
Landseer (1802–73), the son of an engraver. A youthful Landseer
prodigy, he exhibited in the Royal Academy at the age of
thirteen, featuring in the catalogue as 'Master E. Landseer'. His subjects were generally animals, and in his early
manhood he was usually content to depict these in their
natural character. During Victoria's reign, however, he
began to give them an increasingly human quality—a trait
well calculated to appeal to the British public. His works
included such typical productions as *The Old Shepherd's
Chief Mourner* (a picture of a dog pressing its body against
the coffin of its dead master), *Dignity and Impudence* (more
dogs), and *The Monarch of the Glen* (a noble-looking stag in
the Highlands). 'Subject' (or anecdotal) pictures of this
kind were much favoured by the Victorians, and increasingly
so during the third quarter of the century. Towards the end
of his career Landseer also designed the lions in Trafalgar
Square. Reproductions of his pictures by this time decorated

thousands of Victorian homes, and he was knighted for his work. Today his popularity has sharply slumped, though the fine draughtsmanship of his early work is still recognized.

The Pre-Raphaelites

One of the most interesting developments in Victorian painting came in 1848, when half a dozen artists banded themselves together as the Pre-Raphaelite Brotherhood and launched a new movement in British art. They were mostly admirers of Ford Madox Brown, a painter who employed bright colours and built up highly decorative pictures from close observation of contemporary life. In so far as the Pre-Raphaelites had a common purpose, they aimed—like the writers of the Romantic Revival—to disregard long-fashionable traditions and instead to go back direct to nature for their inspiration. Just as the Romantic writers rejected the classical models of the seventeenth and eighteenth centuries, so the Pre-Raphaelites, too, turned back to the later Middle Ages—to the period before the great Raphael, when artists had no acknowledged master of perfection to follow.

The leaders of the Pre-Raphaelite movement were (Sir) John Millais, Holman Hunt, and Dante Gabriel Rossetti, all at this time young men around twenty-one. In this Pre-Raphaelite phase they painted with great brilliance of colour and fullness of detail. Much of their painting was cloyingly sentimental, but technically it was very gifted, and the strong, bright colour was a refreshing change after art's long concern with shadow and subdued tones. The Brotherhood itself did not last long. Millais quickly departed, to take up fashionable portraiture and subject-pictures. However, Rossetti (who was also a poet) passed on much of the Pre-Raphaelite ideal to two young disciples, William Morris and Edward Burne-Jones, whose romantic medievalism was a feature of the next generation.

Other painters

Of other artists, the foremost among those just passing away was William Etty (d. 1849). He painted huge, splendidly coloured pictures on classical themes, with much use of the nude, and was regarded as somewhat lacking in taste. His reputation is now steadily rising once more. Another established artist was the Irishman Daniel Maclise,

Christ in the Carpenter's Shop

From the painting by J. E. Millais. The boy Jesus shows Mary the stigmata on His palm—prophetic of His death on the Cross. The everyday realism of the setting was considered by many at the time to be extremely irreverent.

who specialized in portraiture and historical subjects. Among the young men, a high reputation had been won very early by W. P. Frith, who was soon to turn to subject-pictures of the most crowded and detailed kind, including the famous *Ramsgate Sands* and *Derby Day*. Another young artist was G. F. Watts, who was already painting symbolic or allegorical subjects and striving by this means to impart a moral message.

The desire to imitate earlier ages was even more pro- Architecture nounced in architecture, and was partly caused by the very wealth of Victorian resources and scholarship. All too often the Victorians set out to reproduce the appearance of some great masterpiece of the past. Furthermore, the copying was often not very skilfully done: the Victorian craftsman, though a sound and honest worker, was not the equal of medieval creative artists, and in any case copying usually produces soulless results. All this was a pity, for the second and third quarters of the nineteenth century were a period of extensive building. Public and town halls, clubs, offices for banks and insurance companies, railway stations and churches, all were being constructed in large numbers.

Greek Classical   The most popular style to be imitated in the second quarter of the nineteenth century was the Greek classical. Among nineteenth-century artists Greece often replaced Italy as the place of pilgrimage where the correct models for the architect could be found, especially after the Greek struggle for independence had fanned enthusiasm for that country. British interest, however, had begun earlier, and was much quickened by the acquisition of the Elgin marbles (sculptures from the Parthenon brought to England during the Napoleonic wars by Lord Elgin and later purchased for the nation). This Greek influence on British architecture can be clearly seen in the work of Sir Robert Smirke, who designed the British Museum, and Robert Cockerell, who designed the branch offices of the Bank of England in Manchester, Liverpool and Bristol. Other notable buildings in this style, all built between 1828 and 1850, are the National Gallery and University College, London, both by William Wilkins; Birmingham Town Hall, by J. A. Hansom (the inventor of the hansom-cab) and St. George's Hall at Liverpool, by H. L. Elmes. Both these halls are impressive but not altogether practical. Birmingham Town Hall, for instance, is externally almost an exact replica of a Greek temple, and a building that suited the Greeks for worship in the fifth century B.C. was unlikely to be ideally suited for the municipal business of an industrial town in the nineteenth century A.D. The fashion for Greek-looking architecture shows even more plainly in some fine buildings in Dublin and in Edinburgh, which called itself 'The Modern Athens'. Forms of the classical style were also used even for railway stations (as at Euston and Newcastle upon Tyne).

Victorian Gothic   During the same period the imitators of another style—the Gothic—were growing in popularity. The revival of Gothic was speeded by the large number of churches built in Britain in the first half of the nineteenth century and the renewed interest in the Middle Ages brought about by the Romantic Revival. For churches the classical style was, with a few exceptions, soon discarded. It was felt that Britain

The British Museum

The present front, designed by Sir R. Smirke and built 1823-47, is an excellent example of early 19th century 'classic'—scholarly, heavy, uninspired, impressive.

should return to the Gothic or medieval style, in which practically all her greatest cathedrals and churches had been built, and which was specially associated with the Christian religion. The Tractarians in particular always insisted on churches in the Gothic style. For them, as for most Victorians, a church constructed like a classical temple was too reminiscent of paganism. Gothic, they were convinced, was much more holy.

After the Wyatts[1], the most famous of the early architects who worked in the Gothic manner was Augustus Pugin (d. 1852). His churches are to be seen in many places, a notable example in London being St. George's, the Roman Catholic cathedral in Southwark. His best-known successor was Sir George Gilbert Scott, who designed the Martyrs'

Pugin

[1] Page 236.

Memorial at Oxford, and in the 1860s went on to produce
the Albert Memorial and even a Gothic railway station and
hotel—at St. Pancras. To Scott was also entrusted the
restoration of hundreds of old churches, for the most part
with unfortunate results.

The Houses of Parliament
One of the comparatively few masterpieces of nineteenth-century 'Gothic'.

Pugin was connected, too, with one of the finest secular
works of the Gothic school—the new Houses of Parliament.
The old Houses of Parliament were destroyed on the night
of October 16th, 1834, when officials burning the medieval
tally sticks allowed the fire to grow too hot. It was laid down
that the new design should be in Gothic or Tudor, for these
were considered native styles, whereas Classical was a
foreign importation from Greece and Italy. The design
finally accepted was that of Sir Charles Barry, who was
mainly known at this time for work in the Renaissance
style. It is Barry's Houses of Parliament that stand today.
The building is covered with much detail in the Gothic
style, and for this, Pugin, who acted as his assistant, was in
the main responsible.

Gothic was also used for many other types of building in

the mid-nineteenth century. A number of Gothic castles or abbeys were built as private residences, and a little later the style was also used for the Law Courts in London, for town halls (as at Manchester in the 1870s), and for railway stations (as at Shrewsbury, Carlisle and Perth). Unfortunately few of them, and few of the various classical imitations either, are as good to look at as many of the things the Victorians built when they were not thinking of 'architecture' at all—things like railway viaducts, when they simply had in mind a solid job of engineering.

We have thus far discussed literature, painting and architecture, and during the period 1830–50 nothing much is lost if we end our study of the arts with these. The period was one of rapidly worsening taste in the applied arts of the home: no furniture or porcelain from this period exists Furniture which can challenge comparison with the products of the etc. previous generation or the eighteenth century. In 1850, there was only one sculptor—Alfred Stevens—who posses- Sculpture sed more than a medium talent. And in music, matters Music were even worse: on top of Italian opera had come the great German and Austrian composers—Haydn, Mozart, Beethoven, Schubert and (a frequent visitor to Britain) Mendelssohn—and British musical composition counted for little indeed.[1] Two Irishmen—Balfe and Wallace—wrote rather naïve operas of considerable popularity in *The Bohemian Girl* and *Maritana*; and one Englishman—Sterndale Bennett— showed brilliant promise as a young man, only to submerge his talent in years of teaching and administration. Apart from these, one has to search hard to find any composer now remembered.

Summing up, we find that the period 1830–50 was one of declining merit in all the arts except literature. For this there can be no doubt that the replacement of the old aristocracy as the main patrons of art by a large, wealthy and artistically immature middle class was largely responsible.

---

[1] Mendelssohn was much sought after in Britain, but found the aristocracy for the most part hopelessly unmusical. 'Buckingham Palace', he wrote, 'is the one really pleasant English home where one feels at ease.' Queen Victoria delighted to sing to his accompaniment.

CONCLUSION:

THE GREAT EXHIBITION OF 1851

THE vast advance in science and industry, the immense new range of factory products, the boasted achievements of Victorian art, the intense religious seriousness, found their combined expression in the Great International Exhibition of 1851.

To us the Exhibition may now appear mainly as a display of the national wealth of Britain in 1851, but to its organizers it was a great deal more. Prince Albert, who suggested the whole venture and presided over the Commissioners charged with preparing the Exhibition, wrote this text for the official catalogue: 'The progress of the human race resulting from the labour of all men ought to be the final object of the exertion of each individual. In promoting this end we are carrying out the will of the Great and Blessed God.' Again before the Exhibition opened he said: 'I confidently hope the first impression which the view of this vast collection will produce upon the spectator will be that of deep thankfulness to the Almighty for the blessings which he has bestowed upon us here below; and the second, conviction that they can only be realized in proportion to the help which we are prepared to render to each other—therefore only by peace, love, and ready assistance, not only between individuals but between the nations of the earth.' These were generous ideas, shared by all of progressive outlook at the time.

The idea of a great exhibition was not of course new. In England, exhibitions organized by the Society of Arts had been held in the mid-eighteenth century, and later they had become common throughout Europe. No one, however, had thus far arranged an *international* exhibition. This was the great decision of the Prince Consort when the suggestion was put to him by Henry Cole, a member of the

The Crystal Palace: South Side with Main Entrance

Society of Arts and earlier a helper of Rowland Hill in the introduction of the penny post. As President of the Society of Arts the prince had an appropriate organization behind him and early in 1850 a Royal Commission, with the prince as chairman and including Cole, was formed to execute the project. At a dinner in the Mansion House in 1850 the prince launched the scheme on the country as a whole. The idea was well received, but soon the obstacles began to appear. By intense work, especially on the part of the prince, problems of money and organization were surmounted, only for all the suppressed forces of opposition to boil up over the choice of site. The prince selected a large area in Hyde Park, whereupon there was a great outcry, led by *The Times*. Ultimately the site was approved, but the nature of the building to be erected upon it presented another obvious difficulty. More than two hundred designs were submitted, mostly of ugly brick structures like railway sheds, costly to erect and to remove. But finally the organizers had a stroke of luck in the remarkable project put forward by Joseph Paxton.

Paxton had started life as a gardener's boy at one of the houses of the Duke of Devonshire. He had risen to be manager of the duke's estates and a director of the Midland Railway. At Chatsworth he had built for the duke a huge conservatory and a glass-house to protect a very rare lily. He happened to hear when he was in London that no satisfactory design had been sent in for the Exhibition. He offered to produce one within nine days. The next day he doodled the rough sketch on his blotting-paper during a railway meeting and within nine days the plans were complete. The design was revolutionary, completely discarding conventional styles and materials. It was for an enormous glass-house built entirely of iron and glass, things which the new Britain could produce plentifully. It could be mass-produced quickly in sections, and could be removed with relative ease. Seizing their opportunity, the prince and the Commission accepted the design.

Work on the building began on July 30th, 1850. As it rose, there were further protests about damage to the park; and some large elms had to be included within the building rather than cut down. Conservative forces, including certain foreign monarchs, deplored anything which would bring together a large number of the populace, and so possibly set off a revolution. Protectionists clamoured against the introduction of foreign goods. There were further financial difficulties. But still the mighty edifice rose. Rectangular on plan, with a curved roof, it was 408 feet in width and 1,848 feet in length—three times the length of St. Paul's Cathedral. This long part was known as the nave. Built across the centre of the oblong was a higher part known as the transept. The whole covered nineteen acres, and in its construction employed over 4,000 tons of iron, nearly 300,000 panes of glass, and about twenty-four miles of guttering. The building, at once nicknamed the Crystal Palace, was duly completed and most of the exhibits installed when on the scheduled date of May 1st, 1851, the Queen opened the Exhibition before a vast concourse of people. The story goes that shortly before the ceremony the thousands of small birds which

The Crystal Palace: The Transept, looking South

The iron gates, made at Coalbrookdale, to-day divide
Hyde Park from Kensington Gardens.

roosted in the enclosed trees were causing a great nuisance
inside the Palace. It was impossible to shoot them owing
to the glass, and many other measures had been applied in
vain. The Duke of Wellington, personally consulted over
the matter by the queen, disposed of the problem in three
words: 'Try sparrowhawks, Ma'am.'

Let us now put ourselves in the place of a visitor in 1851
entering the Crystal Palace at the eastern end. The eastern

Machinery in the Great Exhibition

The machinery was shown in motion, powered by steam from a specially
built boiler-house outside.

half was devoted to British goods. At the entrance there was
a large statue of Richard Coeur de Lion and a block of
twenty-four tons of coal, symbols of courage and power.
Inside there were, among many other things: locomotives,
Nasmyth's steam-hammer, photographic apparatus—an
effective camera had first been produced in 1839—balloons,
Whitworth's engine tools, textiles, some glass, and a vast
quantity of furniture and hardware covered with ornate
and hideous designs. The other half—the western—was the
foreign section. Here the biggest exhibition was from
France with her luxury goods—tapestry, silk, porcelain,
and so on. The American section came in for much
criticism, as the Americans had claimed more space than
they could fill. The discerning, however, saw in some of the
American exhibits how British supremacy in machinery
might soon be challenged. There was a sewing-machine
and above all the McCormick reaper, two inventions which
put America far ahead of Britain in those particular fields.
There were, of course, difficulties over the classifying of

A Sportsman's Knife with Eighty Blades
One of the many exhibits equally striking for their
novelty, ingenuity, and hideously over-elaborate
design.

exhibits. A wig-maker was angered when his goods were
placed not in the Fine Arts section but among the Animal
Products. There were also plenty of strange or peculiar
exhibits: the Prussian display included a stove in the form
of a knight in full armour, and the American a piano with
two keyboards at which four people could play at once—
articles both perhaps rather typical of their countries of
origin.

The Exhibition was an enormous success. It was visited
by over six million people from all walks of life, each of

whom had a personal glimpse of Britain's great industrial supremacy. An entrance fee of one shilling made it possible for labourers to come, and railway companies ran hundreds of cheap excursions to the capital. (Thomas Cook first made his name in this way.) Fears of disorder and violence if labourers were admitted and large crowds gathered proved completely groundless. All classes mixed freely without any serious incident, or even an accident. So complete was the triumph that it indeed seemed as if the violence and suspicion associated with the age of the Chartists had ended, and that a new age had begun which betokened prosperity and knowledge for all.

So far as more material results were concerned, the Exhibition in its five and a half months of life made a profit of £186,000. This money, under the guidance of the prince, was used to buy a large block of land in Kensington with the object of forwarding the arts and sciences. On this land have since been built the Royal College of Art, the Imperial College of Science, the Royal College of Music, and all the Kensington Museums—a magnificent legacy. As for the dazzling Crystal Palace itself, this was so much admired, and in itself drew so many crowds, that it was re-erected at Sydenham, where it grew steadily blacker, shabbier and less attractive until it was burnt down in 1931.

Thus the Great Exhibition of the Works of Industry of all Nations, the Prince Consort's own personal project and triumph, seemed to sum up within itself many of the leading features of the Britain of 1851. Here were demonstrated great energy, great enterprise, great wealth—all combined with a remarkable lack of taste in matters of art and design. And here, too was British Victorian idealism: the belief in progress, the conviction that peace between the classes, and between the nations, was at last within sight. Alas for human hopes! Within a few years of this great international display, the Crimea and many other places were to see the nations locked once again in the fury and stupidity of war.

INDEX

(Titles given in brackets were acquired at a date later in the subject's life than the last reference to him in this book)